Social Work in the British Isles

Social Work in the British Isles

Edited by Malcolm Payne and Steven M. Shardlow

Jessica Kingsley Publishers
London and Philadelphia

Thanks to Graham Allsopp for his assistance in providing maps.

First published in the United Kingdom in 2002 by
Jessica Kingsley Publishers Ltd,
116 Pentonville Road, London
N1 9JB, England
and
325 Chestnut Street,
Philadelphia PA 19106, USA.

www.jkp.com

Library of Congress Cataloging in Publication Data
A CIP catalog record for this book is available from the Library of Congress

British Library Cataloguing in Publication Data
A CIP catalogue record for this book is available from the British Library

ISBN 1 85302 763 4

Printed and Bound in Great Britain by
Athenaeum Press, Gateshead, Tyne and Wear

Contents

Chapter 1

In Search of 'British' Social Work
Identity, History and Engagement

Malcolm Payne and Steven M. Shardlow

Images and national identities

At a UK-wide conference, 'Theorising Social Work Research', held in Manchester in December 2000, an English academic commented about policy changes in the Department of Health and the impact these might have upon social work in Britain. At the back, a Welsh attender raised his hand. 'You know you're in England', he started, 'when a speech like that doesn't mention what's going on in Wales, Scotland and Northern Ireland ...' and so the Welsh attender continued. In twenty-first century social work, we need a wider perception than that evident in this partic-ular English academic's comments, about the range of issues, policies and action across the UK needs to be overcome. We need to understand and consider not only what is happening in the different parts of the UK but also in that part of the European Union with which the UK has a land border and an entwined shared heritage – the Republic of Ireland.

When we think about social work in the British Isles, a contentious term if ever there was one, what do we expect to see? A social work that is broadly similar across all component parts, in respect of organisa-tional arrangements, theoretical constructions and practice impera-tives? Perhaps we see a social work that is finely and subtly differenti-ated across the British Isles. Alternatively, a close inspection may reveal large and significant differences. Most important, how does what we expect to see measure up to what we actually find in the social work practised across the British Isles? The forces of nationalism, national identity, regionalism and national self-determination have risen like giants within a Europe that has awoken since the collapse of the communist dictatorships in Eastern and Central Europe. At the other extremity of the continent of Europe, the British Isles have not been unaffected. These powerful forces, linked to notions of national identity, have begun to affect all aspects of the state, including the practice of social work, and will continue to do so as the forces of devolution and regionalism take hold. Questions about the nature of social work within the British Isles that once might have seemed peripheral are now central and cannot be avoided. Working on this book has been a revelation to us. We have been amazed at the answers that we have found and we hope you, the reader, will share that sense of amazement at the extent of difference in social work within the 'Isles'.

Our starting-point for this exploration is not social work but identity and stereotypes. Hence, more questions! What do you think when you hear the following terms? The Channel Islands, England, the Isle of Man, Northern Ireland, the Republic of Ireland, Scotland, and Wales? What are they like? If you know them well, what would you say about them? Here are some of the things you might say: Channel Islands – flowers, cattle, rich people, offshore banking centre; England – first industrial nation, troubled football team; Isle of Man – more offshore banking, motorcycle racing; Northern Ireland – the 'troubles' between the Catholic and Protestant communities; Republic of Ireland – green, rural, potato famine; Scotland – kilts, mountains; Wales – more mountains, coal mining, singing, rugby (not very successfully at the time of writing but we live in hope). All these are images, perhaps stereotypes. If you knew these countries better, you could say more and you would probably want to correct a stereotype. These ideas are, for you, the identity that you give to these countries.

But think harder, perhaps looking at poetic expressions of national identity. Wales is also the words of the hymn *Hen Wlan fy Nhadau* (Land of My Fathers) by Evan James:

Mae hen wlad fy nhadau yn anwyl imi,
Gwlad beirdd a chantorion, enwogion o fri;
Ei gwrol rhyfelwyr, gwlad, garwyr tra mâd,
Tros ryddid collasant eu gwaed.
Gwlad, Gwlad, pleidiol wyf I'm gwlad,
Tra môr yn fur,
I'r bur hoff bau,
O bydded i'r heniath barhau.

O land of my fathers, O land of my love,
Dear mother of minstrels who kindle and move,
And hero on hero, who at honour's proud call,
For freedom their lifeblood let fall.

Wales! Wales! O but my heart is with you!
As long as the sea
Your bulwark shall be,
To Cymru my heart shall be true.
(Evan James[1])

Characteristically, imagery that defines essential elements of national identity often seems to be either pastoral – replete with graphic verbal pictures of the rural idyll – or concerned with the struggle for identity and independence. The latter images are expressed either through celebration at the achievement of freedom or as a lamentation at the loss of freedom; as in this example from Scotland:

> The mark of a Scot of all classes [is that] he … remembers and cherishes the memory of his forebears, good or bad; and there burns alive in him a sense of identity with the dead even to the twentieth generation. (Robert Louis Stevenson, 1850–94, quoted by Scottish Culture, 2001)

These expressions of identity help shape the myths that construct our visions of 'our national selves' and the national selves of others. It is not surprising that the struggle for freedom or the beauty of the national landscape should be significant and possibly even dominant images of 'our national selves'. After all, these images are the very stuff of dreams embedded in romantic attachments to the land and nation. Identities conflict, they are complex, they shift both over time and with our focus. This is a book about social work, so perhaps our starting-point in this chapter was on urban industry rather than the romantic rural. Perhaps in war, soldiers going abroad needed such a song about Wales as a reminder of an idealised homeland far away, but it was an idealisation that few experienced. An identity is for a time and a purpose. The urban assumption we made, writing the first paragraph, reflects the identity that we give social work, because it reflects our priorities and interests – primarily urban – when there are equally serious social issues to be tackled in rural areas. The urban and rural are often related. Quinn (2000), discussing film imagery, argues that the image of Britain is often of 'rose-tinted visions of hedgerows and hills' (p.35), but that the pastoral and the urban are mutually dependent. Both the factory as urban hell and the farm as pastoral paradise are part of the collective vision of Britain.

One important image of the British Isles is their separation because of geography from other cultural, ethnic, political and social identities. Famously separate, as Shakespeare put it:

> this sceptered isle... [T]his fortress built by Nature for herself... [T]his precious stone set in the silver sea, Which serves it in the office of a wall, Or as a moat defensive to a house ... This blessed plot, this earth, this realm, this England. (Shakespeare: *Richard II* ii, i, 40)

Yet these islands, as well as being separate, are also in relationships with continental land masses. Shakespeare's emphasis on the sea as a separation and safety barrier from the rest of the world may just as easily be seen as a risky closeness. In the futuristic world of Orwell's *Nineteen Eighty Four* (1949), written just after and reflecting the experiences of the Second World War, Britain is 'Airstrip One', the aircraft carrier in Europe for Oceana[2] emphasising, as it does, the quality of the relationship of these islands to the United States! This illustrates how geographical images, which we might imagine to be as fixed as land masses, reflect political and social assumptions and experiences. Here, Britain was conceived as connecting with a geographically distant culture and having a proximity to a separately conceived grouping. So it might be with wider culture and with social work. For much of the twentieth century the English language has strengthened a link with the USA in many areas of culture, not least in social work, and there has been a separation from Europe. The editors of this book are not only citizens of the UK and part of (or at least they sit on committees in) Europe and the world. Their identity contains elements of all these entities.

In this way, geographically and perhaps culturally, the British Isles are part of, or just separated from, Europe, and are part of and different from the world, depending how you choose to see it. Therefore, their social work may be part of, but separated from, European social work, and by language may be connected to, but in culture and administrative arrangement distant from, the social work of the USA and the English-speaking world. The people of the British Isles are on the European continental shelf, but on the edge of it, at once *being in, looking in* from the outside, *looking out* from the inside. British social work has connections with Europe, and also links outside, particularly to the USA.

'The British Isles': separate or unified?

What do you know about the British Isles, Ireland, Great Britain, the United Kingdom? The Appendix, *About the British Isles...*, introduces some different ways of understanding the British Isles, all connected, all apparently 'factual', but revealing different interests and focuses. It is not easy to say what these collective terms mean, because they collect many different aspects of identity together in an unhelpful way. The UK includes some of these countries, but not all. Could you be sure whether the Isle of Man or the Channel Islands are part of the UK? If you are clear that the Republic of Ireland is not part of the UK, perhaps you know also that the Republic of Ireland is a part of the British Isles. If Ireland, then, is a separate country, why are they the *British* Isles? This geographical term, the 'British Isles', carries implications of coherence that may be belied by the perceived national boundaries and interests.

What has Great Britain to do with it all? Clearly, these entities have a different identity, perhaps less clear to many of us than the countries.

In summary, the main constituents of the 'United Kingdom of Great Britain and Northern Ireland' are the England of Shakespeare's quotation, Northern Ireland, Scotland and Wales. The 'British Isles' contain, but are not fully part of, the United Kingdom, the Isle of Man and the Channel Islands. The Channel Islands are geographically closer to France than England and contain strong French elements in their language and customs. Wales is a dual-language country; most sign-posts are in both languages, there are Welsh-language schools, there is a Welsh-language television channel. Organisations welcome you in both languages. Yet, the social service system is administratively closer to that of England than of Scotland and Northern Ireland, where there are different administrative organisations. The Scots and Irish languages are not so widely spoken or so apparently vital to the assertion of cultural identity as in Wales. People speak and write English, although with different cultural traditions and varying accuracy, widely throughout the world.

National identity, then, is not a simple concept, but complex and contradictory, made up of many elements. It is cultural, ethnic, gendered, geographical, personal and many other things. It is always contestable. From a social construction viewpoint, an identity is not the essence of someone or a group of people. It is, rather, a historically and contextually formed, socially agreed and contested, constantly re-forming set of ideas about people, where there might be agreement or contestation about the identity and its character.

Hence, it has not been easy to choose an inclusive title for this book. At least not a title that can adequately refer to identities, regions, nations and states, bounded by the geographical regions identified in *About the British Isles...* (see Appendix) – a group of islands, an archipelago on the north-western boundary of Europe (we suspect that we will not have been successful in finding a title that is acceptable to all readers). Most terms that refer to this region are either exclusive in that they only refer to part of the region, or they tend to be unacceptable to a sizeable section inhabitants of some parts of the region for reasons to do with history, culture and identity. For example, the term 'British Isles', in strict *geographical* language refers to all islands that comprise the Republic of Ireland, United Kingdom, Channel Islands and so on. However, like other such terms it is probably not an easy term to accept for some who inhabit one or other part of these islands (particularly Ireland) since 'British' may seem to refer more to non-Irish parts of these islands.[3] Likewise, to use the apparently correct term to refer to the *political* arrangements in these islands, that is, the Republic of Ireland and the United Kingdom of Great Britain and Northern Ireland, is long winded – even this term may not include the Crown Dependencies such as the Channel Islands or the Isle of Man.

The difficulties of finding a correct, suitable and acceptable term for these islands may seem a rather uninteresting and trivial semantic issue. However, the difficulty in identifying a suitable short convenient term indicates a deeper problem. It suggests, indeed confirms, that these islands are not often thought to be a unity, an entity. Rather, they are a fractured and disparate group of islands under the political control of two (or in some respects more than two) separate governments. No matter that the history of all of these islands is interwoven and that for many people, but not all, across these islands the English language is a unifying force. When collective terms are used, such as Britain or Great Britain, they may be used without a clear notion of the extent of the geographical or political territory to which they refer. Wrestling with the same problem of how to refer to these islands, Norman Davies discarded such clumsy terms as 'Europe's Offshore Islands' or the 'Anglo-Celtic Archipelago' in favour of the simple 'The Isles' (Davies 1999, p.xxii) – yet this could refer to any set of islands. Each of these terms makes a claim, asserting an attribute – either the relationship to Europe, the cultural or linguistic history, the present political arrangements or whatever. Therein lies the problem, the very act of attributing a name to these islands is a political act, an act of identity assertion. There are no neutral ways to refer to these islands. Moreover, it is not something that those who inhabit these islands choose to do very often – probably because for most of us, most of the time, our concerns are more regional, local and parochial. When we do need to consider larger entities we seem to prefer the conventional terms that refer to the nation states located with the islands. These examples all serve to illustrate that conceiving of the islands as a unity is something of a novelty – despite their interwoven histories, identities and, dare we say it, approaches to social work. Recognizing that there is no satisfactory solution to the problem of how to refer to these territories as an entity, we have taken refuge in the geographically 'correct', if slightly archaic term, 'the British Isles' throughout this book to refer to all of the islands. We offer our apologies to all who dislike this term and invite them to provide a better one!

People's identities and other identities

Returning to our fundamental concerns about the notion of identity within the British Isles, rather than to our concerns about how to title this book, identities are grounded very differently in the various parts of the British Isles. They do not wholly derive from geography: geographical identities interact with other identities that characterise people in complex ways. Consequently, people see each other in ways that reflect their geographical origins, and those geographical origins become overlaid with other aspects of identity, including ethnicity, class, culture and language.

Hence, for example, some people who do not live in Scotland or Wales, even some people who do, are surprised when a Scots or Welsh person bridles at being called 'English'. Have you experienced the mock horror when some foreigner (like an American or even a Cornish person) thinks a Yorkshire resident might come from Manchester? This city is historically (but administratively no longer) in Lancashire – a deadly rival to Yorkshire in cricket, accent, and historically in war. In which Yorkshire city is there a 'Little Germany'? Where are there Chinatowns – a pagoda, a Chinese Arch? An English city claims the largest number of 'Indian' restaurants in one road in Europe, according to a television programme recent at the time of writing (although most of them are run by people from Pakistan and Bangladesh) – where? These questions suggest that there are ethnic and social identities overlying geography. The identities relate to peoples as well as geographies. These 'people' identities connect with other identities.

Rivalries between aspects of various geographical entities persist, sometimes not wholly serious but perhaps founded in historical conflicts or economic rivalries. Satirically in search of an English national anthem in the 1960s, for example, Flanders and Swann sang of the English being the best (Flanders and Swann 1977, p.78). According to the song, the Scots were mean, ate porridge and (as Presbyterians) had no bishops, unlike the Church of England; the Irish were rebellious; and the Welsh were dishonest, were all miners and sang. Cultural, political, religious, industrial and personal characteristics were all aspects of stereotypes, commonplace to the audience, that the writers call upon. The song could continue with even viler calumnies, extending to the people of the whole world, who even argued with umpires! (Flanders and Swann 1977, p.79)

As in all satire, the exaggeration builds on a basis in perceived truth. The cultural image of the English endorsed in this song is of acceptance of just authority, restraint, amateurishness and 'playing the game' rather than seeking to win. It is an umpire with whom the rest of the world argues! The implication here is that national identity relates to cricket, a middle- or upper-class game, as Norman Tebbit (now Lord Tebbit), the Conservative minister who identified Englishness with supporting the England cricket team, thought. Football, more popular and with a stronger loyalty from working-class people, is refereed, but does not indicate the national identity to the same degree. Identity derives from culture as well as place, class and ethnicity: it derives from many other things too.

Stereotypes that contribute to identities are often the prejudices of the centre for the periphery, the powerful for the oppressed, the large for the small. Even the tiny Isle of Man[4] receives this racism of the cosmopolitan for the naïve, for example in George Bernard Shaw's famous review of Wilson Barrett's *The Manxman*, one of the great rants of all time, including racist stereotypes such as calling Manx people 'aboriginal' and class-based (Rigg 1982). There is an assumption that an intellectual elite is entitled to make fun of the distantly rural in the cause of probably justified criticism of literary merit.

Just so that you know, the editors of this book live on either side of the Pennines, one in Manchester (Malcolm) and one in Sheffield (Steven). Both are English, Malcolm a Londoner by origin, Steven from the Midlands, and both speak with conventional accents – typical of the south-east, although Malcolm deteriorates under stress to the glottal stops and dropped aitches of his London East-End family. Similarly, Steven tends to lapse into the short 'a' and deep 'u' of his home city. Malcolm also lives in South Wales where his wife is based. Steven was educated at one of England's ancient universities, Malcolm at a plate-glass Midlands university; Steven works at an 'old' (pre-1992 foundation) university, Malcolm at a 'new' (post-1992 foundation) one. These terms connote clear identities to many British people, who could and probably would make judgements about class and status based on this information (and in so doing may be tempted to attribute the possession of various sets of values or beliefs to one or other of us). They could identify regions and class of origin from a few words of speech by either of us.

Perhaps you thought that Manchester and Liverpool or Leeds and Sheffield were both sets of twin cities, 35 minutes away from each other on the motorway. To the Merseysider from Liverpool, Manchester is a rival; to someone from Leeds, Sheffield is a less cosmopolitan, more traditional, more parochial city. Here the rivalries are more concrete than historical, although they are also historical – economic competition is a strong force between them. Manchester is about the same distance as the crow flies from Sheffield as from Liverpool, but the two are rarely associated with each other because a range of hills separates them and make travel more difficult and time consuming (not helped by poor roads and slow railways). Regional, city and ethnic identities often derive at least in part from economic as well as historical experience.

Space and time play a part in identity and connections, but are constructed in different ways by economic factors such as employment, income and access to resources. For example, Malcolm's visits to New York this year cost about the same as Steven's to the Czech Republic, but the distance and flight time to New York is far greater. It is cheaper to travel to New York because more people want to go there from Britain than want to go to the Czech republic, so there are economies of scale for the airlines. E-mails and faxes to each take a similar time, unless a contact does not have access to the necessary equipment, through their employer or through having the income to buy for themselves.

Lancashire, Leeds, Liverpool, Manchester, Sheffield, Yorkshire – all these places are within some of the geographical entities referred to above (England, Great Britain, the UK and the British Isles) and represent a complex of identities within these geographical entities. We refer to them here because they are all places that we know, near where we live or have lived. We can ask you the questions without looking up the answers. Similarly, all geographical entities reflect such complexes of identities, that we all perceive them in different ways.

'Near where I live', in the previous paragraph is an example of how identity flows from position and perspective. The local authority where Malcolm lives is Stockport. He would say this to someone from Manchester who asks; to a Stockport person, he would say 'Heaton Moor'. To someone from London, he would say 'Manchester' – they might never have heard of Stockport, or might confuse it with Southport or Stockton. When he worked in London, his American secretary once made an appointment for him in Sheffield two hours after one in Ormskirk. He pointed out to her that they are a hundred miles apart, a two-hour journey, never mind the meeting. 'Well,' she said, 'They're both in the North.' She had looked at the map, but never having been that far north, had no idea what geographical reality the graphic represented. Identity depends on where you are looking from, both socially and geographically. To the Londoner, such as Malcolm's secretary, a one to two hour journey to visit someone living within London might seem to be next door, because it is part of the same city, but a similar length journey travelling outside of London to Birmingham, for example, may seem much further and more distant.

The complexity of factors that have an impact on geographical identities draws attention to how the idea of identity has a richness within it that makes it a useful concept for exploring the complex of ideas that form how a person, place and occupational group such as social work is seen in the cultures which surround it. It will almost certainly be a continuing debate, since identity constantly changes and we refocus our understanding of it as we and those around us change. Chamberlayne *et al.* (1999) contend that that understanding how culture forms the identity of welfare in different countries can be helpfully achieved by looking in detail at the biographies of people. How people experience the impact of the whole national cultural and welfare system on their lives expresses more fully than an analysis of services or policies the identity of welfare and social work in a country. For social workers, who must deal in the individual biographies of the people they work with, the national contexts explored here set out some of the influences of political and economic issues on the social welfare systems that will affect those biographies. The differences discussed between the identities of the geographical entities say something about how they will affect the services that workers will provide and service users experience.

We have been arguing here, then, that while England may have been a dominant cultural identity in the British Isles, the history of the relations between England and the other constituents of the British Isles is one of the factors that shape the differing senses of identities found in different parts of the British Isles. Through these senses of identities, our history is mediated. From our history, our arrangements for the governance of these societies have emerged.

National identities and social work

One final question (at least, direct question – much of this chapter seeks to make you think about your conceptions of these national and cultural entities): is its social work part of your image or stereotype of the identity of these places? If personal identities are partly national identities, and if national identities are factors in the governance of our societies, social work must also be relevant to personal and social identities in any society, because social work is part of the modes of governance in modern societies.

The cynical or depressed social worker/reader might laugh: how could social work be significant? The politically aware British reader might wave the question aside: in early twenty-first century Britain, education and the health service are far more important. Yet Segalman (1986), an American writing about the Swiss, in a passing comment says: 'If you mention the welfare state, you think of Sweden or Britain'. Moreover, Sipilä (1996), discussing Scandinavia, claims that the social care elements of a welfare state are an important feature of its character, although he refers to a wider concept of social care than is common-place in the United Kingdom at the moment.

We argue, then, that social work both forms and is formed by the culture of the places where it is practised. The particular social work of a place contributes to the identity of the people and societies that inhabit it. If this is so, the identity of the social work of the British Isles will be formed by the culture and character of those islands, and how these islands are seen and understood will be in part influenced by the role of social work. However, is there a place, the 'British Isles', to create and be acculturated to its social work? Or must we examine various 'social works' of the British Isles? We examine this question by looking at the historical and constitutional factors creating national identities and national social works in the British Isles.

Historical involvement

The histories of the countries of England, Ireland, Northern Ireland, Scotland and Wales are interwoven and have been so for thousands of years; the various peoples who have settled the British Isles, with their various languages, cultures, religions and forms of social organisation, have left indelible impressions on the current fabric of society within the British Isles. Some of those impressions are now faint and obscured, but they are there none the less.

The British Isles have been continuously settled since the end of the Ice Ages (about 10,000 BC). Since then many different peoples, particularly from mainland Europe, have arrived and settled, sometimes peacefully, sometimes by force. Examples are the Celts in the seventh century BC, the Romans in the first four centuries AD, the Germanic peoples in the sixth and seventh centuries, the Norse peoples in the ninth and tenth centuries, the Norman French in the eleventh century. More recently there have been settlements by other groups, for example those escaping persecution such as Jews in the nineteenth century, or often for economic reasons such as by peoples from outside Europe from the British Empire and later the Commonwealth. A large number of people have also left the British Isles to settle in other parts of the world (for example, New York is the city with the largest number of people of Irish descent living outside of Ireland). These peoples have not settled uniformly across the British Isles, hence some parts of the British Isles may retain the character or culture of particular groups.

The historic period of relationships between these different peoples reveals a development from small independent kingdoms through the formation of nations to the eventual formation of one state lasting a little over a hundred years, during the nineteenth century (even then the crown dependencies had separate arrangements for government). There is no necessity that such a single state should have emerged or that it should have had as its capital London in England. Key elements in the construction of this state were subjugation by the English of the other nations within the British Isles. Wales was conquered by England between the eleventh and thirteenth centuries. It was effectively incorporated within the English constitution and governmental structures with the creation of Welsh counties in 1537 by King Henry VIII. Scotland and England were united in 1707 (Act of Union) to form a single kingdom, to be known as Great Britain – this was a willing union of two states and two crowns, albeit passed by a small majority of votes by the Scottish Parliament. Ireland was conquered in stages by England from the twelfth century, a process of conquest effectively completed violently during the English Commonwealth (1649–1654) and the British Republic (1654–60)[5] by the Lord Protector Oliver Cromwell, although it was not until 1801 that it formally became a part of the same state of Great Britain to form the single state of the United Kingdom of Great Britain and Ireland.

In Ireland and Wales throughout the centuries, systematic attempts were made by the English to suppress culture and language, a policy pursued with great effect in Wales, such that, towards the end of the nineteenth century Welsh was almost obliterated. Although Scotland was never conquered by England in the same fashion as Ireland or Wales, systematic attempts were made to destroy Highland culture with the banning of the use of Gaelic, the land clearances, the banning of the wearing of tartan, and so on, especially during the eighteenth century. The history of the relationships between the peoples of the British Isles is one of rivalry, domination, subjugation and repression in the drive to establish a single state. It is the English who, as the largest nation, sought both to establish the unitary state and dominate the other nationalities and cultural groups within the British Isles. This history has left a continuing effect upon the relationships between the English and other nationalities – the English frequently constructed as aggressors and imperialists, while other nationalities find pride in self-assertion through claims to national identity. This attempt at domination by the English, the largest ethnic group within the British Isles, remains a powerful theme in the history of the British Isles.

We examine this factor in relation to social work more fully in the final chapter.

Constitutional arrangements within the British Isles

The historical entanglement of the countries of the British Isles has left a complex set of interwoven constitutional arrangements. These might seem of little relevance to all but the historian or the constitutional expert. However, the frameworks that define the governance of the British Isles also construct the legal frameworks that contain social welfare policy and social work.

During the years 1801 until 1921 the British Isles were ruled by a single government with a single parliament at Westminster (the House of Commons and the House of Lords).[6] From 1921, the Irish Free State[7] was established as a separate country with its own bicameral parliament, the Dáil, and independent government in Dublin. Political tensions between the governments in Westminster and Dublin were inevitable – given the manner of the Irish obtaining independence (taken rather than granted) and the fact that the constitution of the Republic of

Ireland laid territorial claim to the six counties of Northern Ireland (Antrim, Armagh, Down, Fermanagh, Londonderry, Tyrone). If part of Ireland obtained complete independence from the rest of the United Kingdom, then in the other part significant changes were introduced in the nature of governance. From 1921 onwards, in Northern Ireland the Stormont Parliament and Executive ruled Ulster until 1972 when, due to the breakdown of law and order, direct rule from Westminster was imposed. The other constituent countries of the United Kingdom have not had separate parliaments or elements of devolved government until the late 1990s. There was one attempt in the 1970s to establish devolved governments for Scotland and Wales. A royal commission was held and the resultant Kilbrandon Report (1973) proposed the re-establishment of parliaments in Wales (last independent parliament 1404–5, under Prince Glyn Dwr) and Scotland (last independent parliament 1707). However, the required referendum demonstrated that there was no popular support for such parliaments (of the votes cast 33 per cent were in favour in Scotland, 12 per cent in Wales).

With the election of the Labour Government of the United Kingdom in 1997, there was a new commitment to the development of devolved government for the United Kingdom – it was a part of the government's manifesto pledge. Consequently, two referenda were held in 1998, one in Scotland and one in Wales. This time the results were different (of the votes cast 71 per cent voted in favour in Scotland, 51 per cent in Wales. The Scottish Parliament met for the first time during 1999, as did the Welsh Assembly. Similar developments had also taken place in Northern Ireland following the 'peace process' initiated reluctantly[8] by the Conservative Government of John Major. After the so-called 'Good Friday Agreement'[9] (1998) between both the Dublin and Westminster Governments and political groups and parties in Ireland, a Northern Ireland Assembly and Executive was introduced in 1999 but suspended during the early months of 2000 before being reinstated. Hence, from 1999, the countries of Northern Ireland, Scotland and Wales all had an independent parliament or national assembly with certain devolved powers from the Westminster Government.

This left the constitutional position of England as something of an anomaly as, for example, Scottish MPs could discuss and vote on strictly English matters when these were discussed at the Westminster Parliament but similar Scottish issues would be the preserve of the Scottish Parliament. (This is the so-called West Lothian question named after the constituency of Tam Dalyell the Westminster MP who first posed this issue in the House of Commons at Westminster.) Likewise, while the Labour Government stated a commitment to reform of the House of Lords (the second chamber of the Westminster parliament) by removing some of the hereditary peers' rights to sit in the Lords, no attempt has been made to specify or define the relationship between the House of Lords and the re-established parliaments and assemblies within the United Kingdom. Each of the assemblies is unicameral, therefore it is possible to presume that the House of Lords might remain as a second chamber for all of the United Kingdom. Further, some of the members of the House of Lords hold titles that are rooted in Northern Ireland, Scotland and Wales; what is the relationship of these Lords to both the House of Lords and to other parliaments and assemblies? These measures of reform have neither created a truly federal state within the United Kingdom nor are they truly grounded in established universal democratic principles. Rather, the reforms have all the appearance of power grudgingly, partially and sparingly handed down from the superior government at Westminster.[10] In the words of Davies (1999):

> It [constitutional change] could have diffused the strains of the Union for a season; but in the long term, it could also have encouraged the destabilizing and centrifugal forces of imbalance, nationalism and separatism. (p.928)

Only time will tell. However, it is worth remembering that such forces have unleashed violent separatist movements and the movement of refugees in other parts of Europe. Where this has happened, social workers are in the front line in trying to rebuild civil society – it is to be hoped that will not be necessary across the British Isles anymore than it already has been in Northern Ireland.

The constitutional position of the Isle of Man and the Channel Islands is different again. The crown dominions are self-governing territories that owe allegiance to the British Crown. As such, they are not formally members of the European Union and they have independent governmental structures. For example, the Isle of Man has its own parliament, the Tynwald, which was created when the Island was ruled by Norway, and this parliament predates the parliament at Westminster.

Political and constitutional relationships between the Republic of Ireland and the United Kingdom are being shaped by both bilateral rapprochement and participation in supra-national co-operative and collaborative structures. The constitutional position of Northern Ireland has been an inevitable obstacle to close formal co-operation between the governments of Dublin and Westminster. However, the Good Friday Agreement contained proposals for the creation of 'cross-border' co-operation and the creation of certain cross-border institutions. For some across all of Ireland this might seem to prefigure the first stages of constitutional change and the possibility of the creation of a united Ireland. Yet, the Good Friday Agreement also contained the commitment to such constitutional change being possible only with the consent of the population of Northern Ireland demonstrated through a referendum at some future date. Hence, there exists at least a theoretical possibility of the joint policy development between the two governments of Dublin and Westminster at some future date. The future of the Republic of Ireland and the United Kingdom are bound together through joint membership of organizations such as the European Union[11] or the lesser-known Council of Europe.[12] Ireland entered what was to become the European Union[13] in 1979, the United Kingdom in 1975. The Republic of Ireland embraced membership; its economy has prospered and the country has become one of the founder members of European Monetary Union (EMU) by joining the Euro. Meanwhile, the Labour Government of the United Kingdom publicly espouses its central role within the Union but through ambivalence fails to commit to projects such as the Euro.

Social Work in the British Isles

It is not usual to look at social work across the separate countries of the Republic of Ireland, the United Kingdom of Great Britain and Northern Ireland and the associated crown dependencies such as the Channel Islands – *and* to explore the similarities and differences. The formal titles of the territories seem long winded; they are not the stuff of everyday discussion. The unusual nature of exploring social work across these territories may be because some assume (aside from the fact that the Republic of Ireland and the United Kingdom are different national states) that there is little significant difference between the various countries that comprise the United Kingdom and associated crown dependencies. On the other hand, perhaps there is not even a presumption that there is no significant difference but rather that questions about the similarities and differences in social work across these territories are not even posed.

Recent developments across these territories all invite greater discussion about the nature of the involvement of these various countries with each other and their similarities and differences. Relevant constitutional issues, for example, are the inclusion of the Republic of Ireland and the United Kingdom within the common framework of the European Union; the cross-border involvement of the Republic of Ireland in the recent civilian wars in Northern Ireland; and the devolutionary tendencies in the politics of the United Kingdom.

If we are more inclined to ask about the difference and interconnectedness of these countries in the political sphere we ought also to ask similar questions about the nature of the involvement in the social sphere – in particular in relation to social work. Modern social work conventionally traces its roots to the nineteenth century. Until 1921 the British Isles were ruled from one government in Westminster and investigation may be expected to reveal that the early development of social work in different parts of the British Isles would have been interconnected in some way or another by virtue of being located within the same state. None the less, we might also expect such an exploration to reveal that the existence of significant cultural, linguistic and religious differences within the various parts of the British Isles. These differences might be expected to translate into some significant differences in the nature and form of modern social work practice across the British Isles. Some of the similarities may be surprising. For example, the Central Council for Education and Training in Social Work (CCETSW), a UK body defined by statute and charged with the responsibility for regulating the standards of education for social work in the UK, also had the same responsibility in the Republic of Ireland until the creation of National Social Work Qualification Board, (NSWQB) on 27 February 1997.

Is *national* identity relevant any more? Is it to be defined in political, institutional and geographical borders or by the nature of civil society and the way in which citizenship is formed in any particular country? And if civil society and citizenship is to become a more crucial issue, the social services, formal, informal, statutory, voluntary and private, and the social work which is a part of them, may become a more crucial defining factor of national identity than they have been in recent decades. In the 1950s, having a caring welfare state was a matter of pride in the UK and of attack in the Republic of Ireland (Chapter 3). Social work was increasingly perceived as integral to the point that, in the 1970s, its recognition as the basis for a major local government department marked its institutionalisation in the UK. Nevertheless, as the corporatist welfare state has receded, more diverse structures for the manifestation of citizenship rights than the availability of universal welfare and monolithic social services have arisen. Hence, participation rather than recognition of need has become a touchstone of social work practice – identity is a vital element in the construction of such citizenship rights. Such social changes in separate social states might imply some elements coming together from different directions and others driving the states apart. Similar experiences, such as child abuse, may afflict political and professional decision making in markedly different ways because of different priorities represented in national identities.

Social institutions contribute to national identity. The accumulation and interaction of typical social forms within social institutions create a national society. Social work is a social institution. It is a profession, an activity, it takes place in a set of social institutions called social work agencies, it forms part of the culture of societies in which it exists, it has a role in and is understood as part of that society. The form of social work in any particular society must therefore have some influence on the identity that the society maintains.

Societies change, as do social institutions. Social change impels change in social institutions. As social institutions change, therefore, they mark social changes, and as well as that they may influence the direction and nature of social change. These processes are obvious within social work since demographic, conceptual and administrative changes have all had their impact on social work over the years. This book identifies differing forms of social work in different countries and administrative divisions within the British Isles. The book contains chapters on each of the countries within the British Isles and Bailiwick of Guernsey – as an example of a crown dependency. The purposes of this book are a mixture of the practical and the philosophical. For students and practitioners of social work within the British Isles the book offers an overview of the differing legal, administrative and practice contexts of social work across those islands. This book arose from a variety of work that we have been doing to examine social work in different nations. We found ourselves working on social work activities across Europe and across the globe. In one book (Shardlow and Payne 1998) we included a chapter on social work in Britain (pp.133–150); Malcolm has contributed an article on social work in the UK to an American text (Payne 1998a) and Steven has written about the UK in a book about the fundamentals of European social work (Adams *et al.* 2000). These experiences led us to see how difficult it was to represent social work in Britain in a short compass. This book is therefore a comparative study of social work across the British Isles. It emphasises a complexity and difference that many other texts underplay – that there are major differences in social work practice within the supposed unitary United Kingdom and certainly between Ireland and the other constituent parts of the British Isles. When working on the book we found ourselves amazed at the extent of difference across these islands – we hope you will be similarly captivated.

Notes

1   The hymn was written 1856 in Welsh by Evan James, the English translation is by A. P. Graves.

2   Oceana was Orwell's fictitious name for the US, Ireland and the UK in his novel *1984*.

3   The term 'British Isles' derives from the Roman name for the Celtic settlers of these islands, the Britons – many of whom settled in Ireland as they were pushed further westward by successive peoples invading from the east.

4   We have tried hard to find someone to provide an account of the social services and social work in the Isle of Man, to no avail, but we have left some commentary about Man in the contextual chapters. It is another crown dependency, which has fairly recently shifted towards a 'Seebohm' pattern of provision, and covers a small population.

5   See Davies (1999) pp.591–7 for an account of the constitutional relationships during this period.

6   For a full account of the historical development of parliaments and government in the British Isles prior to 1801 see Davies (1999).

7   In 1936, the Irish Free State changed its name to become Éire and in 1948 it severed all links with the ruling House of Windsor, leaving the Commonwealth to become the Republic of Ireland.

8   Despite taking credit for the development of the peace process the memoirs of Norman Lamont indicate that John Major was personally sceptical if not opposed to the initiative (Lamont 1999).

9   The 'Good Friday Agreement' was approved by 71 per cent in a referendum held in Northern Ireland.

10 By January 2001 the policies being adopted by the Scottish Parliament, notably in relation to charges for higher education, higher pay for school teachers and the intention to provide free care to older people caused embarrassment to the Westminster Government, which gave every appearance of supporting devolution provided no further significant differences emerged between the policies adopted by the countries of the United Kingdom.

11 Throughout its existence the European Union has been known by a variety of different names as its functions have changed: European Iron and Steel Community; European Economic Community (EEC); the European Community (EC) and most recently the European Union (EU). For information about the EU see www.europa.eu.int

12 For information about The Council of Europe see www.coe.int

13 The institutions of the EU are complex but the major bodies are: the European Parliament; a council of ministers (each national government has nomination rights); the Commission; the European Court of Justice and most recently the European Central Bank.

Chapter 2

Social Work in England

Malcolm Payne and Steven M. Shardlow

Introduction: an English identity

The English have a view of themselves as a special and chosen people living in a uniquely favoured country. Thus, Blake implied, albeit in an allegorical poem[1] that the Messiah walked on the chosen land of England. Expressions of England as a uniquely blessed country pepper the cultural, religious and political iconography inhabited by the English. For example, Shakespeare glorified England as 'this scepter'd isle' (Shakespeare, *Richard II* ii.i 40), while Wood suggests that:

> The so-called myths of the English, in fact, are really about the English State and Englishness itself: kings and queens, the Mother of Parliaments, the Tower and Beefeaters, Merrie England and so on. (Wood 2000, p.43)

Here, he equates the people of England with the political state of England with the geographical country of England. The English find difficulty in distinguishing these notions. This is surprising given that the English view themselves as a free and independent people where the Englishman's home is his castle. Yet for many English the combined unified and indivisibility trinity of State, Country and People is a central element of the mythology of England.

The special and desirable notions of England were forcefully expressed on 22 March 1993, the eve of Saint George's[2] day, when John Major, the then Prime Minister of the United Kingdom, concluded his speech to Conservative Group for Europe with the now famous words that encapsulate a romanticised rural portrait of his country:

> Fifty years from now Britain will still be the country of long shadows on country grounds, warm beer, invincible green suburbs, dog lovers and pools fillers and – as George Orwell said – 'old maids cycling to holy communion through the morning mist'.

No matter that John Major used the word Britain, there is no state of 'Britain', and there is no region within the United Kingdom called 'Britain'. As Mikes (1946), himself a Hungarian, perceptively observed, the English have a historic propensity either to confuse or fail to distinguish the country of England, the United Kingdom as a whole or the British Isles. In describing England as he did, John Major was describing an 'England' that is instantly recognisable to the English – even if it does not exist in reality. Moreover, Major's list resonates with similar lists identified by Paxman (1998, p.22) and by writers as diverse as George Orwell (1941 and 1947), Stanley Baldwin (1926), or with the sharply observed commentaries of Bill Bryson (1996). Not a lot has changed, at least in respect of Englishness, since 1946. The English, with a poor sense of 'English identity', still find difficulty in distinguishing the country of England from other countries within the United Kingdom and tend to assume, falsely, that a homogeneity exists across the United Kingdom. In that sense, England and the other parts of the United Kingdom often become synonymous with the English.

A rather less pleasant picture of the English emerges in Home Secretary Jack Straw's warning, broadcast by the BBC in January 2000 during a programme discussing the meaning of being English. He said the English are 'potentially very aggressive, very violent and will increasingly articulate their Englishness following devolution' and that the English had used their 'propensity to violence to subjugate Ireland, Wales and Scotland' (White 2000).

These two strands of English identity, the notion of England as a peaceful rural idyll and the English as a people with a propensity to dominate both near neighbours and those more distant through empire, are but two among many skeins of supposed English identity.

These notions have not often been discussed until recently, because the English have to equate 'Englishness' with the identity of the whole of the United Kingdom.

It is perhaps a little shocking to the bemused English to be faced with questions about defining the nature of English identity – having assumed for so long that such questions belonged only to other peoples of the Isles, the Irish, Scots, Welsh and so on. Separating a notion of England from the other parts of the United Kingdom in terms of culture, identity, constitution, law and social work is not an easy matter for many English to contemplate or to begin to address.

Population, geography

England is the largest country within the United Kingdom, measured by population or geographical area. The population of England is 48,707,000. Between 4 and 5 per cent of the English population are from the ex-colonies of the United Kingdom. Predominantly these groups are from the Indian subcontinent or are African-Caribbean peoples. England comprises approximately 130,000^3 square kilometres – which is 53 per cent of the total area of the United Kingdom. Population density is high for a state within the European Union as there are approximately 350 people per square kilometre.

Economic development

England was the world's first industrial country. It remains a highly urban society; only a small proportion of the population are employed in agriculture which generates less than 1 per cent of GDP. Manufacturing industries are concentrated in the north and midlands with a high concentration of service, financial and new technologies industries in the south-east, centring on London. A major source of the nation's wealth is derived from the financial services industry that centres upon the City of London. The wealth of the country is therefore unequally distributed with the per capita income of the south being on average greater than that of the north. The older traditional so-called heavy industries such as car manufacturing, mining, steel making, shipbuilding and so on are in decline with the loss of markets and jobs.

Full-time jobs lost by skilled or semi-skilled men are likely to be replaced by part-time jobs often taken by women. Disparities of economic development across the country create highly localised economic and social conditions that pose a challenge for social services. According to Hutton (2001), six of the eight English regions have per capita incomes that fall below the European average. The economic needs of the English regions have not been well served by London-based governments that place a higher premium upon the economic conditions that prevail in the south-east of the country. However, the government has created (with effect from 1 April 1999) English Regional Development Agencies (RDAs). These are appointed bodies, consisting of 12 to 15 'regional plutocrats' and councillors, which distribute over £1 billion in total to promote economic regeneration and development. They are not nascent springboards towards regional government.

Governance and political structures – structural arrangements for the delivery of social services in England

The governance of England is complex. Westminster[4] has been a parliament and seat of government for the countries of the United Kingdom since the Act of Union with Ireland in 1800. However, with the establishment of devolved structures of government for Northern Ireland, Scotland and Wales (albeit with varying degrees of power), England, the largest country of the Union, lacks its own national parliament. Rather, England must share Westminster, both parliament and executive, with the other countries of the Union. Some responsibilities have been fully devolved; for example, the Scottish parliament has full devolved powers in respect of education but not employment. Hence, for some matters, the parliament and government at Westminster function as a parliament for the whole of the Union. However, for others it is more of a parliament for England. There is a dormant committee of the House of Commons for English regional affairs – although it has not met since 1978. Yet there is a constitutional anomaly as members of the Westminster parliament who sit for Scottish constituencies may vote on some matters of law concerning England, whereas members of the Westminster parliament who sit for English constituencies are deprived of similar rights in respect of Scotland (cf p.21). Similarly, the constitutional position of the part-reformed, although still unelected and unrepresentative, House of Lords lacks clarity; it appears to be primarily a UK-wide institution. Perhaps rather surprisingly, this apparent inequity and inconsistency in the governance of England has not attracted much political discussion[5]. The phlegmatic English seem curiously unconcerned about an inherently unfair and manifestly unrepresentative constitutional settlement within which England is underrepresented and disadvantaged – all the more surprising given a history of political protest to achieve representation.

The Department of Health is the central governmental department responsible for the provision of social services in England, and its decisions often influence patterns of provision and practice in the other countries, particularly in Wales where the devolved assembly has less independence than in other countries. This influence may well decline in future years.

Local government has been central in the provision of social services within England. There has been and continues to be an uneasy split of responsibilities between central government (principally income maintenance and regulation of national standards) and local government (traditionally direct provision of social work and social caring services but increasingly co-ordination of services and local inspection). Local government in England is complex, consisting of historic structures that have their origins in arrangements that developed several hundred years ago and a more recent overlay of modern structures. The effect is of a slightly chaotic, organic set of structures that are not entirely consistent with themselves or with other structures for the delivery of health and social care. One of these is the City of London[6], described by Cohen (1999) as 'The last rotten borough'. There has been recently significant change in the structure of local government. These major changes to local government were introduced between 1996 and 1998. There are now 34 county[7] councils that provide services such as education, social services and libraries to a mixture of both urban and rural areas. Some of these county councils are further divided into smaller administrative units, district councils (274 of these existed prior to 1998 but the number is now reduced) which provide services such as housing, services for homeless people, the collection of refuse and leisure facilities. In addition, there are 83 'unitary authorities' which provide all of the services for the population within a given geographical area – usually metropolitan areas. (On 1 April 1998 there was a major reorganization of local government when the number of unitary authorities was increased by 19, making a new total of 46 across England. One county council, Berkshire, disappeared altogether.) There are a total of 153 social services departments in England.

Although local authorities provide social services, they are closely connected with other national and local government provision, such as criminal justice, education, health care and housing. The English central government ministry responsible for social services is the Department of Health (DoH), which provides guidance and profes-sional support to the social services, although its main focus is health care and the National Health Services (NHS). Local authorities are funded and influenced by the central government Department for Transport, Local Government and the Regions (DTLR), so this is another route of influence from central government. While legislation provides the fundamental basis for social services, central government controls and influences local authorities through local authority social services circulars that are constantly issued to provide guidance. Central government also publishes an increasingly important range of research, together with practice and policy guidance also seeking to influence how local authority social services act. These are reinforced by a programme of inspection carried out by the DoH Social Services Inspectorate (SSI) on specialist topics, and by the Audit Commission which checks whether they are implementing government policy effec-tively. The SSI and Audit Commission carry out a programme of joint reviews which evaluate the total social services provision of a particular local authority.

Regional co-ordination of social services in England is problematic. In 1986, the government of Mrs Thatcher abolished the existing forms of regional government such as the Greater London Council (making London the only major capital city in the world to have no overall body responsible for the co-ordination of services). Only in 2000 was this situation remedied with the election of a mayor for London and the development of a London assembly – other major regions of England have not been given the opportunity to redevelop regional government.

Social services for adults

The organisation of social services for adults in England derives from the administrative reorganisation wrought by the National Health Service and Community Care Act 1990, mainly brought into force in 1994. This introduced a 'mixed economy of care' into this area of social services, following a similar pattern of organisation in the NHS. This development also made controversial changes to the role of social work that are still being worked out and debated. These changes particularly affect adult services, because there was a political impetus for the changes from the Conservative Government that introduced them. The almost simultaneous changes within children's services were more the product of a professional consensus.

The community care reforms raise several important issues, which we address later in this section. One is the effect of providing for all people over 18 years of age who need social services in a single administrative category ('adults'), rather than in more specific groups. For example, people in their twenties with learning disabilities might have few needs in common with people in their eighties with increasing physical disability. Another is the focus on service provision rather than social work. The third is the professional innovation of 'care management', its effect on the role and practice of social work and its relationship with other innovations, such as advocacy.

However, to provide a context for the debates about these issues, we first review, briefly, the development of adult services, what they consist of and the legislation that underlies them.

Development of adult services

The legislation that governs adult services is mainly of much greater age than the 1990 community care reforms. Major features of the provision derive from the National Assistance Act 1948, one of a group of pieces of legislation that created modern social services from the Poor Law. This Act requires local government authorities to provide welfare services for elderly and physically disabled people, and for others in need, which includes homeless people and families. The Mental Health Act 1959 reformed mental health law, following the Percy Commission (1957) which introduced the term 'community care' to reflect a policy move and professional ideal towards caring for mentally ill people outside hospitals. Local authorities were to develop services in the home and in less institutionalised residential care for mentally ill and learning disabled people.

The community care ideal rapidly spread to other adult service user groups. The Health Services and Public Health Act 1968 which, among a range of provisions, further encouraged this, made mandatory the provision of home help and other home care services. These services were swept up into social services departments (SSDs) when they were created in 1971 by the implementation of the Local Authority Personal Social Services Act 1970, following the recommendations of the Seebohm Report (1968), which aimed to create 'one door' for members of the public to knock at for social services. SSDs were decentralised to varying degrees to make services available more locally. At much the same time, the Chronically Sick and Disabled Persons Act 1970 obliged local authorities to keep a register of disabled people in their area and to provide a wide range of services in the home, including telephones, aids and adaptations of the home to enable people with disabilities to live a more independent life.

With local government and NHS reorganisation in 1974, social work in hospitals was merged with social services departments. Teams of workers usually provide it outposted to the hospital or, increasingly, other kinds of health care establishment. Occasionally, services are provided from the local area team.

The Mental Health Act 1983 reformed the mental health legislation again, giving greater protection to the civil rights of mentally ill people. This Act introduced a new category of social worker, the approved social worker. There are usually several in each local authority area with specialised post-qualification training, a responsibility to maintain continuing professional development and legal powers of compulsion and confinement of mentally ill people based on medical recommendations. This arrangement is under review in 2001.

Legislation after the introduction of the 1990 community care reforms has responded mainly to campaigns by sectional interests. The Carers (Recognition and Services) Act 1995 places a duty on local authorities to assess the needs of carers who provide a substantial amount of care to a social services client. It builds both on the Disabled Persons (Services, Consultation and Representation) Act 1986 which requires SSDs to 'have regard' for carers' needs and also on the policy guidance on the NHS and Community Care Act 1990, which says that carers could request assessments. The Carers (Recognition and Services) Act emphasises the importance of the role that carers play, the burden that they accept and the costs that they save the state. In addition, the Act recognises that carers often have needs and interests that are different from those of the person being cared for. The Community Care (Direct Payments) Act 1996 empowers local authorities to make direct cash payments to disabled people under 65 to enable them to purchase their own services. The aim was particularly to allow younger disabled people to have greater control of the arrangements for their care. It followed experiments and campaigns by disabled people and the experience of the Disabled Living Fund, a short-lived social security allowance with a similar aim which was withdrawn in 1996. There was evidence that local authorities were using a variety of techniques to avoid the limitation on making direct payments. The direct payments legislation relates to the development of advocacy within the social services and social work. It is an innovation since by tradition and long-standing legislative convention (s.29, National Assistance Act 1948 is an example) local authorities are prohibited from making cash payments; this is reserved to the separate social security provision.

The Mental Health (Patients in the Community) Act 1995 is an exception to the general trend of social care legislation in the Conservative era, growing from campaigns by sectional interests. Rather, concerns about the adequacy of supervision of potentially dangerous or at-risk mentally ill people has led to a tightening of procedures. The Act allows patients who have been detained in hospital under various provisions of the Mental Health Act 1983, and who are still at risk or a risk to others, to be made subject to supervision on discharge. It reinforces the duty of the local authority to provide aftercare under s.117 of the 1983 Act by allowing the patient's place of residence to be specified, requiring patients to attend for treatment, education or occupation and by allowing access to the patient's home to the supervisor. Its success is so far unproven, and the series of scandals about patients at risk or committing homicides has continued (Reith 1998).

Range of services

The range of services provided by most local authorities includes universally available residential care for elderly people and less comprehensive residential care for physically disabled, learning disabled and mentally ill people. Most areas also have day care provision and domiciliary or home care (that is, services such as home helps and meals provided in people's own homes) for the same groups. The style of these varies widely. Residential and day care provision for these groups overlaps with hospital day care and nursing home provision in the NHS, with a greater emphasis on medical and nursing care. There is also a social work service for these groups, which would involve visiting and giving support to people with various disabilities and problems. Particularly for people with hearing or visual disabilities, these services are often contracted to historically influential voluntary associations. Aids and adaptations to the home for disabled people are offered. Except in hospital social work and for mentally ill people and for people with learning disabilities and their carers, most of the provision is of a routine, caring nature rather than seeking to provide preventive or therapeutic help.

Until the 1980s the local authority made most of this provision itself, with a minor role for the voluntary sector. However, the Conservative Government of this period pursued more vigorously than previously the long-standing community care policy of closing long-stay provision in the NHS for all adult groups. This particularly affected people with learning disabilities, with mental illnesses and elderly people. At the same time, in pursuit of economic objectives, they constrained local authority social services and especially home care expenditure. A gap in provision therefore opened, which private residential care, paid for by social security grants, mainly filled. As the social security budget expanded, several reports, but crucially one from the Audit Commission (1986), identified a policy failure. That is, the increase in residential care, funded by the social security budget, went against the overall policy of community care because it was increasing the proportion of people cared for in institutions.

The 1990 community care reforms

To sort this out, the Griffiths Report (1988) recommended a new implementation of community care policy, which comprised three elements:

1. Local authorities were responsible for drawing up a 'community care plan' for their locality, including services from voluntary and private sector providers.

2. There would be a 'mixed economy of care' and a 'purchaser–provider split'. Services would be purchased by the local authority for individual service users from private, statutory and voluntary sector providers in the plan. However, the local authority would not be the main provider, and its provider activities would be administratively separated from its purchasing activities.

3. Each individual service user would have what became known as a 'care manager' who would assess the needs of the service user and would purchase from the plan a 'package of services' which would meet the user's needs.

Organisational consequences

After delays in legislating and commencing the changed arrangements, these recommendations were brought into action during the early 1990s, culminating in 1994. A new 'post-Griffiths' system of community care came into being. This led to a reorganisation of most SSDs. In most cases, adult and children's services were divided, whereas previously a functional division had sometimes separated community and domiciliary services from residential and day care. Also most often, purchasing and 'provider' staff were separated. Purchasing staff organised the community care plan and administered the purchasing arrangements for each local authority. Increasingly, this is done in liaison with the health authority, which performs the same function in the NHS. Provider staff worked in aspects of the local authority that offered services, such as day, domiciliary or residential care, including field social work. Health trusts in the NHS provide a similar function. These are organisationally separate from the purchasing health authority, but in SSDs purchasing and providing are split between different arms of the same department. Frequently, private and voluntary organisations in the area gain contracts for providing services. The relationships with health trusts, the providers in the NHS, are to be extended during the early 2000s, with some mergers, particularly in the mental health field, of local authority adult and long-term care NHS services, and other closer joint arrangements.

Within the 'purchaser–provider' administrative split, the position of field social workers became ambiguous. Many were appointed as care managers. Some local authorities regard care managers as providers. In this view, social workers are offering a supportive and therapeutic service to meet the needs of members of the public. Other local authorities, probably the majority, treat care managers as primarily funders and managers of packages of service provided by others, of which a social work service might be a defined element. This gives them a managerial function rather than one in which they relate directly to service users. Some local authorities divided social workers between purchasing and providing functions. Purchasers would then contract with the social work provider units to offer a social work service where it is needed. In other SSDs, care managers carry out both purchasing and providing functions. Here, no one differentiates the social work role into these two administrative elements. In such authorities, care managers might incorporate elements of supportive and therapeutic work as part of the care manager role. This reflects the reality that dividing support, therapy and organising services for the same person is artificial. Alternatively care managers might, in effect, contract with themselves to provide some supportive or therapeutic work, thus dividing care management functions from social work activities in their daily work. This maintains the purchaser–provider split without burdening the service users with relationships with two people with indistinct roles. Doing this makes for clarity of function, but is an artificial distinction in reality. SSDs with this approach leave a great deal unclear.

'Adult services' and adults' needs

Is the post-Griffiths community organisation appropriate to adults' needs? The distinction between children's and adults' services goes back to the break-up of the Poor Law in 1948, when separate legislation was enacted to provide co-ordinated services for children. Further back, from Victorian times children attracted major charitable effort, while adult social needs attracted less support. Many origins of social work lay in 'moral improvement' for families in pursuit of appropriate child care. Adults, except as parents, were left much more to the prisons, the Poor Law and mental health systems.

Of course, there is no real discontinuity for many adult services users between childhood and adulthood. The convention of setting up of a division between children's and adults' services, therefore, needs explaining. 'Children in need' are part of families with problems with disability, mental health and other 'adult' problems. Children with behaviour problems who have suffered a poor upbringing often move on to the mental health or criminal justice systems. Children with learning disabilities and with physical disabilities grow up to become adults with such disabilities and to need services as a result.

The 1971 Seebohm reorganisation sought to do away with administrative divisions in providing for families with multiple problems.

Family doctors do not separate their concerns for children from their provision for the whole family. To some extent, therefore, the 1989 and 1990 children and community care legislation turns its back on the family orientation of the primary health care system and the 1971 social services reforms. As well as being a return to a historic division between children and adults, these changes in structure also result from a reaction to the 1989 changes in child care provision. Child care services since the 1970s have come to focus on child protection, and the professional, legislative and procedural specialisation that this seems to require. This is because children are seen as particularly vulnerable. Therefore, the risk both to them and to the political credibility of social work and the social services needs careful responses. 'Adult services' can thus be seen largely as a residual category – all those services for people who are not covered by the 'child care' legislation. This is evident in the differences in legislation. The Children Act 1989 consolidates most of the legislation on children, while the NHS and Community Care Act 1970 merely established a new administrative system without changing the underlying legislation.

Provision for adults, whether at risk or otherwise, has not attained the same degree of political importance. Yet adults, unlike children, are themselves voters and might have a considerable degree of direct political influence. In addition, they may be vulnerable to all kinds of risk. For example, elderly people may lose their capacity to care for themselves, and the minds of mentally ill people may be so disturbed that they are a risk to themselves and to others. The reasons for lack of political importance given to adult vulnerability can only be guessed at, but they may derive from the assumption that adults have legal and personal capacity for independent thought and action. Adults, therefore, are assumed to be able to arrange for their own care. To intervene, specific legal rights are needed, even if adults may be disadvantaging themselves by their behaviour. Related to this are assumptions that children have a right to provision for their care, education and development, while care for adults is residual, remedial or palliative. For children, a panoply of services will try to make sure they make progress towards independent adulthood. Adults, where problems appear, will be returned to a reasonable state. Hence, provision for children is more personally all encompassing and if necessary therapeutic. On the other hand, for adults, provision comprises mainly services needed to (re)gain a reasonable degree of independence.

Another reason for the categorisation of 'adults' together is the uncertain boundary with the NHS. The largest groups of adults using social services are elderly people and people with mental illnesses. Both groups also receive a good deal of care and treatment from the NHS. They are often first treated and assessed in the NHS before being passed to community services. As a result, adult social services mirror the hospital-based NHS separation of geriatric and psychiatric patients from treatment of the 'nuclear' family in NHS general practice.

Following the NHS for adult user groups also arises because provision in social services often, ideally, interlocks with health care. In addition, the community care reforms introduced purchaser-provider splits in both services simultaneously. Increasingly, particularly for elderly people, health care is seen as acute and hospital based, while SSDs provide long-term care in residential care homes. Nursing homes provide residential care where users need nursing help; geriatric day hospitals provide more intensive and medically-based treatment compared with the more social support of SSD day centres. A visiting district nurse (from the NHS) might provide medication and nursing at home, while a home help (from social services) deals with domestic services. However, service users may not understand the formal differences between the roles because of blurred boundaries between services. All these distinctions are uncertain; many overlaps and local arrangements exist. Discharge from hospital care, which the NHS provides free, has been particularly controversial. Years ago, long-term provision might well have been in a long-stay geriatric ward, also free. Now, it is likely to be in a residential or nursing home for which there is often a charge. A particular difficulty has arisen from the growth during the later twentieth century in house ownership, which means that an elderly person may have a considerable capital resource. However, to use this to pay for care involves losing a home base and liquidating assets that would pass, through inheritance, to descendents. This is a disincentive to accept care, and has engaged the collective mind of the Royal Commission on Long-Term Care (Sutherland Report 1999). Its recommendation that all personal care should be free at the point of delivery (the NHS principle) has not been accepted by the Westminster Government of Tony Blair, but has been accepted by the Scottish Parliament, becoming one of the important differences between the nations in the UK.

Turning to mentally ill people, acute care will usually be in hospital and by outpatient clinic. Services might equally be provided by community psychiatric nurses, a new profession developing in the 1970s and 1980s, or by social workers. To the outsider and to many insiders the roles look similar, except for the approved social worker's function of assessing and authorising compulsory admissions to psychiatric hospital. However, the skills and roles are different, with nurses fitting better with the medical team in providing individualistically based work and social workers having a more outward-looking focus on family and community (Sheppard 1991).

Services, care and social work

Another important consequence for social work of the community care reforms and the creation of the 'adult services' division is the focus on 'services' and 'care' rather than 'social work'. Related to this is a shift in terminology from calling the people who receive social work 'clients' to calling them 'users'.

The community care reforms are primarily concerned with reorganising how services are delivered. Consequently, the role of social workers as care managers, while unclear in government documents, is focused on co-ordinating services rather than on therapy. So, for people with dementia, effective social work might involve reminiscence work to try to stimulate memory and various techniques to help someone with dementia remain connected with their surroundings. Similarly, an adult with learning disabilities might need training in social skills to manage a more independent life, or might need anger management training to control behaviour which challenges carers and others around the adult. In social work, the worker would create an interpersonal relationship with the adult and other important people around, and within the continuing relationship would use such techniques where they were of benefit to the adult. However, such activities have become increasingly specialised, and are also often carried out in multiprofessional settings, so that expecting a generalist social worker to fit them in eclectically to their everyday work is increasingly unrealistic.

Many such useful therapeutic techniques are increasingly seen as 'services', and the purchaser–provider split encourages specialist units or private practitioners to establish identifiable services rather than take on this work within conventional social work. Often people qualified as counsellors or psychologists take up such roles. This leaves social work with an increasingly generic, administrative role which many regard as at a lower professional level than social work education and skills might offer.

Consequently, many of the roles involved are now often described as 'social care' rather than social work. The 'social care' label implies an element of long-term care, with the purpose of maintaining independence, rather than short-term therapeutic intervention designed to bring about a change and improvement in social functioning. 'Social care' also distinguishes care provision from assessment and planning, which inheres in the care management role. The term 'social care' has also developed with the increase in training through national vocational qualifications and levels lower than professional education for social work.

Care (case) management in adult services

Care management is a way of organising social provision that emphasises the coordinating services so that they appear to clients as an integrated whole. It developed in the USA in the 1970s, where it is called case management, and has been refined and extended in its influence since (Moxley 1989; Vourlekis and Greene 1992). Different formulations of it have developed towards an analysis (Payne 1995, p.55, drawing on Steinberg and Carter 1983; Weill *et al.* 1985; Moxley

1989; SSI/SWSG 1991a, 1991b), which sees it as a process comprising five main elements.

The process of care management

The process is circular, starting with an *assessment* of the user's needs. Then, the case manager *plans* with users a 'package of services' from a range of services available and *implements* the package. In the final two stages, the case manager *monitors* how the integration of the services is working; that is, there is a regular check on how the 'package' is working out. Then, periodically, the case manager *evaluates* whether the outcomes of providing the package are appropriate for the user. This evaluation leads to a further assessment and refinement of the plans.

This process is similar to many formulations of social work practice. However, three elements distinguish case management from other forms of social work and professional practice. The first point is that care management is 'needs-led'. Most social work is based on the social worker's theoretical system or the agency's practices and procedures. Needs-led services construct the pattern of services anew in a way appropriate to the particular client's needs. The second crucial element is the idea of constructing a 'package of services' from a range of possible options. The package is adapted to the needs assessed, each element being integrated with the whole. Each 'service user' receives a different package. Changing terminology from 'client' to 'service user' reflects a rhetoric of service provision rather than clienthood in a therapeutic service. The third distinctive element of care management is monitoring and review. Rather than provide services as requested until there is a problem, care management imposes more careful management of resources. Regular monitoring ensures that the integration of the package is working, allied to periodic reconsideration of the whole provision.

Three forms of care management

Beardshaw and Towell (1990, p.18) identified three forms of care management. These have been adapted in different services and for different purposes. In *social care entrepreneurship*, a worker creates and co-ordinates a 'package of services' from the range available, suitable for the service user's needs. Although the package comes from different agencies, the overall service should appear 'seamless' to the client, as though it is one service with different well-coordinated elements. In *brokerage* services, care managers advise and assist users to create a package of services. The worker mediates between the client and the services, perhaps contacting the services to gain their support for services to the client, perhaps helping the client to make the right approaches. With brokerage, the client takes more responsibility and the worker is a supporter and adviser. *Multiprofessional* services organise a service through a 'keyworker' from a range of professionals so that it is delivered consistently. Other professionals work through or refer back to the keyworker, who is usually the main person in contact with the client. Because these different services seem most appropriate for different client groups, they have become associated with different service organisations in Britain.

Social care entrepreneurship

Social care entrepreneurship was adopted by the Government as its recommended model for social workers and care managers practising within the community care reforms. It builds upon the administrative model that British social work generally follows. That is, the concern is with organising provision rather than the therapeutic work that American social work focuses upon. Thus the emphasis is on assessment of service users and, particularly after the Carers (Recognition and Services) Act (1995) discussed above, their carers. 'Assessment' has a legal implication: once someone is assessed as needing services, the local authority has some degree of duty to provide them (Mandelstam 1999, pp.69–147). Users and carers should be involved in assessment and care planning. However, the reality in many places and for many users is that few alternatives are available. The idea of a flexible and specially created package is reserved for people with extremely complex and unusual needs, who receive a full assessment. Examples might be mentally ill or physically disabled people with long-term care needs who are being established independently in the community for the first time, or after a period of institutionalisation. Most people receive a more limited assessment and a more standardised service. Examples might be elderly people who receive home help, day care or residential care services. Increasingly, people in any but the highest priorities receive few, if any, services. Therefore, many workers see the ideal of needs-led services being misdirected towards assessment to ration services.

Brokerage

Brokerage is applicable in any service, and Pilling's (1992) early research on case management in Britain examined some more general brokerage schemes. She found that both sides valued the continuing relationship with clients and that mostly the case managers' advocacy on behalf of their clients was accepted and did not interfere with priority systems in agencies. Good packages of services were achieved. However, where access to particular services was difficult, the brokerage model did not ensure that they were provided. Similarly, Bland's (1994, 1996) studies of a case management scheme with brokerage elements for elderly people identified a problem in getting unwilling professionals to deliver services if they were dubious about case management as a technique. She comments that the brokerage and advocacy elements of case management were less important in Britain than in the USA.

In spite of its general applicability, brokerage has become particularly associated in Britain with direct payment schemes, particularly for physically disabled people. Brandon (1998, p.148), for example, defines it as 'a system set up to arrange for the direct payment of money to an individual or individuals with a disability'. This came about because it was adapted from Canadian models used for this user group (Brandon 1998, p.149–50) and because its availability as a technique coincided with the development of the powerful Independent Living Movement. The movement originated from the formation of the British Council of Organisations of Disabled People (BCODP) whose membership was of organisations of disabled people themselves. Previously existing organisations were mainly of their relatives or professionals and volunteer helpers. Independent Living organisations argue that disability arises not from the impairment which the disabled person suffers but from environments designed for able-bodied people. The philosophy of the movement is to promote the empowerment of disabled people to make choices in asserting control over their lives and to participate fully in society (Morris 1993b). Morris's (1993a) research study identifies, as a way of promoting such empowerment, direct payments to disabled people to employ their own personal assistance.

Multiprofessional care management

Multiprofessional care management has become particularly influential in services for mentally ill people. This has occurred for three reasons. First, services for mentally ill people have traditionally involved a range of professionals in hospitals, and this arrangement has continued as mentally ill people are discharged from hospitals or are mainly dealt with in the community. Second, the process of moving people out of mental hospitals usually requires co-operation between hospital and community services. This is because it has to bring housing, social services, nursing and medical care together with occupation, which may involve education, leisure and work provision. Finally, many such patients need risk assessment and careful monitoring from a variety of professional points of view to reduce risk of violence or suicide. Because of the risk, brokerage is inappropriate. Social care entrepreneurship is not ideal because it is mainly concerned with the delivery of separate services rather than services integrated with medical and other therapeutic treatment.

The risk incurred with many patients has raised public anxiety about this user group. One early case, the killing of a social worker, Isobel Schwartz, by a mentally ill client in the late 1980s led to the adoption of the 'care programme approach' which is a form of multiprofessional case management, using a keyworker (Reith 1998). Government guidance (DoH 1996) requires the approach to be applied where certain risk factors exist: it encourages multiprofessional working and careful planning to avoid danger. Although the requirements are similar to care management in the community care system, the multiprofessional element gives it a different focus. In addition, the mental health team usually undertakes it, led from the health service, whereas the social services lead community care. The care programme approach was introduced earlier than care management in community care. However, services to mentally ill people are provided through care management in the community care system, and the two approaches often overlap and conflict. Therefore, the existence of the two approaches can cause the same confusion that the care programme approach was introduced to avoid.

As this form of care management has developed, 'assertive' services have been emphasised: 'assertive outreach', 'assertive community treatment', clinical case management and intensive case management. Here, the service actively seeks out and tries to engage the user. Users are not allowed to reject the service or drift away. They are sought out and actively brought back into contact. This is considered crucial to reducing risk of suicide and violence, and reducing deterioration in behaviour and quality of life that arises when users stop taking medication or lose social contacts.

Social work roles in adult services

The purchaser–provider split creates in adult services work the possibility of three different field social work roles which overlap with each other (Payne 1995). Two are the conventional social work roles described by the Barclay Report (1982) on social work roles as 'counselling' and 'social care planning'. Counselling involves interpersonal work, with individual service users and both their families and their social network, to help them deal with problems and change their surroundings. Social care planning focuses on promoting services and community support, involving service users collectively in these activities. The third role, care management, is a more recent innovation. It is important because of its integration into the community care reforms and because of the more specialised uses reviewed in the previous section.

Care management is a controversial innovation because of its effect on the established professional role of social work. There are three positions in the debate (Payne 1996). One view, strongly expressed in Payne (1995), considers care management as a form, or implementation, of social work. In this view, care management practice includes the therapeutic and interpersonal elements of social work. The second view sees conventional social work in the British social services as having weaknesses that in some ways are corrected by case management. The third view sees care management as an example of the influence of 1980s managerialism on social work. In this view, effective social work has been damaged by the influence of care management.

The argument for the first view, that care management is a form of implementation of social work, lies primarily in the origins of care management and the range of possibilities that it offers. It originated as a development of social work methods in the USA, and early implementations of it in the UK, for example, stress its role in clarifying and developing the social work role. Comprehensive accounts of care management show how it relies on continuing interpersonal relationships between worker, service user, carers and others involved. It also calls on the social work skills of effective liaison and co-ordination. All of this relates directly to conventional social work roles. However, against this view it can be argued that care management has not been implemented like this in British community care. The heavy government prescription of social care entrepreneurship as the basis for care management practice prevented, as we have seen, the full use of care management possibilities for flexible work. For example, Hadley and Clough's (1996) research found that many workers experienced the changes as bureaucratic and obstructive to effective interpersonal relationships with users. Assessment was treated as a way of rationing services rather than of creating new types of provision. To cope with this, a formalised system of care management was adopted, with heavy use of structured multi-page forms with many tick-boxes. This made care management seem more bureaucratic rather than more flexible, as the ideals of case management propose. Research by Stalker (1993) found early on that over-complex forms discouraged flexibility and sharing with service users. Lewis and Glennerster's (1996) comprehensive study of the implementation of community care in four local authorities found a lack of clarity about the model of care management to be used and how it might be developed. Instead, the focus was on achieving the government's cost constraint and privatising organisational objectives.

The second view of care management, that social work has weaknesses that care management addresses, proposes that social work is often not based on clear assessment and planning and on effective agreements with users and carers. In addition, social work has often avoided concern for controlling costs and achieving purposeful aims with users. To the extent that care management enforces this kind of clarity and objective setting, it is a useful addition to conventional practice. Clark and Lapsley's (1996) book focusing on planning represents this position.

The third view of care management, that it damages many important aspects of social work, is reviewed by Sheppard's (1995) study. In some ways the mirror image of the second view, this position identifies the New Right political origins of managerialism, which focuses on control of professionals and costs through processes like care management. Pollitt (1993) argues that this often introduces organisational methods that are inappropriate to the role and responsibilities of the public sector. In this view, the individualisation of care management and involving users and carers is not concerned with achieving social work values of empowerment, but is another method of social control. It co-opts users and carers into the system to pursue their individual interests rather than being concerned about the needs of all, and uses them to control professional discretion, which would reveal inadequacies in the services.

Beyond field social work, where care management has drastically changed social work roles, day and residential social work have also changed. In some respects, community care seeks to displace residential care as the preferred way of providing care services. However, residential and day care are more appropriately seen as part of a range of provision from which choices and combinations are made to create the package (Wagner Report 1988; Davies 1998). So, a particular service user might have some domiciliary care with some day care, perhaps on different days of the week, combined with residential care to provide respite, such as a holiday, for home carers from the stress of constant caring. Because of the purchaser–provider split, use of private sector residential care, purchased by care managers in the local authority, has increased. However, Davies (1998) argues that a range of flexible types of 'shelter-with-care' is beginning to emerge. This places residential and day care on the borders of community provision, with an increasing range of possibilities for practice (Jack 1998). However, it may be that this will be seen as a form of social care, with the term 'social work' reserved for individual, family and group work in the community.

Social Work with children and families

The current framework for the provision of social work to children and families in England derives from the Children Act 1989[8], implemented in 1991. This was both a consolidation Act, incorporating the bulk of previous children's legislation and also an Act that created a radically new legislative framework. This Act was introduced in response to a series of perceived difficulties in the provision of social work for children and families during the 1970s and 1980s. According to Packman and Jordan's (1991) near-contemporaneous account, these were:

- the legacy of the debates surrounding the 'permanency movement' which drew on research such as that by Rowe and Lambert (1973), which highlighted the damaging effects upon children of not being placed with families but being left in institutional forms of care

- the findings of a significant body of research into child care – much of it commissioned by the Department of Health, for example the increasingly common use of emergency measures to remove children (Place of Safety Orders) reported by both Millham, Bullock *et al.* (1986) and Packman, Randall *et al.* (1986)

- all too apparent failures in social work practice evidenced in a succession of reports into child deaths, in particular those of Jasmine Beckford, Tyra Henry and Kimberley Carlile.

Reform of the child care system in England has always been more responsive to the 'stick' of disaster than the 'carrot' of genuine desire to reform the lot of deprived and vulnerable young people. Lord Mackay (Lord Chancellor), during the progress of the Act through Parliament stated that this piece of legislation was 'the most comprehensive and far reaching reform of child care law in living memory' (Hansard).

These oft-quoted words emphasise the importance of the Children Act. The primary importance of the Act derives from the attempt by those who framed this piece of legislation to redefine the nature of the relationship between three parties the state, the family and the child. According to Fox Harding (1991), the Act gives expression to a desire to reconcile a series of ideas that are inevitably radically opposed to each other in respect of: the needs of children; the protection of children from harm, damage and abuse; according due weight and value to children's rights; while preserving, promoting and enhancing family and family ties, roles and responsibilities. Commenting upon the Act in relation to the reconciliation of the rights of families, children and the role of the state, Packman and Jordan (1991) wrote, in a perceptive comment written soon after the Act was passed, as follows:

> It [the Children Act] treads a tightrope between children and parents, the state and families, courts and local authorities, and where power is unequal it tries to safeguard the weak. Thus the needs of children come first, because of their dependence and vulnerability, but the role of parents and other significant adults in their lives is given increased respect and consideration. (p.324)

These tensions find expression in three major principles that are embedded in the Act and find expression in the development of children and family social work in England during the years following the passing of the Children Act.

1. Paramountcy

> If a child comes before a court, the child's welfare must be 'paramount', throughout his or her childhood, that is, up to the age of 18, in any decision made about that child. Courts will consider a variety of factors to help establish the

paramountcy of the child's welfare. These include: the wishes and feelings of the child – having due regard for the age of the child; the physical, emotional and educational needs of that child – including any harm that the child has suffered or may suffer; factors such as the age, gender and background of the child; and, importantly, it is enshrined in the legislation that consideration must be given to the child's racial background.

2. Parental responsibility

Prior to this legislation, the responsibilities of parents toward their children were not clearly stated. The Act has introduced the notion of 'parental responsibility' to encompass the variety of rights, duties and obligations that parents owe to their children. Most importantly, these obligations are not dissipated if the child is no longer living with the parent either through divorce or because the child is in the care of a local authority. In these situations, parents still have responsibility for and obligations of care towards their children.

3. Partnership

Although the term 'partnership' does not appear in the Act the 'partnership principle' appears to be fundamental to practice under the Act in that social workers are expected to involve parents and families in all aspects of their children's lives when the state intervenes in a family – wherever this is possible. New ways of working that have the potential to promote greater involvement by families and also encourage a partnership approach by shifting power away from professionals are being introduced in some parts of the country. One such development is the introduction of family group conferences (Morris and Tunnard 1996).

The significance of the Act for the provision of services to children in need and children in need of protection cannot be overestimated.

During the 1980s in England the predominant emphasis within children's services had been on the protection of children perceived to be at risk of some kind of harm. The provision of support for families and the protection of children have frequently been conceptualised as distinct and contrasting activities. Funding or effort placed in one direction inevitably entails that the other is being ignored. The pressures of fears of child death have often persuaded local authorities to place more emphasis on protection than support. The Children Act encourages a refocusing of effort to provide more family support and earlier intervention (Department of Health 1991). A range of different forms of services are suggested, including: family centres that can provide a local base close to and accessible for families; respite care for children and families; practical services as well as longer-term counselling and therapy for families. There is evidence that in some parts of England attempts were made to develop preventative services in line with the sprit of the Children Act even as early as the first few years after the passing of the Act: see, for example, the discussion of schemes to provide respite care for families under stress (Bradley and Aldgate 1994) are of work which has been described as a substantial are of growth and one that is now regulated by the provisions of the Children Act (Robinson and Stalker 1993). These efforts to develop preventative services have been reinforced by government policy circulars[9] following the publication of an influential summary of major recent research projects on children and families (Department of Health 1995a), the upshot of which was to call for a more substantial refocusing of services for children and families (see below).

Quality protects

In September 1998 the then Secretary of State for Health, Frank Dobson, launched the Labour Government's three-year programme to modernise (the Government's catchword) and reform children's social services (Department of Health 1998). The main or most important elements of this programme, as highlighted by Government itself, were:

- to set clear new national objectives for children's services that specify outcomes for children; precise targets for local authorities to achieve will also be set in some policy areas

- an emphasis upon partnership between central and local government with policy development originating from consultation with other interests, such as the voluntary sector

- an enhanced role for local councillors, strengthening their responsibilities and increasing their accountability to ensure that the interests of children come first and that children in public care are given as good a start in life as possible

- a requirement for all local authorities to produce a Quality Protects Management Action Plan

- a new grant to £375m payable over three years to improve adoption services; support to care leavers; information management; assessment care planning and record keeping; quality assurance systems; and to enable the views of young people to be better heard.

The importance of the Quality Protects Programme lies in the creation of new ways for government to manage and control the activities of local government in respect of children's services. This is achieved in three ways: first, by strengthening internal controls on service provision through the increase in responsibilities of local councillors; second, Government-specified targets; third, by making the public aware of the performance of councils through the publication of league tables and statistics. Hence, one year later, in November 1999, the Government introduced the 'performance assessment framework' that ranks the performance of social services departments across some 35 nationally applicable performance indicators (www.doh.gov/paf). Despite claims that this would introduce 'league tables' Denise Platt, Chief Inspector of Social Services, said 'We published performance indicators to encourage authorities to ask questions about differences in their services. It's unfortunate that it was misinterpreted in the macho way that it was' (News 2000, p.9).

It may not have been the intention to set up a competitive league table, but John Hutton, Minister of Health, announced the day before the publication of the framework that social services departments in some 17 local authorities had been identified as delivering unacceptably low standards of service, were officially designated as being 'at risk', and may at some future date, if no improvement is apparent, lose the right to run social services in their area. He placed these local authorities on 'special measures' because of poor performance in certain areas. Reporting this state of affairs in the *Guardian*, of the five indicators published, four related to children and families (Brindle 1999). It is early days as yet, but this approach by Government to manage and control services better for children and families may herald the future not only for services for children and families but more widely across the social services. This identification of underperforming public authorities, seen most strongly in education, may be balanced by the Government's intention to identify 'beacon councils' (akin to the beacon schools in respect of education) that will share expertise, policy and practice. (For example, in January 2000, in respect of services to care-leavers four authorities: Suffolk, Wakefield, Kensington and Chelsea and Westminster were identified as beacon councils).

Assessment of children in need

A new framework for the assessment of children in need (replacing the so-called 'Orange Book' (Department of Health 1988)) has been introduced as official guidance, with effect from April 2001, by the Department of Health, the Department for Education and Employment and the Home Office (Department of Health, Department for Education and Employment *et al.* 2000). This new framework represents an unusual example of government interdepartmental co-operation – in current jargon, an example of 'joined-up thinking'. The jointness of the approach is suggestive of a desire by Government to take a holistic approach to children in need evidenced by policy statements to end childhood poverty within 20 years and to tackle problems of social exclusion as they affect and blight the social, educational and employment opportunities of the young. It is envisaged that in the fullness of time this form of assessment will become standard across education, social services and youth justice, possibly avoiding some of the damaging divisions of the past where 'the deprived' have been assessed and treated differently from 'the depraved' and both differently from 'the disabled'. As the accompanying practice guidance seeks to establish, this new framework is 'grounded in knowledge' (Department of Health 2000). In particular how theory, research and practice can be used to generate an understanding of the meaning and significance of how the three 'domains' or 'systems' (these are: the child's developmental needs, parenting capacity and family and environmental factors) of the assessment framework 'contribute to the understanding of human growth and development and the interaction between internal and external factors which have an impact on the lives of individuals' (p.1).

The model proposed for the assessment of children in need combines an emphasis upon children's developmental needs combined with an ecological model of the social and familial phenomena that surround the child.

If successful in shifting practice, this assessment framework may have a powerful impact upon the practice of social workers in the way that the needs of children and families are conceptualised and may represent a step forward in the use of knowledge to inform social work practice.

Child Protection

From the 1970s until the present date, a national system for the identification and management of child abuse has continuously evolved. It was the death of Maria Colwell in 1973, and the consequent enquiry report (*Report of the Committee into the care and supervison provided in relation to Maria Colwell* 1974) that presaged the creation of an ever more complex system of structures, guidelines and government circulars. The then newly created 'Seebohm' structures (Seebohm Report 1968) inspired social services departments to welcome the process of bureaucatisation of child protection as the belief permeated all levels of social services thinking that if only the perfect system could be found then the problem of child abuse would be conquered. Hence, as one high-profile inquiry into one child's death followed another (see, for example, Department of Health 1991) successive accretions of guidance and circulars from the Department of Health left a rich series of sedimentary layers of policy and structures. During the 1980s, the deaths of Jasmine Beckford (*A Child in Trust* 1985) and Kimberley Carlile (*A Child in Mind* 1987) were particularly significant in shaping the evolution of the child protection system. So was the débâcle over the manner and extent of removal of children from their families in Cleveland, due to the suspicion that these children had been sexually abused by a member of the family (*Report of the Inquiry into Child Abuse in Cleveland* 1988).

By the early 1990s these various forces resulted in the construction of a child protection system that included child protection registers, regional interdisciplinary child protection committees and a plethora of mandatory procedural guidance emanating from the Department of Health, resulting in a situation in many parts of England where social workers have been concerned to follow procedure blindly in the misplaced belief that procedure alone will protect children. The nemesis of this belief in procedure can be found in the conclusions of the Department of Health review of research published up to 1995 (Dept. of Health 1995). Here, it is recognised that many children and families have been subject to unwarranted and unjustified intrusions into their lives through the investigation processes of the required child protection procedures. In addition, there is strong evidence that families have become afraid of any kind of involvement with child protection agencies through fear of their children being removed to care. This belief among families remains strong even though less than one in a hundred children referred to the child protection procedures are removed from their family. The Department of Health has recognised that considerable energy and resources are ineffectively employed or wasted by all professional organisations in the mechanisms used to identify child abuse. Hence, in response to the findings in the 'Messages from Research', the Department of Health (1995a) has called for organisations to 'refocus' child protection work. This refocusing should both provide more preventative services and a greater emphasis on meeting the needs of all children in need – not just those seen to be at risk of abuse. There is also a shift of emphasis towards a reliance upon the 'professional judgement' of the individual social worker to counteract the belief in procedure. This may mean that social workers make more informed judgements grounded in evidence-based practice or that social workers are held even more strongly to account for failure than has been the case in the past – a fearful prospect!

Turning around the monolith of child protection procedures in England is rather akin to turning around a large ocean-going oil tanker – corrections to the set course are small and slow to take effect. Moreover, it will be interesting to see for how long the refocusing agenda is maintained in the light of further child deaths such as those of Adjo (Anna) Climbie (aged seven) who died of hypothermia in St Mary's Hospital, Paddington on 25 February 2000 after a period of sustained abuse by her great aunt and her great aunt's boyfriend[10]. The death of Anna Climbie aroused much media attention, an extensive report will be produced in due course and the London Borough of Haringey, where Anna lived, has been made the subject of 'special measures' on account of the poor level of service provided to Anna. Will other local authorities seek to revert to the management of child protection by procedure as a consequence of this and other child deaths?

Substitute family care

A significant issue during the 1990s has been the approach toward the transracial placement of children. In practice, this has always entailed the placement of black children with white parents. Policy in respect of trans-racial placement of children in England has been varied, ambiguous and often contentious. Views about the desirability of placing children in a different race family to that of the child's own birth family owe as much to ideology and belief as to validated empirical research about outcomes for children (see, for example, Bagley 1993, Rushton and Minnis 1997, Thoburn, Murcock et al. 1997). Current policy seems to emphasise the importance of considering the needs of the child holistically rather than identifying any single characteristic of the child as the sole or dominant factor that determines placement.

ADOPTION

The 1990s saw the publication of a considerable body of research about family placement, providing the backcloth for more informed discussion about policy and the implementation of policy that is grounded in a thorough understanding of research. Some of the most important research explores the needs of children and outcome of services in meeting such needs (Fratter, Rowe *et al.* 1991). During 1999, adoption became a major national issue in England, receiving much attention in the national media; the immediate cause being the illegal abduction of two foster children. Jennifer and Jeffrey Bramley spent four months in hiding in Ireland, having fled their home in Ramsey, Cambridgeshire with their two foster children Jade (aged 2) and Hannah (aged 4) when they were refused permission by Cambridgeshire Social Services to adopt these children.[11] Just as the media interest in the 'Bramley' case was subsiding another rose to national prominence when in January 2001 Flintshire Social Services removed (EPO under Children Act 1989) two six-month twin girls, Kimberley and Belinda, from the care of Judith (aged 47) and Alan Kilshaw (aged 45). The Kilshaws had previously paid £8200 to a Tina Johnson, head of Californian internet-based company, 'A Caring Heart Agency', to adopt these children. The children were adopted in Little Rock, Arkansas. Subsequent to the adoption, it was revealed in the press that the children's mother (Tania Wecker) had previously arranged for the children to be adopted by another couple, resident in USA, Richard and Vicki Allen. They are reported to have paid £4000 to adopt the children and the children had been living with Richard and Vicki Allen. The twins are reported to have been taken by Tania Wecker from this family whence they were given to Judith and Alan Kilshaw. In a bizarre twist, the Kilshaws and the Allens appeared together on the Oprah Winfrey chat show – something that can have little relevance to settling this complex dispute. It is not usual for adoption to become a matter of media concern. It is questionable whether the interest of the media in the 'human interest' of such cases promotes the interests of the children involved.

In the light of such cases it may not be surprising that adoption has become a matter of concern in the highest political circles, possibly in response to these high-profile cases. Unusually for a prime minister, Tony Blair has taken a considerable personal interest[12] in the development of policies and strategies for adoption. In February 2000 he commissioned the Cabinet Office's Performance and Innovation Unit to conduct a review of adoption in England and Wales. This unit produced a consultation document, *Adoption,* (July 2000) and in December 2000 the Government published a White Paper, 'Adoption – a New Approach' (Department of Health 2000), with a foreword authored in the name of the Prime Minister. This White Paper identifies a series of problems associated with adoption at present, significant among these being the following:

- the process of placing a child with potential adopters and completing the adoption is too slow, on average the time taken is almost two years from a child being first 'looked after' to being placed

- likewise the process of recruiting adopters is too slow

- perhaps most importantly, the outcomes for looked-after children are poor, with poor educational attainment for the majority and a significant number experiencing mental health problems

- and of these looked-after children only 4.7 per cent in 1999 were offered the opportunity of a permanent substitute family.

A clear policy directive is emerging from the White Paper, a drive to increase the numbers of looked-after children who are adopted. This policy drive is grounded in an ideology that rests upon the belief in family life as an 'insulator' against these and other problems. The White Paper proposes several significant modifications to current adoption. These include:

- national standards for adoption practice, specifying the standards expected of local authorities

- a new Adoption and Permanence Taskforce will be created and charged with the functions of disseminating best practice and working to tackle poor performance

- the introduction of timescales for 'continuously looked-after children'; a plan should both be made and implemented within six months of the commencement of a child being continuously looked after. Where appropriate a substitute family should be found for the child within the next six months

- a National Adoption Register (England and Wales) will be introduced to assist the matching process between children and families.

These initiatives will be linked to both a targeted increase of 40 per cent[13] of the number of looked-after children who are adopted by the year 2004–05 (an example of target setting under the Quality Protects Programme) and earmarked funding of £66.5m during a three-year period (again from the Quality Protects Programme). The significance of these proposed changes lies in the shift towards providing permanent families for more looked-after children than at present.

FOSTER CARE

A series of critical reports concerning the state of fostering in England was published during the 1990s. For example, in 1996, the Social Services Inspectorate Report (SSI), *Inspection of Local Authority Fostering* (Social Services Inspectorate 1996) identified significant failures in respect of fostering provision by all of the six local authorities inspected. According to Warren (1999), the most worrying aspect of this report was that 'many looked after children had not had a comprehensive assessment of their needs – and only a third had individual care plans' (p.49). The report also identified a number of other significant failings in the provision of foster care. Early in 1997, the Association of Directors of Social Services (ADSS) published a report based on a survey of some 84 directors of social services and over 500 foster carers (Association of Directors of Social Services 1997). This report found deficiencies in the provision of foster care and called upon the Department of Health to develop national frameworks for the provision of foster care. In a report published soon afterwards, the National Foster Care Association (NFCA) highlighted considerable variations in the quality and nature of foster care services across various local authorities, based on a survey of the vast majority of social services departments in England (Waterhouse 1997). Towards the end of 1997, the Utting report was published concerning the safety of children who live away from home. In addition, Berridge (1997) reviewed published research on foster care. These various reports created a climate in which significant change was possible, such that in September 1998 the UK Joint Working Party on Foster Care was established, under the chairmanship of Tom White, with the intention of developing national standards for foster care across the UK, not just for England, involving voluntary bodies, the Department of Health, the Northern Ireland, Scottish and Welsh Offices. Following an extensive process of consultation, a set of consultative standards were published and adopted in 1999.

Criminal and youth justice

During the 1990s one of the distinctive features of English social work was the progressive disconnection of social work with offenders from other forms of social work practice. Since the mid nineteenth century and the work of the 'Court Missionaries' (the founders of the probation ideal) a primary aim of the probation service has been to divert offenders from custodial sentences and to provide social work in the community to encourage and assist offenders not to re-offend. This approach to offenders has been grounded in welfare principles: the provision of professional help to ameliorate the social causes of much petty crime. However, in one of the characteristic last breaths of a dying and decaying Conservative Government, the then Home Secretary Michael Howard, against professional advice, forced through legislation to change the function of the probation service (Home Office 1995, 1996) the aim being to transform the probation service to a vehicle to control and punish offenders in the community rather than to divert offenders from custodial sentences. An important strategy to achieve this aim has been to change the background of those employed in the probation service. Hence, from 1996 onwards, probation officers have no longer been educated as social workers but have their own qualification (Diploma in Probation Studies) using employment-based training routes, significantly increasing the control that employers have over the nature and form of education for the probation service. This shift in philosophy of the probation service towards becoming a community-based criminal punishment agency has been maintained by the Labour Government (1997–2001). Hence in England, by purpose and design, social work with offenders was legislated and organised out of existence during the 1990s.

Since 1995 there have also been major changes in the policies and structures adopted in England for the management of youth crime. As with much social policy in respect of social work the response of Government to the media's moral panics has been highly significant. The sustained coverage in the media of all elements of the murder on 23 February 1993 of James Bulger (aged two) by two young people, almost always referred to in the style reserved for adult criminals as 'Thompson and Venables' (then aged ten years)[14] demonised these young people and set a climate for change in the English youth justice system.

Following a significant gestation period the Crime and Disorder Act 1998, which came into force on 1 October 1998, has introduced a wide range of changes for the management of youth offending. One of the most significant changes has been the creation of a National Youth Justice Board for England and Wales, charged with the dual responsibility of setting required national standards in all areas of youth justice work to monitor the implementation of these standards. So, for example, from April 2000, the government introduced a new system for the management of quality in respect of secure placements for young offenders[15]. From that date the Youth Justice Board has been given the responsibility of purchasing places in secure accommodation from the ten Young Offender Institutions (YOIs) in England and other providers of secure accommodation such as local authorities. The purchasing of places is dependent on the provision of places where quality standards, such as young people can lead a 'purposeful day' and can be taught according to the prescriptions of the national curriculum can be met. The overwhelming majority of secure accommodation is provided through the YOIs, and it is likely that some of the smaller units will find it uneconomic to continue to provide places to the required standards. Not that the standards of care provided previously in the YOIs have been high or have met the needs of children and young people – as can be seen from the report by the Chief Inspector of Prisons, Sir David Ramsbotham, into Portand YOI (Ramsbotham 2000), which was criticised for the scandalous conditions in which young people were living. There is and remains considerable room for improvement in the quality of care provided in what seems to becoming known as the 'secure estate' for young people. Relative to other EU countries England imprisons a large proportion of offenders, often in very poor prison accommodation. Possibly the attitude of the English to those incarcerated in secure accommodation – whether the young or the old – is less than sympathetic.

Another major change introduced by the Crime and Disorder Act 1998 has been the requirement to create interdisciplinary teams (consisting of educational workers, social workers, police and probation officers) in all local authority areas to develop and provide a co-ordinated response to youth crime across conventional professional boundaries. These new Youth Offending Teams (YOTs) have range of new orders to recommend to the courts and to implement, orders such as the 'action plan order' (an order detailing a plan of action to help the young person avoid offending in the future); 'reparation order' (requiring the offender to make reparation for the crime either to the victim directly or to the community at large). It is not yet possible to provide any evaluation of the impact of these various changes to the management of youth crime. They do represent a shift in philosophy. There is an emphasis on being 'tough on crime'[16] and being seen to be tough on crime, rather than on the welfare needs of youth offenders. For example, cautions by the police can no longer be used. These were effective in diverting a significant number of young offenders from the youth justice system; many who were cautioned did not re-offend. Similar types of cases to those that would have received a police caution in the past are likely, under the new arrangements, to have a court hearing.

Social work education

Social work education in England has a long history in the higher education system, building on courses introduced in universities in the main urban areas during the early part of the century. Government took a hand during the 1930s in probation and later in the 1940s and 1950s, in setting up specialised courses for child care, and welfare work in the 1960s. These courses were all brought together after the implementation of the Seebohm Report in 1971, when local authority SSDs were formed to incorporate most forms of local government social work. Shortly afterwards, the Central Council for Education and Training in Social Work (CCETSW) was formed to develop and validate professional social work education. Validation involves a judgement about whether the organisation and curriculum of a programme are a valid preparation for the qualification awarded and, in the case of social work, for beginning practice.

A number of disparate qualifications were brought together, and with the introduction of the Certificate of Qualification in Social Work (CQSW) in 1972, a standard qualification was introduced for social workers. It provided two-year courses for non-graduates, one year for postgraduates who had a social science degree. Both included placements in field practice. These were based in universities and other higher education institutions. A considerable amount of curriculum development work was done, and documents from this period reviewing aspects of the syllabus content for social work were influential.

An important innovation, also bringing together a previously existing range of specialist courses, was the creation of the Certificate in Social Service (CSS), a part-time course for serving staff which was generally used to second existing residential care staff for training. CSS was generally provided by consortia of agencies and further education colleges, whose main work is at a lower educational level than the universities where CSQW was based. This proved to be an important management model, since it recognised that SSDs formed a larger and more powerful interest group which was more enthusiastic to influence the organisation and curriculum of courses than agencies had previously been. Although at the outset CSS was regarded as a lower-level qualifi-

cation than CQSW, it was eventually recognised as an equivalent qualification.

In the 1980s a review of the system proposed a three-year qualification leading to a general social work qualification, with a specialised
final year (CCETSW 1987). However, the Government rejected this
proposal as too costly, and a two-year qualification was continued, the
Diploma in Social Work (DipSW) which incorporated an element of
specialisation in the second year (CCETSW 1989, 1993). All DipSW
courses at all levels were two years long. The management model
adopted was derived from the CSS, which was merged with DipSW.
Thus, social work courses are provided by consortia of agencies in 'partnership' with local further and higher education institutions. In some
areas, these include all the possible colleges; in others there is more than
one consortium, each with a different character and partners.

CCETSW has always had significant influence on curriculum
development, and a feature of the new requirements for the DipSW was
a significant focus on anti-racist and anti-discriminatory practice. This
was encouraged by development projects (CCETSW 1991), but proved
controversial in the New Right political environment of the Conservative Governments of the 1980s and 1990s (Jones 1993). Jones (1996)
argues that there is a tension between the objectives of academic education in social work and the wish by governments to subvert and control
its practice in pursuit of social ideologies. At the time of writing, a major
review of the DipSW has been conducted by a consultancy firm, JM
Consulting, on behalf of the Department of Health. Significant
changes in the curriculum and organisation and delivery of social work
education at professional qualification level are expected (www.doh.
gov.uk), in part to halt the considerable decline in the numbers of
people coming forward for professional education. In April 2001, a
government statement announced that the main element of the new
system was to be a three-year undergraduate degree as the basic social
work qualification.

Post-qualification training for social workers has had a chequered
history, and a variety of models has been adopted, none of which has
really stimulated a substantial provision. A number of masters courses

have developed at various universities, offering elements of specialised training associated with the opportunity to complete a small research thesis. Since the 1970s, post-qualifying courses have been accredited by CCETSW. In 1990, post-qualifying consortia were established to accredit and manage the development of post-qualifying training in regions of England (CCETSW 1990a). These have been of varying success, and are being reviewed at the time of writing in early 2001.

Three elements of the present post-qualification framework have, however, become widespread. The first is the provision of a qualification and training for practice teachers. Most universities have provided courses for beginning practice teachers and continuing support since the 1960s; some earlier. This was formalised in the mid 1990s through regional consortia providing a nationally recognised qualification. It is also associated with the accreditation of agencies as placement providers. Post-qualifying training, assessment and continuing development for approved social workers who have power to arrange the compulsory admission of mentally ill people to hospital is also universal. A post-qualification course in child care law was also introduced in 1999, accompanied by considerable pressure for widespread participation.

While this provision exists for social workers, other staff in social services agencies have had very few training opportunities. This problem was addressed by CCETSW's joining the social care 'industry' into the Conservative Government's development of National Vocational Qualifications (CCETSW 1990b). These are designed to cover all areas of employment. Occupational standards are set by consultation among employers, and 'competencies' are defined. Workers are assessed to see whether they meet the standards at various levels; the professional qualification is set at level 5. Training is provided, often in-service, to assist employees to meet the standards. Because it is part time, because competencies require detailed definition and therefore assessment is highly structured, and because most workers at a lower level would therefore not receive college-based training and qualification, there has been criticism that this process is mechanistic and excluding. In particular, there are fears that many workers in residential and day care, who offer daily care to some of the most deprived and oppressed service users, would lose the opportunity to progress to higher education and professional qualification. Moreover, while the system is widely available, few workers have progressed very far and there are signs of poor commitment to all training by social services employers in public, private and voluntary sectors. However, the recognition of existing skills and informal training, the ladder of competencies and qualification, and the wide coverage of the system offer some training opportunities to staff who in the past have had no training at all.

The system was further strengthened by the new Labour Government, with the establishment of national training organisations, NTOs, led by employers, to map training needs, develop occupational standards and strengthen training provision at all levels. There are several relevant to the social services, including TOPSS (Training Organisation in the Personal Social Services) and similar organisations in pre-school and health care, the voluntary sector and criminal justice. The Labour Government has also established general social care councils in each UK nation, with different titles, outside England combining this role with the NTO role which will establish codes of conduct and registers of practitioners with recognised qualifications, and validate and manage social work professional education. As these are established, in the early twenty-first century, CCETSW is being wound up. Consistent with the devolution of government, both TOPSSs and GSCCs will be established in each of the four countries of the UK, with some UK-wide co-ordination.

Conclusion

The period from 1989 until the present date has seen major changes in the nature of provision of social work in respect of both adults and children and families. We have indicated the wide range of provision available, and the importance of its interrelationships, especially with health care in relation to adult services. Closer links are also evident between social care provision for children and the education system, and services for young people and the new Connexions service, drawing on elements of careers guidance, youth provision, education welfare and social work (re SEU website). During the 1990s, adult services were the centre of many of the debates about the nature and role of social work in Britain. They have been the focus within the social services of the development of the Conservative government's policy of seeing local government and government more generally as an enabler of private and independent sector provision, rather than being a provider in its own right. Consequently, adult services have borne a burden of increasing managerialism (Payne 2000), as New Right policies have implemented auditing and control processes through management initiatives, rather than professional developments. The major professional development of care management, with its potential for improving standards and flexibility in adult service provision, has only been implemented in a limited way through the community care reforms. However, in some more specialised adult services, some elements of its creativity have been developed through brokerage and multiprofessional assertive care management. There may still, therefore, be opportunities to strengthen the professional and creative elements of care management in the future.

Many of the changes introduced in services for children and families derive from the major changes introduced as part of the Children Act 1989. Some of these changes have had a chance to bed down and become part of established practice. Yet the pace of change is relentless and social workers, working in the field of children and families social work, constantly have to adapt to new guidance about good practice. However, much of this development also has an impact on the perception of the role of social work. We have noted how public perceptions of social workers as 'removers of children' from parents have led to difficulties in gaining acceptability for social workers to intervene in family situations. Social work with children and families has become a 'media issue', and changes in practice and policy have been made to be responsive to moral panics. Hardly a month seems to pass without some high profile media issue. Through this media attention and high exposure, the effectiveness of social work has been thrown into question, and has led to managerialist demands for compliance with performance indicators and evidence-based practice. There has been a questioning of professional expertise, and a priority to alternative interventions, welcome in themselves, such as Surestart, to improve children's progress at an early age, and a focus on education in the early years, and on preventing child poverty. Such macro-level approaches to social problems raise questions about an appropriate role of social work. Moreover, so much of recent policy change seems inspired if not fully driven by the pressure of media coverage of what may or may not be major issues in social care. The pace of change is likely to intensify as the new quality control bodies, the GSSC and the Social Care Institute for Excellence (SCIE), to mention but two, come on stream in the years 2001–2003. It is likely that some of the forces seen in the construction of English social work will become more significant as greater divergences become apparent from other countries in the British Isles.

It has been possible to write an account of social work in England without much reference to the impact of the other nations in the Isles. Thus far, at the beginning of the 21st century, awareness of alternative models of social work and social care provision in the other countries is minimal in England. The structural differences, where probation is part of social work departments, and social services are part of health trusts in Northern Ireland, may be known in England in some professional circles, but have had little impact on professional or political debate. The legislation and service policies discussed here are so far regarded as the 'main' description of social work and the social services in Britain, from which the other systems are regarded as deviations, arranged to respond to particular local exigencies. The English assumption of centrality, and dare it be spoken, 'superiority' in social services provision is, as yet, undented.

Yet, signs of gathering impact of devolution are there to see. The possibility that Scotland may take a different approach to community care costs and the possibility of different education and training provision and priorities may stretch differences between England and other countries in the UK. The growing strength of regionalisation in the UK suggests that the next decade may prove to be a period in which social work in the Isles may have an impact on the social care services of the dominant English. Accepting a wider range of ethnic, cultural and national differences among people in the UK seems a natural corollary of growing awareness of racism in relation to migrants and asylum seekers moving to the UK.

Notes

1 Jerusalem was later to become a famous hymn set to music by Parry.

2 Saint George is the patron saint of England, although reputed never to have set foot in the country.

3 Statistical information from a variety of sources including: Comptons Encyclopaedia (1997) (CD ROM); Central Office of Information (1996) Britain in 1996: An Official Handbook. London: Central Office of Information.

4 The House of Commons was first established in 1346 and was initially a parliament of and for England.

5 Various members of the Conservative party have attempted to raise this matter but with little success.

6 The City of London Corporation is governed by a curiously named body, the Court of Common Council. Voting rights to elect the aldermen are by possession of property rather than residence; as such, it remains an undemocratic and archaic relic from the past. Uniquely in England, those who vote for the local government in the city have two votes in local elections as they may also vote for the government in their place of residence – almost always in another local authority. This is not entirely of academic interest as the City of London does provide social services.

7 A 'county' is an historic division of the country that dates back to the Middle Ages.

8 The Act refers to England and Wales.

9 A 'circular' is a letter from Government providing advice or mandatory guidance to local authorities.

10 On 12 January 2001, Marie-Thésèse Kouao (aged 44) and her boyfriend Carl Manning (aged 28) were sentenced to life imprisonment for the murder of Adjo Climbié (known as Anna). According the *Observer* (14 January 2001) Anna had been: 'starved, tied up, beaten, left naked in an empty bath, and forced to eat scraps of food "like a dog" and the post mortem examination found 128 visible marks of abuse' (p.9).

11 On 21 December 2000 Mr Justice Hogg in the Family Division of the High Court made an adoption order to Mr and Mrs Bramley in respect of these two children. An unusual case of abduction, where the charges of abduction were dropped and the abductors were awarded full parental responsibilities!

12   This personal interest may derive from the fact that Tony Blair's father, Leo, was fostered when his parents, who were travelling entertainers, left Leo with another couple that they had met while on tour.

13   An increase promised by Tony Blair on 21 December 2000

14   The English legal system normally requires anonymity for young offenders except, curiously, when the offences are very serious, in which case young offenders can be treated as adults, and the case can be publicised and heard in adult courts according to adult rules – hence this case was heard in the Old Bailey.

15   This incorporates the purchaser–provider split seen since 1989 in the care management system.

16   A phrase used on many occasions by Jack Straw, Home Secretary (1997–2001) based on a parliamentary statement by the Prime Minister, Tony Blair, when he was Shadow Home Secretary.

Chapter 3

Social Work in Late-modern Ireland

Harry Ferguson and Fred Powell

This chapter maps out the broad parameters of how social work is organised and delivered in late-modern Ireland. It does so in the context of offering a critical analysis of the complex forms and meanings of social work in late-modern societies. The island of Ireland is made up of 32 counties, 26 of which comprise the Republic of Ireland as constituted by the formation of the Irish Free State in 1922 – hereafter referred to as 'Ireland'. The other six counties remained under British rule in the United Kingdom and are not featured in the analysis in this chapter. Ireland is a small country with a population of 3,626,000 (1996 census). Social work in Ireland is perhaps unique in the context of islands covered in this book to the extent that civil society and the state were dominated by the Catholic Church for most of its history. Only since the 1990s has Catholic hegemony finally begun to crack in a welter of scandal and public outrage. Though the seeds of destruction of Catholic power in Ireland were sown in the 1960s, when the country began the process of modernisation, the changes that were subsequently unleashed have been momentous. Modernisation has meant secularisation, generating a cultural shift that has eclipsed traditional Ireland. In this momentous period of change social work has emerged as a significant profession, albeit one heavily preoccupied with child welfare, protection, and the management of risk.

As we show in what follows, it is not possible to understand the nature of social work in contemporary Ireland without grasping its past. The welfare state emerged in Ireland in the teeth of clerical opposition (Powell 1992). The 'social', in the sense of a public sphere has had to discover itself within a traditionalist context, determined to look backwards. Paradoxically, the collapse of traditional Ireland has generated a heightened sense of not only crisis but also new possibilities. Yet it is not clear what direction Irish society wants to adopt, other than economic rationalism as the perceived source of prosperity. This chapter analyses the unique context out of which Irish social work has emerged, the wider issues it raises and the new challenges posed by (post) modernisation for social work (Ferguson 2001; Powell 1998) and for Irish society as a whole.

The history and development of social work in Ireland

It is essential to set the emergence of social work in Ireland within the context of the emergence of Irish society as a whole from a traditionalist pre-modern culture to a postmodern one. Social work, as a component of civil society, was effectively shaped by the Catholic Church, which reduced the Irish state to a subsidiary role in the provision of social services and completely dominated civil society for the first fifty years of the state's existence. The roots of Irish social work date from the nineteenth century. Kearney (1987, p.7) notes that the first trained social worker was appointed to a position in housing management in 1899, and records the establishment of a settlement movement at Trinity College in 1901, known as the Dublin University Social Service Union. Others have placed the beginnings of 'modern' social work slightly earlier with the child protection movement following the foundation of the first Irish branch of the National Society for the Prevention of Cruelty to Children in Dublin in 1889 (Ferguson 1996, p.7). In fact, 'scientific charity' can be traced to the mendicity associations, dating from 1818, notably the Dublin Mendicity Association (Powell 1992, p.8).

The establishment of the Irish Free State in 1922 was followed by the Catholicisation of civil society. The only secular voluntary organisation to retain a significant role in the provision of social services was the Irish Society for the Prevention of Cruelty to Children, as it became in

1956 when it finally split from the UK Society. The national network of N/ISPCC Inspectors dealt with in the region of 2500 cases a year and was the only national casework agency of its type in the country. During the years under UK management (1898–1955), some 478,865 children were involved with the NSPCC in the Republic of Ireland (Ferguson 1996). Nowhere was the profound influence of Catholic social teaching on the Irish Free State and social policy more evident than in the 1937 Constitution (Whyte 1980). Article 41 'recognizes the Family as the primary and fundamental unit group of Society, and as a moral institution possessing inalienable and imprescriptible rights, antecedent and superior to all positive laws' (Bunreacht na hEireann 1937). The use of discretionary powers to protect children was often in opposition to the principle of minimum intervention into the family prescribed by the Constitution and the Catholic hierarchy (Ferguson 1995a). Meanwhile, those children who were removed from parental custody were placed in Ireland's large network of industrial schools which were run by religious orders and where many experienced horrendous abuse which is only now beginning to be disclosed (Raftery and O'Sullivan 1999). This kind of division of labour between the Church and voluntary sector typified the minimal role of the state in the provision of social services before the 1970s.

It was not until the Health Act 1970, which established eight regional health boards, that the state became the main employer of social workers and the professionalisation of welfare services proceeded in Ireland (Ferguson 1996, p.13). Since 1970 the role and task of professional social work in Ireland has been transformed from a peripheral activity into a key statutory service mainly engaged in child protection and probation work. It was only in the early 1990s that professional social work qualifications became fully regulated by the Irish state. The establishment of the National Social Work Qualifications Board (NSWQB) in 1997 meant that social work education ceased to be administered from the UK by the Central Council for Education and Social Work. The NSWQB has proven to be a very important development in the professional emergence of Irish social work. It validates four professional courses, two at masters level and two at undergraduate level, in Dublin and Cork. Four years is the minimum period for training in social work. This aptly reflects something of how the Irish social work profession is still in a state of emergence and self-definition. This must be understood against a background where the forces of traditionalism and modernity have struggled for hegemony, with the forces of modernity ultimately being successful. Professional social work has, therefore, emerged at a point when Irish society has reinvented itself as a secular postmodern state, with all the ambiguities and challenges that implies. However, the roots of Irish social work remain deeply embedded in a rich tradition of voluntarism and community development that continue to play a vital role.

The social policy context

The historical development of social work in Ireland – or in most respects its relative *under*-development until recent years – must be placed in the context of the general approach to social policy. The postwar world sought to put to rest the spectres of mass unemployment, hunger and destitution, which had characterised the 1930s. Keynesianism provided the economic strategy that underpinned the welfare state. The welfare state has been described by Offe (1984, p.147) as 'the major peace formula of advanced capitalist democracies for the period following the Second World War'. The welfare state not only guaranteed a modicum of social rights but also gave trade unionists economic rights and influence over policy making in return for a disciplined and collaborative approach to economic management. This was the essence of social democratic politics, which dominated postwar Europe.

In Britain, the welfare state had been associated with the Beveridge reforms introduced by the Labour Government between 1945 and 1951. The Beveridge reforms were denounced in Ireland by the Catholic Church, which caricatured the welfare state as 'the servile state'. The controversy was known in Ireland as the Liberal Ethic debate. The leading spokesperson for the Catholic point of view was Fr. Phelim O'Briain, Professor of Philosophy at University College, Galway, who, in a series of articles published in the *Irish Independent* in

1952, castigated the welfare state as 'a variant of the cruder methods of Nazism, Fascism and Communism'. He referred to 'Welfare totalitarianism' and the 'dehumanisation that State paternalism is bound to achieve'. This attack on the idea of the welfare state had a defensive ring about it, being delivered in the wake of the 'Mother and Child' controversy in 1951. The controversy, which was essentially about how the Church managed to secure the rejection of a state health service, brought to an end one of the most talented and promising ministerial careers in the history of the state, through the forced resignation of the Minister for Health, Dr Noel Browne. It damaged the Church's standing among the poor, who re-elected Dr Browne with an increased majority – a rare act of defiance for the time. Catholic opposition to the welfare state was in the final analysis about power and ownership. The demarcation line of Church–State relations in the sphere of social policy had been firmly established, with welfare defined as a touchstone for ideological controversy in the modern Irish state.

In the 1960s the social liberalism of the Second Vatican Council softened Catholic opposition to the welfare state, provided that it did not intrude upon the Church's power and ownership over a significant proportion of the means of welfare. The state, cast in the role of financier, served to ensure the continuation of Catholic control over schools, hospitals, children's homes, etc. Ironically, economic development, which transformed Ireland after 1960 from a rural traditional society into a modern urban one, vastly extended the scale of social provision. However, it did so in a manner that ensured Catholic hegemony over social policy was not only retained but also augmented.

Catholic social thought gradually was reshaped. The former enemy of the welfare state became its vocal champion, albeit that church power was not to be surrendered. A new politics of social concern allowed the Church to occupy the moral high ground, remonstrating with the politicians for their failures to deliver an adequate quality of life for all. Taxation was the unpopular task of the secular power in Irish society. Redistribution increasingly became the province of the Church as educational opportunities and health care expectations expanded geometrically. Even poverty as a social issue could be rehabilitated by the

Church as the demand for class equality weakened with the decline of Marxism. The levelling ambitions of Marxism had proven utterly unacceptable to Catholicism because they suggested that God and humankind were equal. Marxism was always a profoundly heretical doctrine in Ireland. Yet its decline opened the way for a radical humanist Catholicism – liberation theology. Liberation theologians ironically took over where the Marxists left off, harrying Government over its blatant hypocrisies. As the Labour Party aimed its message increasingly at the better off majority, the vacuum was filled by campaigning priests and nuns, most notably Fr. Sean Healy and Sr Brigid Reynolds of the Conference of Religious in Ireland (CORI) (Healy and Reynolds 1999). Genuine conviction and concern breathed new life into an institutional Church deeply compromised by an innate conservatism and over-identification with the interests of the better off at the expense of the socially deprived faithful.

The pursuit of the welfare state ideal itself began to become more problematic as postwar growth began to falter during the 1970s. The emergence of a postmodern culture challenged the core beliefs of social democracy, the political credo upon which the welfare state edifice precariously rested. Postmodern culture produced a more atomised and individualised society. Economically, deindustrialization occurred with traditional manufacturing industries relocating to the developing world, where labour costs were much lower. Politically, class solidarity began to break up. Into the vacuum stepped the New Right, appealing to a new mood of acquisitive individualism.

The New Right was skilfully to exploit the politics of crisis during the 1980s in order to bring about structural reforms in the welfare state and the labour market with a view to curtailing social and economic rights and redistributing wealth to the rich. Attention was concentrated on the welfare state as the fundamental cause of the economic malaise. As the *Irish Times* commented, 'tackling the financial crisis comes first' (20 July 1987). This New Right inspired critique was to shape Irish public policy throughout most of the 1980s. It associated the origins of 'the crisis' with rising expectations in terms of living standards and growing welfare dependency. Its protagonists contended that competition between interest groups (i.e., trade union, the farmers and industrialists) had de-established the economy and made the country ungovernable because no administration in recent decades could reconcile these warring interests whose ambitions conflicted with the common good. In reality, this ungovernability thesis was a coded attack on trade unionists. Democracy had gone too far!

At the core of this New Right critique is a belief in the superiority of the market as an economic regulator and method of allocating and using scarce resources. In essence, citizenship would be better served by an emphasis on duties and obligations than through the provision of social and economic rights. The emergence of the Progressive Democrat Party in the 1980s, whose 'espousal of the tax cuts, privatisation, and fiscal rectitude ensured that their appeal was predominantly to the bourgeois and middle-class, was indicative of a trend to the right' (Breen et al. 1991, p.200). After the 1987 General Election 146 out of 166 Dail Deputies were members of parties favouring public expenditure cuts (i.e., Fianna Fail, Fine Gael and the Progressive Democrats). Little wonder then that, as we show below, the scale of social problems like family poverty, child abuse and drug addiction increased significantly over this period. There was no corresponding growth in social services. The Irish state was conspicuously unaccountable and disinterested in providing more social work services.

The national debt more than trebled between 1980 and 1986, rising from under £6 billion to over £24 billion – the ratio of the national debt to GNP also increased, from 88 to 148 per cent. The debt repayment problem was exacerbated by the weak performance of the economy in terms of output during most of the 1980s. There was virtually no growth in the economy from 1980 to 1986 compared with the annual growth rate of nearly 4 per cent in the period from 1975 to 1980. There can be little doubt that action was required to correct the serious imbalance in the public finances. The reintroduction of property taxes (i.e., 'the rates', first introduced to finance the Poor Law in 1838) and the imposition of a meaningful corporate tax along with a wealth tax would have solved the problem. A strategy of public expenditure cuts based on a principle of equality of sacrifice was adopted instead.

The relative political powerlessness of the poor was the decisive factor in determining this regressive strategy.

In a society beset by poverty and mass unemployment, equality of sacrifice served to mildly reduce the living standards of the majority and severely exacerbate the poverty of the underclass while sharply increasing the living standards of the rich. The New Right have insisted upon swinging cutbacks in public expenditure to finance tax cuts for the rich in the name of wealth creation. Public expenditure cutbacks drastically reduced the quality of Irish social services between 1987 and 1992 at the expense of the poor. The local authority house-building programme had virtually come to a halt by the end of the 1980s. By 1992 there was a housing waiting list of 23,400. The pupil–teacher ratio in many primary schools rose to 30.1 and in some cases over 40.1 as a result of the public expenditure cuts, the worst in the European Community. Long queues for vital health care operations and surgical procedures were created, depriving the poor of the basic right to health care. In 1992 there were 36,421 people waiting for essential hospital treatment. Cuts in social welfare during the same year added further hardship to the miserable lot of the poor.

Tragically, there is little evidence that all the sacrifice imposed on the poor has produced any results in terms of economic improvement. Fiscal rectitude simply redistributed wealth to the rich and eroded the hard-won social rights of the poor. For the poor the crisis was a disaster. By January 1993 the fiscal rectitude strategy of the New Right had pushed unemployment to a record of 302,000, or 21 per cent of the labour force. The long-term unemployment figure stood at 104,000. Between 1986 and 1991, 137,000 Irish people emigrated, most of them for reasons of economic necessity. This period witnessed the fourth major wave of Irish emigration since the Great Famine of the 1840s. It is no coincidence that similar types of economic and social policies were employed during these two disastrous periods in Irish history. In November 1992 the Irish electorate passed its verdict on five years of uncompromising New Right politics, with its emphasis on acquisitive individualism, by transferring their loyalties in large numbers to the Labour Party.

The discovery of a 'New Left' project in the 1990s represents a sea change which, according to its advocates, promised to reconstruct politics. At the heart of this task is the redefinition of citizenship in postmodern society. The welfare state, the great political project of the postwar Left, sought to define citizenship in terms of social rights. The New Right in the 1980s changed the emphasis to the duties and obligations of citizenship. It is notable that in the USA, the Democratic Administration has declared its opposition to welfare dependency and Labour in Britain has pursued welfare reform. Politics in both countries moved beyond the traditional left collectivist conception of citizenship as membership of the welfare state to embracing a form of progressive individualism. The Rainbow coalition of the mid 1990s comprised of Fine Gael, Labour and Democratic Left infused a sense of optimism for change in a more egalitarian direction. The National Anti-Poverty Strategy epitomised this change. Nevertheless, in 1997 Ireland once again moved to the political right with the return of Fianna Fail and Progressive Democrat government. A succession of political scandals involving systematic tax evasion scams by leading banks, as well as corrupt links between business and politicians, have created a deep sense of public cynicism. The so called 'Celic Tiger' economy of the late 1990s has produced unprecedented growth rates. It has also sharpened social inequalities, producing a substantial underclass excluded from wealth and participation in late modern society.

Modernisation, fragmentation and polarisation

It is a paradox that Ireland is modernising in a postmodern world characterised by fragmentation and polarisation. The term modernisation is generally associated with the transformation in western society wrought by the industrial revolution and emergence of welfare states over recent centuries. This process involved a fracture with the traditional feudal social order amounting to a fundamental transformation of society, characterised by reflexive modernisation at the advent of the twenty-first century (Crook et al. 1992, pp.1–2; Beck et al. 1994, p.6). Ireland, which belatedly adopted a modernization project in the 1960s, has had to overcome an economic and cultural gap at a point when the

rest of the developed world is moving on to new forms of social organisation. Yet the pace and scale of economic development, which now
promises to overtake that of the United Kingdom, places Ireland in a
barometric position in terms of reflexive modernization. Thus, in contemporary Ireland, the paradoxes of modernisation have acquired
increasingly extreme form. Greater wealth stands in marked contrast to
endemic poverty. Substantially increased diversity and choice in terms
of 'lifestyle politics' has been accompanied by more fragmentation and
polarisation. As rural life has declined in response to the forces of industrialisation and urbanisation, inner-city ghettos, characterised by
poverty, drugs and crime, have come to dominate the social landscape.
Cultural and political life is no longer organised in terms of traditional
identities and shared values, partly because contemporary inequalities
of income, wealth and power do not produce the homogenous classes,
such as business, small farmers, and workers, that shaped the social and
political geography of traditional Ireland. Instead, new social movements have organised around issues as diverse as gender, environment,
urban inequalities, traveller issues, refugees and asylum seekers. Social
conflicts have become more pluralistic, representing a much wider
variety of interests, and involve a different set of targets including the
state, bureaucracies and professionals.

Dramatic increases in public awareness of the problem of child
abuse, and child sexual abuse in particular, through public enquiries
(McGuiness 1993; Keenan 1996; North Western Health Board 1998),
and the outing of clergy who molest children, have become a metaphor
for the historic transformation that Ireland is undergoing. The political
fall-out over the Fr. Brendan Smyth case (a cleric whose sexual abuse of
children was covered up by his superiors for forty years and whose
extradition to Northern Ireland in 1994 was delayed seven months)
even brought down the Coalition Government in 1995 (Moore 1995).
Ireland is going through a very robust exorcising of traditional values
that put the institution of the Catholic Church and the family first
regardless of the rights of the individual and/or child. The 'paedophile
priest' has become a potent symbol of the detraditionalisation of Irish
society (Ferguson 1995b). The rapidity and scale of the change has led

one commentator to liken the events in Ireland to those in Eastern Europe following the collapse of Communism (Ardagh 1995). This comparison may be overstated but there is little doubt that Catholic hegemonic control is being fundamentally rejected in a climate where, since 1990, Ireland has decriminalised homosexuality, passed a constitutional referendum in favour of freedom of travel and information in cases of abortion and legalised divorce, through another constitutional referendum.

The shape of social work in late-modern Ireland

It is against such a background of extraordinarily rapid social change in Ireland that the needs of vulnerable citizens and the state of Irish social work must be analysed and understood. There are presently a total of 1493 social workers in Ireland, 1281 of whom are qualified. The service provided by these social workers in Ireland today can usefully be mapped out according to three main sectors: the state/statutory sector, the voluntary sector and the informal sector. The eight health boards are the main state agencies and by far the largest providers of social work services. These are delivered through three programmes: the community care programme, the general hospitals programme and the special hospitals programme (McGinley 1995). The hospital programmes provide important medical social work services in specialisms such as maternity, mental health, oncology, addiction and children. These cater for a number of service user groups. For instance, social workers attached to psychiatric units in hospitals provide some of the child guidance services offered in the state, while child and family psychiatric services are increasingly also being developed in the community through the community care programme.

Generic social work services – which in reality, as we show below, have become child care services – are provided through the community care programme. Doherty (1996) estimated that the Mid-Western and Midland Health Boards combined employed a total of 104 social workers, servicing a population of 500,000. This averages out at around 15 per county, providing a range of community services including work in fostering, adoption, child psychiatry, youth homelessness, domestic violence and family support, as well as child abuse investigation, assessment and management. Some 40 per cent of social workers are in their twenties and 70 per cent under the age of 40. The vast majority of frontline social workers – 85 per cent – are female (Doherty 1996), while the management structures of health boards are distinctly male dominated (O'Connor 1998). The number of child abuse cases officially processed by such community care teams increased by 526 per cent between 1989 and 1997 (Ferguson and O'Reilly 2001).

Probation and welfare officers are the second significant strand of state social work and were in fact the first statutory social workers in Ireland, the first one being employed in 1961. Their primary role is to provide an advisory service to the courts, preparing pre-sentence reports, supervising offenders in the community, and organising and administering Community Service Orders. After a review of the service in 1969, three senior officers and 27 probation officers were appointed and it has developed from there into a modern service. By the 1990s some 250 were employed around the country. In 1980 the service produced 777 pre-sentence reports for the courts and a total of 1712 new cases were placed under supervision. By 1994, 3587 pre-sentence reports were being produced and 2060 community service reports presented to the courts, while some 2633 offenders were placed under the supervision of the probation service (Cotter 1999).

The growth of the probation and welfare service arises from developments that have contradictory implications. It reflects an increase in schemes to keep offenders out of custodial institutions, such as the Intensive Probation Scheme, where offenders have to agree to undergo an intensive period of group work to change their offending behaviour and attitudes as an alternative to custody. On the other hand, the growth in social work resources in the criminal justice area is part of a new 'politics of enforcement' (Jordan 1997). Crime in Ireland has become a site for politicians to whip up populist support by getting 'tough on crime' – building more prisons, putting more police on the beat, more probation officers to mop up the criminals. Meanwhile, the roots of crime continue to lie in the growing inequalities in wealth in Irish society, and must be understood as a social problem arising from particular economic conditions (Bacik and O'Connell 1998). Its solutions, therefore, go well beyond attempts to develop effective probation work and a just penal system (O'Mahony 1993; McCullagh 1996).

A further, and much more modest, arm of the statutory sector is the social work service provided by 'the Corporation' to local authority housing tenants. While all social work services interface with the marginalised, this is perhaps the most clearly focused on the special needs of the travelling community, the most vulnerable and socially excluded minority in Irish society.

Within the voluntary sector, as suggested above, until recent years the ISPCC was the leading social work agency in Ireland. It now employs a small number of social workers and child care workers in community projects, as well providing its flagship service, Childline, the telephone help line for children. The Catholic Church continues to be the main 'voluntary' provider of social services, delivering the bulk of services in this state to people with disabilities (Quin and Redmond 1999) and in residential child care. In the light of falling vocations and scandals concerning the abuse of children in their care, some Orders are withdrawing from residential child care which being is replaced by the state (Clarke 1998).

The informal sector relates to care in the community, most often through the family – the unpaid domestic labour done by women – of the elderly, infirm and people with disabilities. There is growing evidence of a vibrant self-help movement as found in such diverse areas as child abuse survivors groups and initiatives (Fahy 1999; McKay 1998), action against drugs, and Alcoholics Anonymous. More and more people in Ireland are also turning to counselling and psychotherapy services to find 'help' for personal troubles. While not usually included in standard assessments of social service provision, the informal sector warrants inclusion because of its increasing significance as part of an entire network of 'helping' services and practices in advanced modern societies where the boundaries between the state and civil society, expertise and lay people are in a process of re-definition (Giddens 1998).

Community development

Community development in Ireland is deeply rooted in the rural communitarian movement that emerged during the 1930s. It was deeply traditionalist in its world view and closely connected with the overweening influence of the Catholic Church. The influence of Muintir na Tire, founded by Father John Hayes in 1937, typifies the traditionalist element in the communitarian movement in Ireland. Forde (1996) has underlined its role as a cultural defender, observing that 'Muintir na Tire was established at a time when urbanisation was impinging on rural life, when communism was considered an international threat, and when the State began to play a more active role in social planning' (p.9). Muintir na Tire started as a co-operative but mutated into a system of parish councils. It was ideologically a deeply conservative movement. As it has been noted, 'Muintir na Tire refused to acknowledge the possibility of class or other conflict in its parish councils, which are organised on a vocational basis with representation from all the main class groupings in the parish' (Forde 1996, p.9).

In 1958, Muintir na Tire adopted the UN definition of community development that emphasised partnership between the state and local communities (Forde 1996, p.9). Following the Irish modernisation project, initiated in the 1960s, the pace of rural decline was sharply increased, weakening Muintir na Tire. In order to combat this decline Muintir na Tire embarked on a programme of reorganisation in the 1970s, and parish councils were replaced by democratically elected community councils. Forde (1996) has assessed the strengths and weaknesses of community councils as follows

> It could be argued that the strengths of community councils lie in their ability to provide local amenities, such as community centres, in the organisation of leisure activities, and in lobbying the State for improvements in local facilities. Their weaknesses include their failure to develop sufficiently to offer employment to professional workers, their inactivity for large periods of the year and their inadequacies in planning and managerial terms. (p.10)

The decline in the role of Muintir na Tire continued. The number of parish councils fell from 300 in the 1970s to 120 in 1990 (Forde 1996, p.10). This decline was primarily due to the onward march of rural decay. However, there has been a concomitant shift in the direction of community development. As Crickley and Devlin (1990) have noted, 'during the last decade, community work shifted its emphasis from an overall concern with issues in a geographical area to a focus on specific interests and communities of interest, e.g. training, employment, women, youth, traveller and minority groups' (p.54).

As Ireland began to redefine itself as a multicultural society, community development emerged as a significant social profession. European structural funds and the National Anti-Poverty Programme (NAPs) have provided substantial funding for community development initiatives. Training courses have been developed at three of the constituent colleges of the National University of Ireland: Cork, Galway and Maynooth. Professional recognition is provided for the four courses at Cork and Maynooth by the UK National Youth Agency. A buoyant labour market provides a diversity of careers for community and youth work graduates, largely in the voluntary and community sector.

The voluntary sector and civil society

The position of the Church as a social services provider was established as early as 1844 following the Charitable Bequests Act. This law gave the Roman Catholic Church a very powerful position within Irish society through ownership and control of many of the schools, hospitals and social services, a control which it continues to exercise to the present day. Thus Christian or, more precisely, Catholic values and principles became synonymous with social work values (Skehill 1999, p.31). The Irish Government's Green Paper on the Community and Voluntary Sector (Department of Social Welfare 1997) acknowledges this powerful religious role in civil society:

> It is notable that the voluntary sector in Ireland not only complements and supplement State service provision, but is the dominant or sole provider in particular social services areas. In this context, Roman

Catholic religious organisations and these of other denominations have played a major role in the provision of services. Many services have been initiated and run by religious organisations, for example, services for people with a mental and physical disability, youth services, the elderly, residential child care services and services for the homeless. (p.31)

The role of the Roman Catholic lay religious organisation the St Vincent de Paul, which has 1000 branches in Ireland and approximately 11,000 members, in providing welfare and various financial services has been acknowledged by the Green Paper as operating a 'shadow Welfare State' (Department of Social Welfare 1992, p.31). This is a remarkable admission in an official report. On the same page, the Green Paper makes its position clear by stating that 'the Government greatly values the vital role played by these various organisations and acknowledges the enormous contribution made by them in assisting individuals in need, the communities in which they live and work and society as a whole'. This statement is a striking testament to the enduring power of the religious in Irish society and the role of the voluntary sector in maintaining that power. It also raises the problem of 'assistencialism', which Friere criticised for ignoring dialogue with the poor and imposing silence on them. He viewed it as an antidemocratic strategy. Moreover, as Regan recently noted, 'assistencialism' prevents the poor 'from entering history as active critical agents of change' (*Irish Times*, 7 June 1997).

Given numerous recent allegations of breaches of trust and abuse of power by the Roman Catholic clergy, leading to many criminal convictions, the Government's ringing endorsement of its role would seem to be somewhat inappropriate. It also sits uneasily alongside the Green Paper's (Department of Social Welfare 1992) assertion that 'an active voluntary and community sector contributes to a democratic and pluralist society' (p.24). The Roman Catholic Church is not democratically accountable. This lack of accountability raises questions about a democratic deficit in a voluntary sector where it is probable, though this is not disclosed in the Green Paper, that the bulk of funding goes to the Roman Catholic Church. Furthermore, it is difficult to see how pluralism can be achieved within a denominationalist framework that is its very antithesis.

The Green Paper (Department of Social Welfare 1992) opines that 'the role of religious organisations in relation to the voluntary and community sector is changing', citing a decline in vocations and the 'withdrawal of religious personnel from some services' (p.31). For instance, the ownership of Our Lady of Lourdes Hospital, Drogheda has recently been transferred to the North Eastern Health Board. This development might be seen as symptomatic of a trend in which the religious surrenders institutional control to the state. However, that would be a simplistic analysis. The Green Paper (Department of Social Welfare 1992) notes that 'religious personnel have increased their role in, for example, community based services and are redressing their mission' (p.31). In a study of voluntary organisations in the Eastern Health Board (by far the largest in the country, including Dublin City in its boundaries), Faughnan and Kelleher (1993) found that 57 per cent of these bodies displayed multiple form of religious involvement, which included religious personnel being founder members, providing significant finances, occupying the position of director and providing premises.

Religious involvement in the voluntary sector is mutating and evolving from its traditional ownership of the institutional voluntary sector to community participation, frequently in a leadership role. It appears that rather than a decline in religious influence in a more secular society, there is evidence of a remarkable ability to adapt and to continue to exercise a hegemonic role. The underlying aspiration of the voluntary and community sector to promote democratic pluralism is fundamentally challenged by this on-going religious hegemony that remains the most durable influence in civil society in Ireland. It defied the long-term trend toward secularisation and secular values within Irish society as a whole. What is evident is that traditionalist influences continue to be highly influential in defining the concept of community in Ireland.

Nonetheless, voluntarism in Ireland is changing. Powell and Guerin (1997), in a national study of the voluntary sector, found evidence of significant change in the nature of civil society in Ireland. The UCC

Social Studies Research Unit survey provided evidence that 'many voluntary organisations are increasingly adopting the philosophies of community development and empowerment and mutating into democratically based bottom-up communitarian organisations, and that attitudes supportive of civil society are widely held among the Irish population, particularly among those who have had involvement with voluntary organisations' (Powell and Guerin 1997, p.174).

The evidence from the survey of voluntary organisations is that professionalisation has made a big impact on the voluntary sector. Despite this trend, however, there is also evidence that much of the employment within the voluntary sector is of a 'secondary labour market' or workfare nature – poor career structure, low pay, long hours and temporary employment. The growing confusion between workfare (under the guise of community employment schemes) and voluntarism threatens to violate the basic ethic on which the latter rests.

Increased resourcing of the voluntary sector is an indicator of emerging models of statutory intervention in civil society (transition from simple welfare pluralism to the partnership model). Despite the changes in the way the state is working with the voluntary sector (in the form of EU-funded regional partnerships) and the diversity of funding available from statutory sources, traditional barriers are still firmly in place in many areas, as evidenced by the results of the UCC research. The survey of voluntary organisations showed that there were strong preferences for increased state funding and an increased statutory monitoring role. However, difficulties still exist in relation to influencing statutory policy. The Green Paper on the Voluntary Sector also raises the possibility of formalising funding arrangements based on an approximation of the contract system, as used in the UK. The introduction of the approach raises a complex set of question relating to the introduction of commercial values into social services. The UCC survey of organisations identifies difficulties faced by organisations in attracting donations. At the same time there would appear to be an acceptance that the demands of the public are already stretched by numerous appeals for donations. The majority of organisations estimated that the

National Lottery had no effect on their fund raising activities, although their detailed responses suggested a more ambivalent view.

The evidence would also indicate that a very strong positive perception of the voluntary sector is held by the general public. The research found that the voluntary organisations recognised that there were problems in relation to the existence of adequate accountability to funders (both public and private). The association between the voluntary sector and democratisation and civic participation is quite pronounced in the literature. The majority of organisations believed that clients and volunteers had considerable influence on their policy making.

The voluntary sector is at a crossroads in terms of its role and direction. The 1997 Green Paper outlines a strategy for the voluntary sector by which its relationships with its statutory counterpart are based on the emerging principle of 'social dialogue'. This presupposes the development of an enabling state, which is engaged in dialogue, and partnership, and which allows bottom-up responses to emerge from voluntary organisations and community groups. This ideal form of a responsive and enabling state envisages a realistic transition in the relationship from 'separate dependency' to 'integrated dependency'. The implication of such a relationship is that it represents an incorporation of the voluntary sector by the state, with the attendant dangers of formalisation, based on the necessity of consensus politics. The future contribution of the voluntary sector to an enhanced civil society in Ireland will depend greatly on the ability of the voluntary sector to respond imaginatively to the challenges posed by both closer co-operation and dependence on the state and the encroachment of for-profit principles derived from the influence of the commercial sector. The relevance of many voluntary organisations in contemporary Irish society will also be tested by their ability to adjust to a late-modern society, where the requirements of reflexive modernisation are increasingly felt in demands for accountability and user-led initiatives from within organisations.

In the transition to an advanced modern society, the challenge of social policy is to respond reflexively to changing needs and demands.

The challenge to universalistic welfare is based on the particularism associated with identity politics and social movements – including neoconservative elements stressing the primacy of the market, the communitarian aspects of social obligation and the alleged inefficiencies of direct state intervention. The dilemma facing a disparate voluntary sector is how to reconcile its existence with the demands of common citizenship, previously associated with universalistic welfare measures.

Child protection and Irish social work

Although it has undergone a period of unprecedented growth, in many respects the personal social services in Ireland remain underdeveloped. The creation of the health boards in the early 1970s was meant to provide the basis for a generic social work service. However, two forms of rationalisation have occurred. Within the personal social services, child and family social work soon came to dominate; while further rationalisation is evident in that child protection has come to dominate child and family social work. The net effect is that social work with other vulnerable groups is either non-existent or seriously underresourced in Ireland. Services to the elderly are confined to relatively small numbers of medical social workers, even though this has not prevented some from pioneering the development of awareness and practice with problems such as elder abuse (O'Loughlin 1999). Nor do social workers employed by the Irish state provide any kind of meaningful service to persons with disabilities, while mental health services are confined to medical social workers based in a small number of hospitals and community-based services. This situation is a product of two main factors: The continuing influence of the voluntary sector – especially through the Catholic Church – in providing social services, and a series of public disclosures of system failures in child abuse cases and the particular demands on the state from a newly politicised civil society to be accountable for the protection of children (Ferguson 1994, 2000).

By the mid 1970s, community care social workers employed by the eight health boards had effectively taken over the primary responsibility for child protection and displaced ISPCC social workers. During the 1980s the numbers of child abuse referrals made to health boards increased by almost tenfold: from 406 cases in 1982 to 3859 in 1991. These referrals were investigated by more or less the same number of social workers and the scope for providing a more generic child care service was rationalised by cutting back in preventive child welfare areas. The emergence of child abuse guidelines in the late 1970s and their increasing importance (Ferguson 1996) meant that social workers were losing their traditional discretion to work with families in whatever ways they felt were best (Walsh 1999). In the process, child *care* was largely reframed as child *protection* (see Ferguson 1995, pp.26–7). Reports of child abuse grew relentlessly in the 1990s as public awareness increased and inter-agency co-operation was strengthened in the light of the child abuse inquiries. Cases handled by health boards rose from 3,856 in 1991 to 7,312 in 1997, an increase of almost 100 per cent. By now, however, these increases did reflect, at least in part, the availability of greater resources.

Some £40m was injected into the system to implement the 1991 Child Care Act, with relatively large increases in the numbers of staff and services available to report suspected cases and to respond to them. This included the creation of child care development officers in each of the health boards, social work team leaders and additional posts in frontline social work, community child care work, psychology, child psychiatry and family support work. The numbers of social workers employed in child care in the health boards increased from 309 in 1987 to 821 in 1995. In 1998, in the Eastern Health Board Region – covering Dublin – alone, 221 social workers were employed. The contrast with the late 1980s, when it was not uncommon for as few as five social workers to constitute the entire social work service covering two counties of Ireland is striking. In a real sense, it is only now possible to speak of Ireland as having the human resources and infrastructure needed to constitute a modern social work service. Even today, many social workers have to work in very unsuitable office accommodation, where it can be difficult to even find space to conduct an interview.

The impact of child protection on Irish social work has undoubt-edly been profound (Richardson 1999; Walsh 1999), but the precise implications require careful judgement. Some have argued that these developments have (re)constituted Irish social work as a bureaucratic, forensically driven enterprise where the onus is on gathering evidence of 'abuse' to the neglect of helping the socially excluded (Buckley 1996, 1999; Buckley, et al. 1997; Thorpe 1997). Thus Irish social work is held to have gone the same way as its near neighbours in the UK and to have lost its essential humanist base as it has had to become a investigative, intrusive service focused on policing dangerous families rather than supporting children and parents in need.

However, this view is flawed and simplistic in some crucial respects. While it is true that child protection has become the dominant discourse in Irish social work, the precise implications of this depend on the meaning of child protection in this cultural context. While Ireland is certainly under pressure from external globalising processes and the influence of limited and limiting notions of child welfare, the concept of child protection and welfare being constructed here is not the same as in the UK and other Western nation-states. Nor have commentators paid due regard to the impact of the new resources and full implementation of the Child Care Act on practice. Recent research (Ferguson and O'Reilly, 2001) has shown that, unlike the UK (Gibbons, et al. 1995; Department of Health 1995), very few referrals are in fact screened out of the system by social workers without an investigation. Moreover, the proportion of cases that receive little more than an investigation into child abuse without the provision of follow-up services is relatively low. The cases dealt with typically include very low levels of actual injuries to children but relatively high levels of adversity in terms of behaviour problems, addiction, neglect, parents under stress and domestic violence. Social workers are actively striving to include 'child welfare type' problems and a broader definition of need in their casework. The continuing welfare orientation of Irish social work reflects, in part, how notions of the integrity of the family are still powerfully enshrined culturally and in Irish social policy, resulting in a child protection service in which notions of family support remain significant (Murphy 1996). It is also a product of how the 1991 Child Care Act placed obligations on health boards to promote the welfare of children in their areas by providing family support as well as child protection services. Thus social workers themselves remain the key providers of long-term therapeutic services in substantiated cases, work which is increasingly done in conjunction with other services, such as community child care work and psychology.

Greater resources and an increased network of child care professionals providing services under the Child Care Act has meant that social workers are also increasingly acting as case managers rather than doing the actual case work themselves. Such developments have made social workers in Ireland acutely aware of the pressures they face to perform a role which is valued as much if not more for administrative competence than therapeutic effort and skill (Howe 1992). These pressures arise in part from the impact of more procedures and the law, and the more managerial culture that has developed since the early 1990s. Health board social work teams now *have* a management structure, of team leaders, senior social workers and child care managers, all of whose work with child abuse is regulated by a senior management group which constitutes the 'Child Protection Notification System'. In some respects, these structures limit the capacity of social workers to construct and develop practices based on core humanistic values. Yet, in other respects, Irish social workers generally value the increased accountability and protection offered to them through child abuse guidelines and management structures (Ferguson and O'Reilly 2001).

It is crucial to see this in a context where, prior to the 1990s, social workers worked in relative isolation with little public or professional interest in or value given to their work. This included a distinct lack of interest in the profession within the health boards themselves, which were (and in many respects remain) dominated by the medical profession. Thus, while child abuse and system failures in child protection have contributed to a more bureaucratised managerial culture in Irish social work and generated great fear and anxiety among practitioners and managers, the benefits to the profession have also been significant. There remain huge pressures, however, in the context of public pressure arising from child abuse inquiries, to aspire to some notion of safe practice that does not take account of the often difficult realties social workers face in doing their job. This includes high caseloads involving extremely complex, often intractable, problems for children and families, high proportions of involuntary and often threatening clients, overstretched resources and poor working conditions. Too often the outcomes for service users is a failure to have their needs met.

Opportunities, dangers and the future for Irish social work

For some commentators a professional crisis now exists in Irish social work, and it is quite common to find this view expressed in the media. For instance, the *Irish Times* social affairs correspondent has noted that 'it is increasingly difficult to recruit social workers and it may be necessary to train mature students for the job' (Padraig O'Morain, *Irish Times*, 8 October 1999). O'Morain, citing a major employer as his source, explained the deficit in the social work labour force in terms of two factors: 'not only are young graduates attracted to other jobs, but social workers are leaving because of the stress of child-protection work and violence or threats'.

On the other hand, the interest in social work as a profession has never been higher and demand for professional training courses far outstrips the places available. Rather than simple 'crisis' talk, we prefer to characterise the situation in terms of the new opportunities and dangers which constitute late-modern social work. Social work has always been beset by crisis tendencies because society has always had contradictory expectations of what it wants the profession to achieve – the care versus control dilemma. Nor is the pervasive sense of anxiety surrounding social work unique to Ireland, but a global phenomenon. For example, Jim Ife (1997) writing in an Australian context, has observed:

> Living with contradictions and having to make difficult moral choices is nothing few for social workers, but the political context of economic rationalism and the organisational context of managerialism have made the job much more difficult and have forced social workers to make major reassessments of where they stand, and the nature of the social work task.

Arguably, three basic factors can be identified that challenge the integrity of the social work task and threaten both professional and personal empowerment. First, the crisis in the welfare state, which is being undermined by a resurgent market, makes it difficult for humanistic social policies and humanistic social professions to survive. Essentially, the idea of welfare is being de-legitimated by market values that are anarchic and subversive of all values. Economic rationalism, which in Ireland is epitomised by the 'Celtic Tiger' economy, asserts that good public policy is that which makes sense in market terms, and that a healthy economy 'lifts all boats'. In reality, there is a redistribution of wealth going on but there seems to be a 'trickle-up' rather that a 'trickle-down' effect. A spate of recent tribunals have investigated corruption and wrongdoing by politicians and financial institutions, and have underlined the moral consequences of unregulated markets and the implications for politicians who get too close to business. Public opinion is outraged and the morale of public servants (like that of social workers) who subscribe to a humanistic value orientation is threatened.

Second, the impact of the market has led to the emergence of quasi-markets in the public sector. This has given rise to the so-called 'new managerialism' in the belief that good management can solve all problems and make the public services more efficient and effective. As shown in this chapter, the 'new managerialism' has created many new positions for social workers in Ireland. As the 1991 Child Care Act has been implemented and the reforms of the expert group on the probation and welfare services are introduced, a welcome career structure has opened up for the social work profession. The downside is that the trend towards managerialism has been accompanied by a devaluation of the traditional discretion inherent to the professional role of social workers in the public sector. Some social workers are reported to be seeking alternative futures in the voluntary sector, where humanistic values find a more congenial and respectful environment. The problem is that human beings cannot be equated with 'goods'. Nevertheless, the consequences for social workers of constant restructuring and organisational 'development' are the creation of an environment of permanent uncertainty and insecurity. This chronic organisational instability saps professionals' morale. The impact on service users is rarely considered, since management is governed by top-down rationality rather than bottom-up democratic accountability (Ife 1997; White 1999).

Third, the emphasis on rationality has led to a demand for a competency-led approach to training by employers. The competency movement (as witnessed in the UK) is guided by the logic that occupational roles should be defined according to the competencies required to perform them rather that through a system of professional accreditation. The intention of the competency movement is to break the power of professional monopolies. The recruitment of social care managers in the UK from a variety of professional backgrounds is indicative of the trend towards a competency-led labour force. On the positive side, a competency-led labour market opens up wider employment horizons to social workers and promotes choice and opportunity for many public servants. However, it can lead to a very technically based view on training. Social work education has always been defined by a combination of humanistic knowledge, values and skills. While we cannot of course claim to speak for all social work educators in Ireland, our sense (and hope) is that Irish social work education is managing to hang on to the importance of critical theory and an education for practice which goes beyond the limited pragmatism of inculcating technical skills. We are also conscious of the risk of caricaturing the meaning of competency-led education which, if done with imagination, can and should produce critically reflective competent social workers (O'Hagan 1996). The danger is that a competency-based approach to training is likely to increase managerial power at the expense of professional power. At a more fundamental level, the competency movement can be perceived as a threat to the core identity and future integrity of social work as a professional activity, since it incorporates a basic objective of the deconstruction of professionalism in the light of labour market rationality. The competency to discharge the task rather than the professional qualification is the guiding rationality. However, one real value of a competency-based approach is that it provides a common language, universal targets and learning objectives for students and educators, and in that respect Irish social work education does need to be clearer.

Almost undoubtedly, social work in Ireland, and beyond, will have to address multiple realities in its future. It will need to continue to assert and reassert its values in humanistic practice, which is popularly regarded as equivalent to humanitarianism. At the same time it will need to equip social workers to face the challenges of working with the growing numbers of involuntary clients coming to the attention of statutory services (Barber 1991; Ferguson and O'Reilly 2001). Furthermore, it will need to reflect on the relationships between the state and civil society if practice is to be more empowering. Finally, the profession will need to redefine itself in more inclusive terms to broaden its base in Irish society. This is especially the case as the country is having to face the reality of the depth of racism among the Irish, not only in terms of its traditional target in the traveller community, but also as it becomes a more multicultural society.

The requirement is for anti-discriminatory practice, which is rooted in multiculturalism, and defined by Thomas and Pierson (1995) as:

> A term used widely in social work and probation work, and in social work training, to describe how workers take account of structural disadvantage and seek to reduce individual and institutional discrimination particularly on grounds of race, gender, disability, social class and social orientation. (p.16)

Thompson (1997) observes: 'A basic feature of anti-discriminatory practice is the ability/willingness to see discrimination and oppression are so often central to the situations social workers encounter' (p.238). He views the need to be sensitive to the existence of discrimination and oppression as a basic social work concern. The power of human agency vested in the social worker offers a choice between transforming or reinforcing discriminatory practices within the social system through promoting social justice, equality and user participation. Jordan (1995) views anti-discriminatory practice as a moral imperative in an unjust society. This view suggests that social workers cannot simply be technicians of state power but should become moral arbiters of justice in the social order.

Social workers employ anti-discriminatory practice methodologies through enabling individuals to overcome individualised and institutionalised prejudice. They also seek to empower service users to tackle the social context that embeds and defends institutionalised discrimination. However, anti-discriminatory practice – at least in a systematic sense – has been slow to develop in Ireland. By decontextualising practice, traditional individualised social work in Ireland fundamentally ignored discrimination. It was viewed as beyond the remit of the caseworker. This served to reinforce monoculturalist 'Anglo conformity'.

Essentially, it is impossible to disentangle anti-discriminatory and anti-oppressive practice from political ideology. The multiculturalist perspective that informs anti-discriminatory practice shapes its form and content. Inevitably, statutory social work settings are more likely to adapt liberal multiculturalist perspectives. In civil society voluntary and community groups are likely to be more directly influenced by social movements and adopt a critical multiculturalist perspective.

Social work is quintessentially a humanist activity. In a society that is increasingly materialist and governed in terms of economic rather than social values, humanism is challenged as never before. It has two sources of legitimacy. First, humanism is rooted in the professional association, the Irish Association of Social Workers and specifically in its Code of Ethics. This gives professionals an alternative source of authority in the face of managerial pragmatism. Second, humanism is legitimised by practice that is genuinely democratic, respectful of difference and socially inclusive. This means placing social justice and empowerment at the centre of social work practice and struggling to reconcile them with the increasing demands of risk management and checklist practice.

Achieving this must involve renegotiating the relationship between the voluntary and community organisations that constitute civil society and state. As part of the National Anti-Poverty Strategy, the Green Paper on the Community and Voluntary Sector (Department of Social Welfare 1997) set out 'to suggest a framework for the future development of the relationship between the State and community and the voluntary sector and to facilitate a debate on the issues relevant to the relationship' (p.ii). The lack of response from social workers to the Green

Paper was disturbing. It contains the basis for a democratic bottom-up dialogical approach to social work that emphasises user rights and a genuinely empowering practice based upon active citizenship. It offers a legitimate response with which to counter the hierarchical practice of the 'new managerialism' in the public sector (see Powell and Guerin 1997). There needs to be a new emphasis on client participation, community engagement and socially inclusive forms of practice. Social work education in Ireland will need to move beyond its orientations towards work with individuals and social groups.

Ife (1997) characterises this alternative approach as critical practice:

> An important aspect of the critical approach is that it accepts and validates wisdom and expertise 'from below' as well as 'from above' ... The essence of practice from a critical perspective is that both sets of wisdom and expertise are valued and brought together. This is essentially a dialogical relationship. (p.137)

Such critical approaches find a particular relevance in the rapidly changing world of late-modernity. This is a 'Runaway World' (Giddens 1999), a reflexive global order where popular wisdom constantly challenges and reforms professional expertise. Increasingly 'scientific' top-down management is being discredited in favour of participation, dialogue and empowerment. The paradigms of 'risk' and 'trust', which Giddens has fruitfully explored in his work on modernity, must shape the future of social work (Giddens 1990; Ferguson 1997). While risk management dominates the concern of employers and lay people alike, trust and confidence building in the community should dominate the concerns of the profession. Social work needs to rethink its relationship with volunteers, community activists and view service users as citizens. This involves nothing less than constantly asking what we mean by the social work profession in the new millennium.

Chapter 4

Social Work in Northern Ireland

Jim Campbell and Mary McColgan

Introduction

Social work practice in Northern Ireland takes place in the context of an unusual set of legal, administrative and societal contexts. Historically, geographically and politically, Northern Ireland has an ambiguous position within the British and Western Isles, and these particular circumstances have affected the development of the social work profession. This chapter will examine, critically, the way in which social work is affected by the interplay of law, policy, practice and education, in a part of the United Kingdom which has experienced profound levels of social and political violence. In conclusion, it is argued that recent political change in Northern Ireland potentially offers social workers new ways of engaging with clients and communities, and that in doing so enables social workers to fulfil a more progressive role than has been hitherto possible.

Politics, society and the management of conflict in Northern Ireland

It does not seem possible fully to understand how social work functions in Northern Ireland without first considering the nature of the state in a society often described as the most violent in Western Europe. Since the advent of the most recent 'Troubles' in 1969, over three thousand people have died and tens of thousands have suffered physical, psychological and emotional injury as a result of intercommunal, paramilitary and state violence (Fay, Morrissey and Smyth 1999). Political and constitutional arrangements in Northern Ireland have always marked it out as a 'place apart' within the United Kingdom. The Government of Ireland Act 1920 partitioned Ireland and left the north-eastern six counties a contested geopolitical space (Map 4.1).

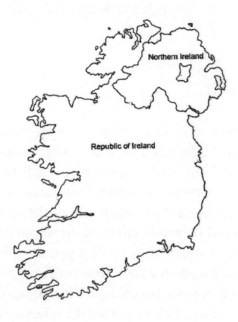

Map 4.1 Outline Map of Ireland: Northern Ireland and Republic of Ireland
Source: CAIN Project, Incore, Northen Ireland

Since 1921 many Catholics, who constituted a large minority of the population of Northern Ireland, perceived themselves as nationalists 'trapped'; their political aspirations to be part of the new Republic of Ireland in the southern 26 counties were hardly recognised. Conversely, most Protestants saw the union within the United Kingdom as a guarantee of civil and political rights, and felt threatened by what appeared to be an alien and hostile culture in the South. Simplistic notions of national identity, religious affiliation and ethnic difference cannot, however, fully explain the history of the political conflict in Northern Ireland. There have been, for example, various moments in this history when nationality has not been an organising principle around which politics revolve. For example, the motivation of class interest can help explain the revolt of the United Irishmen in 1798, the Poor Law Relief riots in Belfast in 1933 and the rise of the Northern Ireland Labour Party in the 1960s, and perhaps the politicisation of paramilitary groupings in the 1990s. An interesting development in the recent 'peace' talks was the role of the Women's Coalition as a mediating influence on the process, thus suggesting an increased interest in gendered politics. Although some academic and political discourses reinforce the notion that the conflict in Northern Ireland is essentially one of 'two warring tribes', the role of the British, and to a lesser extent, the Irish political establishment, in the management and at times exacerbation of the conflict, should not be ignored (Whyte 1991; Gaffikin and Morrissey 1990).

Despite the complexity of these social structures, constitutional arrangements between Northern Ireland, the rest of the United Kingdom and the Republic of Ireland tend to be preoccupied with problems raised by the 'national question'. For example, in 1972 full legislative and executive powers were removed from Stormont, the local parliament, and placed in the hands of Westminster. Described as 'direct rule' this mechanism has meant that Northern Ireland has been administered through a newly created Northern Ireland Office, headed by the Secretary of State for Northern Ireland and small number of ministers of state with responsibilities for numerous portfolios. Some attempts have been made to change these arrangements over the last 27 years. The Sunningdale Agreement led to the setting up of a power-sharing executive in Northern Ireland and all-Ireland institutions in 1974. After a short period of months, power was once again returned to Westminster after civil unrest led by workers and loyalist paramilitaries. Arguably, the next most significant attempt to change constitutional arrangements took place with the signing of the Anglo-Irish Agreement between the British and Irish Governments in 1985. For the first time since partition, the Government of the Republic of Ireland was given a degree of input into the policy-making processes of Northern Ireland (Hadden and Boyle 1989). Most recently, *The Agreement* (NIO

1998a) provided a structure in which a power-sharing executive, a North–South body and a body representing the islands of Britain and Ireland could be formed. Arguably this is the most significant constitutional development since the formation of Northern Ireland.

The weakness of the local economy is also a contributory factor in this political instability. Although the industrial activity had dynamic periods during the nineteenth century the manufacturing base went into almost continuous decline throughout the twentieth century (Borooah 1993). The result has been that the Northern Ireland state has depended upon subventions from Westminster in order to deliver upon a wide range of spending commitments on social security, health and education, agriculture, industry, and security. The political economy of Northern Ireland since 1921 has been characterised by high levels of unemployment, poverty and a range of unmet social and health needs. Even during the relatively stable period of the paramilitary 'cease-fires' of the past few years, the gap between the Northern Ireland and the UK average has remained. For example, in February 1997 unemployment stood at 8.8 per cent compared to 6.2 per cent for the UK as a whole (SSI(NI) 1997). In addition, considerably more people are unemployed for longer periods in Northern Ireland and men are more likely to be unemployed than women. Mallett (1997) highlights the extent to which poverty is endemic in this region through long-term unemployment and low wages. The contextual background of the political conflict has served to intensify the interplay between these factors, which have given rise to high levels of both social and economic deprivation. He concludes that low pay perpetuates both the experience of poverty and lower expectations of the workforce, and dependency on inadequate state benefit encourages a poverty trap. The deregulation of the labour market in Northern Ireland has led to more part-time work and a loss of entitlement to employment protection.

When these statistics on inequality are disaggregated, some groups are even worse off. For example, a tension continues to exist between the injustices, real and perceived, which many Catholics and Protestants feel. Fair employment legislation has done little to change the disadvantaged position of Catholics in the labour market. Both indirect and direct discrimination have been used to explain why Catholics continue to be more than twice as likely to be unemployed as Protestants (Teague 1993, McGarry and O'Leary 1995). On the other hand, Protestants tend to view the period of direct rule as a time when perceived allegiance to the United Kingdom state has paradoxically resulted in less power and influence. Disregard by Westminster of the internal affairs of Northern Ireland since its inception in 1921 has allowed a form of politics to develop which is typified by sectarian conflict (Brewer 1991). Even the geopolitics of the region reflect such divisions, with Catholics tending to live in the west and Protestants in the east (see Map 4.2).

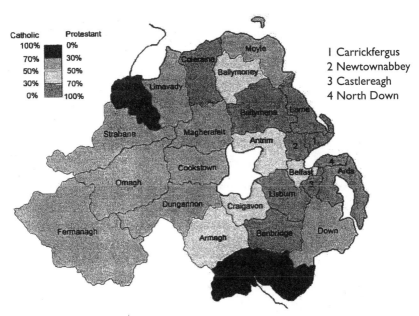

Map 4.2 Catholics and Protestants as a Percentage of the Population, District Council Areas, 1991
Source: CAIN Project, Incore, Northern Ireland

These structural problems create particular difficulties for other sections of Northern Irish society. Mallett's 1997 study, echoing earlier research (Spence 1996), pointed to a link between unemployment, lone parenthood, stress and ill health. A similar story is documented in studies of areas of poverty within Northern Ireland. For example, the report *Children of Creggan* (Foyle Health and Social Services Community Trust 1997) focused on a community in Derry, a city which has endured much civil unrest throughout the Troubles and one which has suffered a combination of endemic poverty and unemployment. The study found a community experiencing great levels of psychological stress, proportionately high numbers of families and children in need, and a generalised 'legacy of distrust and fear' of statutory intervention (p.44). The report concludes by arguing that statutory services should use alternative community development approaches as a way of targeting and resolving inequalities. The caveat was 'that community development is not a "quick fix" nor a cheap solution to meeting the health and social needs of the under fives' (p.49). Given the high levels of poverty, social need and intercommunal conflict in Northern Ireland, there is a growing recognition by Central Government of the need to look beyond individualistic approaches to solving some of these problems, and towards a more fuller engagement with groups and communities (DHSS(NI) 1996).

Organisation, policy and practice

Social work in Northern Ireland has developed against this backdrop of civil unrest and political uncertainty. In an early account of the way in which social workers responded to the conflict, Williamson and Darby (1978) described how practice was adjusted to deal with large-scale population movements, intimidation and the influence of paramilitary organisations. A few years later professional social work emerged within a particular, and unique, administrative structure known as the 'integrated service', established by the Health and Personal Social Services (NI) Order 1972 (DHSS(NI) 1972). The rationale for the creation of the integrated service can best be explained in the context of the decision to introduce Direct Rule by the Central Government at Westminster. It has been argued that this was an administrative arrangement which attempted to resolve conflict through a number of political, social, economic and military strategies (Ditch and Morrissey 1992). One of the consequences of this intervention was that systems of welfare were bureaucratised, with responsibility for health and personal social services, alongside other services such as education and housing, placed in the hands of quasi-autonomous agencies. These agencies have had a significant impact on social work practice because, quite unlike the system in the rest of the UK where health and social services organisations are split, they employ health and social services professionals under the same unified structure.

This technocratic strategy had both positive and negative consequences for social work in Northern Ireland (McCoy 1993). Four health and social services boards were established in 1973 under the direction of the Department of Health and Social Services. The service was administered by a hierarchy of professional groups, including medics, nurses, professionals attached to medicine, administrators and social workers. These boards had access to considerable financial resources and substantial decision-making authority to plan and provide for services. During the 1980s, however, there was an increasing move towards systems of general management and devolution of power and budgets away from boards, with smaller units of management given greater responsibility for the running of services. The last developmental phase mirrored the changes in social and health services in Britain following the publication of the Griffiths Report in 1988. Since the early 1990s boards have devolved many of their earlier general and statutory functions to community and hospital health and social services trusts, using the Health and Personal Social Services (NI) Order 1993 (DHSS(NI) 1993). In the last five years welfare bureaucracies in Northern Ireland have been preoccupied with policy themes which are common throughout the UK:

- the split between of purchasing and providing
- the principle of needs-led assessment
- GP fundholding
- deinstitutionalisation
- the consumer rights of service users and carers
- general rather than professional management.

The boards' overall responsibility is now to purchase services for populations in their areas and for trusts to both provide and purchase services. These processes are exceedingly complicated because four boards and 19 trusts organise health and social welfare for a population of only 1.6 million people.

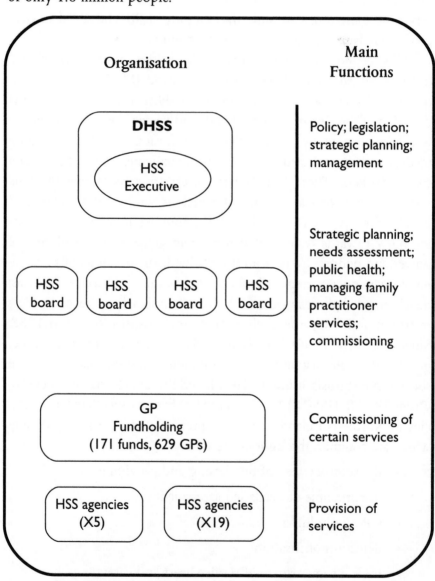

Source: DHSS (NI)

Figure 4.1 H&PSS structure in Northern Ireland

The government has recently published a white paper, *Fit for the Future*, which proposes to substantially reduce these organisational units (DHSS(NI) 1998).

Although there were benefits gained from the integrated service, particularly around multidisciplinary working and the efficiencies gained from common budget usage, there were also limitations. From the start, the prevailing organisational discourses within the integrated service implied the need for professional detachment from political issues and involvement in conflict resolution. Although professionals continued to deal with the problems that resulted from the Troubles, until recently few attempts were made actively to engage with political issues and work to resolve community conflicts (Campbell and Pinkerton 1997). Death, and the fear of death and injury, taken together with the social cleavages created by violence, have inevitably affected social workers; there should be no surprise in this, given that social workers themselves are mostly drawn from these communities. Sectarianism is pervasive in all aspects of life in Northern Ireland, at personal, familial and societal levels. A major difficulty in trying to deal with the fear associated with sectarianism is the subtle mechanisms that serve to reproduce oppression. These include the identification of social markers which help reinforce stereotypes about the 'other', for example through identification of the names, the use of language, schools attended and areas lived in (Brewer 1991).

Although there have been some attempts by social workers to reconsider their role in working in this context of violence, social welfare organisations in Northern Ireland do not encourage practitioners to think through the 'politicisation' of practice and the impact of political violence and sectarianism on their practice. This is partly because the issue is so difficult and dangerous to deal with in the workplace, but also because the agencies themselves are designed to operate *above* the conflict. As a result, Smyth and Campbell (1996) have argued that the social work profession has remained 'largely captivated by an ideology of benign attachment, one which fails to address the insidious effects of sectarianism on practice' (p.90).

This reality has posed tensions and challenges for the delivery of social work services, education and training. An example of such tension is illustrated in the way in which the probation service for Northern Ireland has grappled with the issue of 'political prisoners'. Early in the Troubles, a debate took place within the organisation about the appropriateness of providing reports to courts for clients who declared their actions to be politically motivated. Since then probation officers have had little formal, legal contact with such clients, although the service has in the 1990s increasingly engaged with schemes that aim to rehabilitate such prisoners. At the heart of such tensions are the positions that social workers occupy between the state and civil society. Because of nature of these relationships in Northern Ireland, it could be argued that social workers have to face greater problems than counterparts elsewhere. The professional requirement to analyse discrimination in society and to challenge pervasive forms of subordination have contrasted sharply with the very real fears associated with delivering a service to clients who are often from the 'other' community. The resultant professional dilemma is captured in Traynor's (1998) assessment of the 'no-win' situation faced by many social workers:

> The worker, therefore is faced with a choice: to confront sectarianism and face possible defensiveness, or collude in the interest of service development and meeting community need. The dilemma is starker if workers come from 'the other community', seek acceptance, feel they have something to prove, feel guilty for the past oppressions of their own community, are afraid of accusations of discrimination or fear for their own safety. (p.2)

Law and practice

A distinguishing feature of the political administration Northern Ireland has been the relative ease with which laws and departmental agendas are introduced. Sometimes important policies are implemented without parliamentary process. For example, the equivalent to the Community Care Act for England and Wales is a policy paper, *People First* (DHSS(NI) 1991) issued by the Department of Health and Social Services. Even when parliamentary processes are used to introduce law for Northern Ireland, the mechanism is usually the Order in Council, often criticised because it allows little time for scrutiny and local debate (Hadfield 1989). Orders in Council have tended to be similar to equivalent British Acts, but are usually introduced some time after the Act and are occasionally shaped by local circumstances.

Thus, the principles of child protection legislation and policy in Northern Ireland were largely determined by a principle of 'parity' with other UK legislation. Sometimes, however, local circumstances have been taken into account as demonstrated in the history and drafting of The Children (Northern Ireland) Order 1995 (DHSS(NI) 1995). A failure to introduce a review of legislation for children's welfare during the previous 25 years was the result of a complex interplay between social policy, social reform and social unrest (Kelly and Pinkerton 1996), and the particularities of personal social services organisations (Horgan 1997). The Order introduced a new emphasis on parental responsibility and the duty of the state not only to intervene to promote and protect the welfare of children, but also to work in partnerships with parents to help them support their children (McColgan 1995). The workings of family support systems in Northern Ireland have been found to be diverse, and include respite services, day centre and day care facilities as well as domiciliary services which families receive in their own home (Higgins, Pinkerton and Switzer 1997).

Article 66 of the Order sets out the statutory responsibility of health and social services boards to carry out investigations where there is reasonable cause to suspect that a child is suffering or is likely to suffer significant harm. The boards have delegated responsibility to local trusts to carry out such investigations and to co-ordinate, develop and monitor child protection work. These processes are regulated through Area Child Protection Committees (ACPCs). A recurrent theme in child protection services has been the refocusing debate which realigns protection within a broader continuum of family support for children in need. In some respects at least, statistics on the child protection register over a ten-year period (1986–1995) suggest downward trends in this area (Switzer 1997). However, the Department of Health and Social Services have emphasised that the confirmed cases of child abuse account for only 40 per cent of the total registered; it would appear that the remaining children are not registered because child protection plans are deemed unnecessary (DHSS(NI) 1997a, para 8.10). These statistics are supported by boards' data on reductions of numbers of children on child protection registers (Northern Area and Western Area Children's Services, and Children's Services Plan 1999–2002), with a number of associated explanations used to account for these trends. It may be that clearer assessment thresholds and multiprofessional co-operation are contributory factors (Western Area Board, Children's Services Plans 1999–2002, p.60).

This apparent achievement belies tensions inherent in the shift from protection to supportive services to children in need and their families. There are indications that patterns identified in the wake of the Children Act in 1991 will be replicated in Northern Ireland. Higgins, Pinkerton and Devine (2000), for example, have concluded that there had been no dramatic shift towards family support within the first year of the introduction of the Order. In effect there have been concerns that the predominance of child protection activity as evidenced in England and Wales would limit a broad definition of children in need and restrict the strategic development of supportive services. Spratt (1998) has discussed the impact of common regional guidance in joint protocol procedures, pointing out that there are ambiguities around the use of police in child protection practice and in the development of a culture of risk management:

> If assessment of 'need' means multi-disciplinary checks in the guise of 'liaisons', multi-disciplinary meetings become a substitute for case conferences and the resulting 'provision of services' consists of visits by the social worker to 'monitor and advise', then a mirror image of the child protection system is in operation. (p.99)

A professional culture which emphasises prevention is required to counter-balance these tendencies. Higgins *et al.* (1997) and Cavanagh (1998) have argued that collaboration with the voluntary sector and local communities may redress some of the limitations in the implementation of policies on parental participation in child protection work. Other evidence (Hayes 1995; O'Hagan 1997; McColgan 1998) suggests that legislative intent has yet to be realised in practice, especially in the context of case conference settings (Dunlop 1999).

The introduction of mandatory children's service plans in April 1999 seeks to provide a strategic focus for a range of services to children, including children subject to child protection investigation. A key feature of this development has been the creation of a children and young people's committee, which is comprised of core group representation from a range of statutory and voluntary bodies involved in service provision. Although potential benefits should emerge from these processes of negotiation with the community and voluntary sectors, new organisational changes proposed in *Fit for the Future* (DHSS(NI) 1998) may reinforce existing reliance on risk assessment to the detriment of an holistic, interagency approach to assessment of need.

The ways in which adult services have developed also reveal local differences from national policy and legislation. For example, The Mental Health (NI) Order 1986 resembles equivalent British legislation in that it provides a substantial legal role for the approved social worker (ASW), yet there are also differences. In the review of the previous mental health legislation, the MacDermott Committee (DHSS(NI) 1981) argued for the exclusion of personality disorder as a condition for compulsory admission to hospital, and it was agreed that compulsory admissions to hospital should be carried by general practitioners, not psychiatrists, alongside an ASW or nearest relative. These 'compulsory' admissions are a novel feature of the Order, because clients are not detained until a period of up to 14 days, during which a multidisciplinary assessment takes place. A client may then be either kept in hospital for a further period, or regraded to voluntary status. This mechanism allows for the protection of civil rights in terms of immigration and employment law (Potter 1997). An additional feature of the legislation was that it provided the Mental Health Commission for Northern Ireland with extensive powers of inspection in the community and access to voluntary as well as detained clients. It has been argued that, as a result of these deliberations, the legislation is more protective of patients' rights and affords the ASW a greater role than their British counterparts (Prior 1993; Campbell 1998).

The particular legal and organisational context has also shaped various forms of multidisciplinary working. In mental health, health, learning disability and elders programmes of care throughout Northern Ireland there has been a tendency for social workers to be employed alongside nurses, professionals associated with medicine and, to a lesser extent, medics. New opportunities for cross-disciplinary working have also increased with the advent of care management – there is some evidence to suggest that the integrated service has encouraged innovative and flexible practice and that social work has had a part to play in these new arrangements. However, blocks to multidisciplinary working remain. Many boards and trusts have been unsuccessful in modifying interprofessional rivalry, and the relative power of the medical profession has never been fully challenged. Caul and Herron (1992) have argued that this imbalance led to the marginalisation of social work with the introduction of general management. For example, in the early years of the integrated service, a professional seam ran right through the organisation from basic grade practitioner to director of social services at board level. With financial retrenchment in the 1980s and 1990s, and the introduction of general management, this system of line management has been gradually eroded. In many cases social workers are now managed by other professionals, particularly nurses; the reverse is also the case. This is not, however, the case for medical practitioners who have had their system of line management and professional accountability left more or less intact.

The Probation Board (Northern Ireland) Order 1982 (NIO 1982) established the current Probation Board for Northern Ireland (PBNI). Prior to this date, the service had been administered by central government. The Board has gradually has established position which takes account of the political and social context of Northern Ireland and is thus different, in some respects, from its counterparts in the rest of the UK. Although the service has statutory responsibility for the supervision of young offenders from the age of ten years, it has never supervised released parolees. Unlike its UK counterparts, PBNI has no role in a social work service to the divorce court; this responsibility was passed on to health and social services boards in the late 1970s (Gadd 1996).

The Board comprises lay members of the community and is enabled by legislation directly to fund voluntary organisations and community groups to undertake supervision of offenders and the prevention of crime (Lindsay 1998). The introduction of the Criminal Justice (Children) Order 1998 (NIO 1999) effectively replaced training school orders with juvenile justice centre orders. These are targeted at the most serious offenders, have a shorter duration, and comprise a significant non-custodial component. It is anticipated that this shift in policy will have an impact on the need to develop a range of community rehabilitative and support services for the majority of young people who will otherwise receive a community sentence. The government's juvenile justice strategy for Northern Ireland is premised on four principles.

1. Corporate responsibility for agencies to reduce criminal proceedings is achieved by targeting responses to juvenile crime.

2. Diversionary strategies need to be based on effective interagency co-operation and co-ordination.

3. Minimal custodial sentencing, and a range of non-custodial options, should be used.

4. In exceptional situations, time-limited custodial sentences for serious offences should be closely supervised in the community.

Despite such measures, it has been difficult to establish accurate statistics about the numbers of children and young people involved in offending behaviour. This arises from differential frameworks for recording statistics and the realities of high levels of juvenile crime in certain localities in Northern Ireland where paramilitary-style justice is dispensed. Paradoxically,

>...the erosion of legitimate law enforcement and the unacceptability of the security forces, largely but not exclusively in Republican and Nationalist areas, has left a vacuum. This has been filled by a form of 'community policing', that is, policing by paramilitary organisations.

However, this is policing which extends beyond detection and arrest to trial, sentencing and delivery of punishment. (Lindsay 1998, p.14)

Restorative justice has emerged against this backdrop of alternative justice systems. Based on Breton laws, it adopts an approach which focuses on the relationship between victim and offender and is underpinned by principles of collaboration, community reintegration, reconciliation and inclusion (Auld 1997). It remains to be seen whether such radical approaches to policy and practice will affect the nature of probation work practice.

The introduction of new mixes in the economy of welfare in the 1990s has encouraged new forms of partnerships between statutory, voluntary, community and private agencies in Northern Ireland. Traditionally very strong voluntary agencies increasingly employ qualified social workers, although increased professionalisation brings with it some dilemmas. Such agencies have had to strike a balance between a traditional commitment to innovative practice and more recent pressures to develop and provide services purchased by the statutory sector. An example of this is the case of the Bryson House Family Support Service, which has been operating since 1978. It is currently providing five schemes across Northern Ireland and is aimed at providing practical and emotional support to families under stress. Several themes have emerged from evaluations of the service (Bogues and McColgan 1997; Bogues and Lindsay 1998). Although resources have been retracting, the service provided a focused response to children at risk and need.

- There was a strong partnership ethos that was evident in partnership with both families and statutory workers; this was reflected in the positive feedback from service users and referrers.

- The service allowed for the development of open, trusting relationships underpinned by a value base of support, respect and equality that mitigates against labelling and poor self-esteem experienced by families under stress.

- A major limitation of the support provided was the absence of reliable, valid frequency measurements to record change in children's behaviour or parental functioning.

Aspects of training

Despite of the unusual administrative arrangements which flowed from the imposition of Direct Rule, there are close relationships between social work education and training in Northern Ireland and the rest of the UK. In the early years of the service there was a period of expansion in training and employment which coincided with the growth of the profession in Britain, post-Seebohm. Northern Irish social workers share a common knowledge, values and skills base with counterparts trained in Britain, under the auspices of the Central Council for the Education and Training of Social Work (CCETSW). In all of the fields which social work is practised – adult services, criminal justice, family and child care services – common, cross-national themes emerge.

In Northern Ireland there are three diploma in social work programmes delivering five different routes to social work qualification – two postgraduate, one non-graduate, one undergraduate and an employment-based route. The diploma in social work, which was introduced in 1990, is also the professional qualification for probation officers in Northern Ireland (Reilly 1997). The Central Council for Education and Training in Social Work (CCETSW) requires social work education and training to be organised and provided by collaborative partnerships of universities, colleges, statutory and voluntary sectors. Bamford (1996) describes the experience of partnership and the concomitant tensions and conflicts of the 1990s. He outlines the difficulties in the politics and psychology of partnership as well as the achievements gained. The developmental model of collaborative systems, procedures and mechanisms for curriculum delivery is set against the competing fragmented professional interface of academics and agency personnel. The hard-won achievements were testimony to the time, energy and commitment involved in establishing complex systems, which were based on mutual understanding and trust. He argues that a 'partnership chemistry' was created which had its roots in a constructive planning process. Some partnerships engaged in jointly funded lectureships with agencies, while all have been involved in the production of regional and national curricula (Smyth, Schlindwein and Michael 1993; Gibson, Michael and Wilson 1994).

The additional benefits of partnership included the creation of expertise to problem solve issues such as assessment regulations, practice learning dilemmas and curriculum resources and, crucially, relationships which were 'highly productive in terms of defining much more closely what is important in delivering the curriculum to students' (Bamford 1996, p.26). Synchronizing the 'fit' between training and the experiences of newly qualified workers (NQWs) was the focus of the *Readiness to Practice* study for Northern Ireland (Rea 1996). This research sought to examine the perceptions of the cohort of new social workers qualifying in 1993 and their managers. They were questioned about levels of skills, knowledge and values, and their capacity to meet employers' expectations in their first year of employment. The study generally found high levels of satisfaction among NQWs and line managers about the overall extent to which their social work training had prepared them for practice, although specific criticisms were made about some aspects of training in the criminal justice field. Interestingly, the profile of respondents reflected a predominantly mature, female Catholic cohort with prior experience of employment in social work or social care settings across voluntary, statutory or private sectors.

This profile of the people drawn to the profession in Northern Ireland has been broadly confirmed by other small-scale studies (Smyth and Campbell 1996; Bogues and Falconer 1998). Research into the Northern Ireland workforce (NISW 1997) has provided valuable insights into the activities of social work managers, community-based social workers and residential social workers. The results have drawn attention to high levels of stress compared with the general population. Managers and residential social workers tended to report higher levels of stress and lower levels of job satisfaction. Recent organisational changes have affected different tiers within the profession. Thus, managers tended to focus on problems created for them through restructuring while basic-grade practitioners highlighted financial retrenchment as an impediment to job proficiency and satisfaction. In Northern Ireland, social work education and training has taken place against the backcloth of political uncertainty, sectarian conflict; and major economic and social deprivation. The NISW study found that some staff, particularly Catholics, experienced incidences of sectarianism. The challenge of addressing sectarianism in the context of social work education has been explored by Smyth and Campbell (1996) who argue that antisectarian training for qualifying social workers is hampered by institutional and personal resistance.

Apart from the probation service, which is an independent organisation responsible to the Northern Ireland Office, all other statutory social workers are employed within recognisable programmes of care: mental health, family and child care, learning disability, older people, and health and disability. Forms of multidisciplinary working have allowed some opportunity for training with other professionals. For example, during the implementation of the Children Order unprecedented multidisciplinary and interagency training programmes took place, focusing on three levels – foundation, comprehensive and specialist. 25,000 members of staff, across the statutory and voluntary sectors, were trained in 1996/7 (SSI(NI) 1997). Apart from disseminating pertinent information about the legislation, the training forums reflected agency emphases on partnership and sought to lay the foundations for enhanced co-operation and integration across professional boundaries. In particular, the operational requirements of child protection procedures were predicated on closer liaison and core group working between relevant professionals.

At the start of the new millennium, the future of social work education, training and employment faces new challenges. The quinquennial review of CCETSW alongside the emergence of a National Training Organisation (NTO) for the personal social services has important implications for social work education and training in Northern Ireland. The focus of the second stage of the CCETSW review may lead to considerations about rationalising the numbers of qualifying programmes and reviews of the content of diplomas in social work. In an attempt to promote consistency and agreement about key aspects of diplomas in social work training, several regional initiatives have involved collaborative ventures, which has had significant impact on the quality of placement provision, practice teaching and the assessment of competence. For example, the allocation of placements is undertaken by a regional placement allocation group which meets twice a year to allocate resources across all the programmes, and local initiatives have influenced the development of practice assessment panel procedures and the content of pathways teaching.

Discussions about the complementary roles of NTOs undertaking promotional and developmental activities in tandem with the General Social Care Council functions for regulating education and training have raised concerns about the necessity for local representation. If the integrated health and social services provision remains the model for service delivery, it is recognised that the introduction of a Northern Ireland NTO would need to liaise effectively with existing networks across government departments and relate to voluntary and private sectors, as well as maintaining UK alliances. However, an equally pressing issue for social work education has centred around the validation of the diploma in social work in the context of training and education in the Republic of Ireland. Since 1997, professional standards for social work education and training have been set by the National Social Work Qualifications Board (NSWQB) in the Republic. These standards have been established in line with the European Directive 89/48, which has stipulated professional education and training of at least three years duration. As a consequence, there are issues about the transferability of the diploma in social work into the Republic of Ireland, particularly the content of academic teaching, the length of placement experience and academic levels. To this end, CCETSW (Northern Ireland) has undertaken a collaborative study of the social work qualifications and employment requirements in both jurisdictions. The anticipated outcome of the report will contribute to cross-border discussions and initiatives aimed at achieving comparability of qualification within a European context.

Funding of higher education has been another significant factor in social work education and training. The cessation of mandatory grants and the requirement for tuition fees will have an impact on undergraduate and non-graduate programmes. Despite efforts to advocate for similar special measures for other professional groups, it is not yet clear if the government will support this parity principle. Recent indications of reduced applications for social work training, coupled with the profile of mature entrants, may lead to a decline in the quantity and quality of future social workers in Northern Ireland. It may be that in the long term this development will affect the social work labour force and that social work programmes may be forced to select students who have the ability to provide personal funding for training. This prospect would reinforce existing patterns of exclusion for disadvantaged groups and exacerbate poverty among social work students.

These tensions in qualifying training have to be set in the context of a broader continuum of social work training. Northern Ireland has the distinction of being the first consortium approved by CCETSW to establish a post-qualifying framework through local partnerships of educational institutions and social services agencies. The post-qualifying framework has been in operation since 1991 and has developed a consolidation programme as well as a range of award levels through portfolio submission. This enhanced focus on professional development has taken the lead in promotion of professional standards. The importance of evaluating research in the field of social work in Northern Ireland has been given some impetus by the recent establishment of a Research and Development Office (RDO) for the Health and Personal Social Services in Northern Ireland. The Office has a declared remit to establish a strategy for the combined areas of adult and children's health and social care, with a particular emphasis on promoting interdisciplinary, interprofessional and interinstitutional research. As well as facilitating collaborative research projects, the RDO aims to develop a coherent strategy which targets specific research areas for potential contribution to developing or enhancing international standards. This has coincided with the creation of the Centre for Child Care Research, which has set itself three major objectives, to:

1. identify and conduct original research into child care needs and services

2. provide access to a wide range of child care research findings

3. offer training and consultation on undertaking and applying child care research.

Recent developments

Just as the Troubles have inevitably affected aspects of policy, practice and training in Northern Ireland, the series of ceasefires that first emerged in 1994 may offer opportunities for new forms of social work. It may be that the shifting political attitudes created by a series of recent ceasefires will create a greater willingness by this society to engage in more cross-community peace-building initiatives. The Agreement (NIO 1998) implies a realignment of political relationships within the UK and between the UK and the Republic of Ireland. It is reasonable to assume that social workers, like other professionals, will have to change their practice, given these rapidly changing circumstances. For example, one consequence of the recent political negotiations has been the possibility that the administration of health and social care, for the first time in 30 years, will be the responsibility of local, democratically accountable politicians and institutions.

In the past, social workers have had to face many challenges created in a society that has suffered much violence and social upheaval. It may be that in this changing environment social workers will play a more active role in engaging with clients and communities whose needs were often neglected. In doing so they will be supported by a number of recent key policy documents, *Health and Wellbeing: Into the Next Millennium* (DHSS(NI) 1996) and *Well into 2000* (DHSS(NI) 1997a), which place considerable emphasis on a number of important health and social welfare themes, such as addressing social exclusion, assessing need, interventions which are preventative, and working in partnership with local communities.

Departmental strategies for the next five years suggest that social workers will have to rethink the way they practice with communities and disadvantaged groups. The emphasis of these policies on decentralised, user-friendly services implies that traditional statutory, casework approaches are less likely to be required. For example, the theme of user empowerment has found its way into the discourse of most social welfare organisations. Social workers and their agencies can make professional choices about whether this is driven by a consumerist or more genuinely empowering ideology (Forbes and Sashidharan 1997). A recent piece of research in Northern Ireland helps illustrate the choices that can be made by social services organisations and their staff. Campbell and Donnelly (1996), in their survey of a mental health social work service in Belfast, found quite high levels of overall satisfaction among service users, but that the social role and function was unclear. Respondents were generally ignorant about how to complain, and there was no evidence of any systematic attempt to involve users in planning or providing services. Since the survey was carried out, a service user advocate has been employed by a local trust to initiate more participation by clients in the delivery of mental health services.

A similar argument can be made about the way some social work agencies in Northern Ireland have embraced, or rediscovered, community work. Despite the reservations of some community workers in the voluntary and statutory sectors in Northern Ireland, there is a tendency by the state to re-examine the value of community development as a method for delivering welfare services, reflecting a parallel rapprochement in the rest of the UK. A wide range of different projects in Northern Ireland is currently sponsored by the Government in areas of child and family welfare, community care and the criminal justice system. Such developments might be viewed as the cynical manipulation of disadvantaged communities, but at the same time organisational changes might offer social workers new agendas which can help them move away from the technocratic approaches that were a feature of the service since 1973. The Shankill health and social care project in Belfast uses a multidisciplinary and cross-agency approach to solving social and health problems. It is jointly funded by Central Government, the local trust and European Union monies, and involves close working relationships between a variety of stakeholders – statutory workers, local communities and agencies. The probation service for Northern Ireland is also attempting to alter traditional approaches to working with prisoners and ex-prisoners by employing youth and community workers in disadvantaged areas in out-of-hours work. Although court work remains part of the agency's statutory function, there is a realisation that prevention must involve some recognition of the impact of the Troubles on the criminal justice system, and the role of local communities and influence of paramilitary organisations in the resolution of social problems.

Although sectarianism appears to be the historical site of oppression and subordination in Northern Ireland, the existence of racism is a phenomenon which many social workers have failed to acknowledge. Mannkler's (1997) study revealed the structural nature of racism, which is often hidden by the overemphasis on the conflict between Protestant and Catholic. Consequently, discussions about the needs of minority ethnic communities are often marginalised. One significant aspect of change in the social life of Northern Ireland in recent years is the increasing awareness and visibility of ethnic minority groups. In the past, it was often mistakenly assumed by policy makers and the wider public that issues of racism did not exist in what was an apparently homogenous society; the continual focus on sectarianism exacerbated this form of social myopia. Although some health and social services trusts in Northern Ireland have, traditionally, provided social work services to the travelling community, to date services to all minority ethnic communities has been at best patchy. There is now a gradual recognition of the centuries-old racism carried out against the travelling community and new forms of oppression faced by newer minority ethnic communities living in Northern Ireland. It is some indication of the 'colour blindness' of Northern Irish society that it has taken a full 22 years to introduce race relations legislation after the British equivalent (DHSS(NI) 1997). This event has provided some impetus to antiracist social work training and practice in Northern Ireland in recent years. The introduction of the Race Relations (Northern Ireland) Order will offer social workers, and other professionals, new opportunities for working with these communities. The Order has profound implications for a social work culture that traditionally often ignored the needs of minority ethnic communities. It may be that the experiences and lessons of antisectarian training may help social workers examine their attitudes to racism and explore new ways to empower these disadvantaged groups.

This context of political and social change may also allow new policy agendas to create opportunities for new forms of antisectarian social work practice. It can be argued that the inability to address this issue was an understandable response to the anger of the past and fear of the present. There are, however, a number of encouraging signs that institutions and staff are being 'freed up' to speak more openly about the issue. Correspondingly, CCETSW in Northern Ireland have recently commissioned research into how social care agencies have tried to address sectarianism. Their aim is to construct a range if standards in practice and training which might allow agencies to examine aspects of sectarianism in a more open, yet safe environment.

A major problem faced by Northern Irish society is in coming to terms with the traumas of the past and in addressing very high levels of physical, psychological and emotional needs (Fay *et al.* 1999). In their review of services available to 'victims' of the conflict, the Social Services Inspectorate have identified many gaps and inadequacies in ways in which professionals dealt with these issues in the past (DHSS(NI) 1997). The authors of the report argued that the community and voluntary sectors are well placed to deliver services close to where need is most felt, but that they should be offered the financial and professional support hitherto not afforded to them. They also recommended that counselling services should be much more closely regulated and accredited in order that clients traumatised by violence could trust those who offer help. This reassessment of the importance of the 'victims' has been given further impetus by the Bloomfield Report, (NIO 1998c) which argued for the political and social recognition of victims' needs and the establishment of a commissioner for 'victims'.

It is clear that, given the position which social work has in the organisation of health and social welfare in Northern Ireland, these developments imply changes to practice. What appears to have happened in the past is that statutory services have tended to avoid the very difficult political problems, which are usually associated with violence to their clients. Instead they tended to focus on less controversial services which could be delivered in more technical ways. There are signs that the profession is embracing some aspects of change. In the aftermath of the Omagh bomb in which 29 people lost their lives and hundreds were traumatised, social workers have played an important role, alongside other professionals, in assessing need and providing service. For the first time a regional training course has been organised to help social workers and other health and social welfare professionals to develop their knowledge and skills base in dealing with the impact of such traumas. As the levels of trauma caused by 30 years of political and social conflict slowly emerge at a time of relative peace, then these new skills will be essential to social workers.

Conclusion

The history of social work in Northern Ireland reveals a number of contradictions. These social workers share a common training, skills and knowledge base with professionals working elsewhere in the United Kingdom, and have to deal with many of the social problems that are commonplace throughout the British Isles. On the other hand, the political and social violence, which led to the creation of the integrated service, has profoundly affected practice. Participation in a centrally planned and financed service has allowed for innovative ways of multidisciplinary working, but there remains a question about whether social workers have managed to preserve their professional identity in the midst of organisational change and competing policy agendas.

Perhaps it is because of the nature of the organisations in which social workers practice, and the relationship these agencies have with the state, that the profession has to date not been well equipped to deal with the underlying problems of social and political conflict which permeate Northern Irish society. However, it may be that new political developments and social movements will create opportunities to resolve the problem of the state. In this context, social work will need to change if it is to offer responsive services to those who have suffered most because of the Troubles.

Chapter 5

Social Work in Scotland
After Devolution

Lorraine Waterhouse and Janice McGhee

Introduction

This chapter traces the development of the political, economic and social landscape of Scotland. It outlines the legal and governmental structures that diverge from the rest of the UK. It offers an overview of the delivery of social work services and the philosophy behind them. Key policy areas for service provision, including criminal justice social work, children's services and community care, are identified and recent research findings explored. Adequate resourcing and interdisciplinary co-operation emerge as the main challenges for future development in all three areas. The devolution of power to the Scottish Parliament presents an opportunity to provide services that match the needs of people living in Scotland. At the same time, devolution poses a question about the longer-term symmetry of social work policy and service provision within the UK as a whole.

Political, economic and social structure of Scotland

Economy

Approximately five million people live in Scotland, with women representing 52 per cent of this population (*Scottish Office* 1998b). Many of the wider social and economic trends affecting the United Kingdom (UK) are found in Scotland. Over the last 40 years, Scotland has seen an expansion in non-manual employment associated with a decline in manual and heavy industry (McCrone 1992). There has been a growth of self-employment to a level of approximately 10 per cent in 1997 (Mackay *et al.* 1999, p.55).

Looking at average incomes across the UK, Scotland is overrepresented at the lower end of the income distribution scale although ahead of the North of England and Wales (Goodman *et al.* 1997, p.110). Within Scotland, there is an east/west divide in the distribution of income (Hills 1995). Glasgow, situated in the west of Scotland, for example, scores highly in league tables ranking deprivation (Hills 1995, p.80). Poverty remains a major social problem in Scotland, with more than one in three Scottish children estimated to be living in poverty (Scottish Poverty Information Unit 1998). The children of lone parents are especially vulnerable, with three-quarters dependent on income support (Scottish Poverty Information Unit 1998). More than one-third of all live births in Scotland in 1997 were to unmarried mothers (*Scottish Office* 1998b, Table IB3) and, as in England and Wales, there has been a dramatic increase in the divorce rate[1] over the last 40 years to around 40 per cent (Mackay *et al.* 1997, p.94).

Housing and health

In postwar Scotland public-sector housing dominated but decreased from the 1970s with a significant growth in owner occupation between 1981 and 1995 – about 80 per cent compared with 33 per cent in England (English 1998, p.123). This was mainly due to the sale of council housing under the right-to-buy legislation introduced by the Conservative Government. However, in Scotland public renting remains higher and owner occupation lower compared to England and Wales. Housing associations play a major part in the provision of social housing in Scotland, where there is a high proportion of households dependent on social security benefits (English 1998, p.130). Homelessness continues to present problems, and it is estimated that there are 33,000 children in Scotland affected (Children in Scotland 1995).

The Chief Medical Officer for Scotland reported recently that there was a growing health gap between Scotland and England as illustrated in mortality rates for men and women under age 65 (Scottish Office 1996). The explanation appears to be found in the differential social and economic status of the two countries rather than in differences of medical efficacy (Scottish Office 1996). These global figures hide regional variations within the UK. Despite higher levels of public spending on health care in Scotland, there have not been the expected health gains (Turner 1998, p.57).

Social deprivation is seen as a major causal factor in Scotland's health deficit, although poor lifestyle including the incidence of smoking and a high-fat diet are also implicated (Scottish Office 1996). There are also variations in mortality rates within Scotland with an overconcentration in the Greater Glasgow area that has high levels of social and economic deprivation (Carstairs and Morris 1991). The Chief Medical Officer for Scotland concluded that Scotland's health compared badly to other Western industrialised countries (Turner 1998, p.54). Only 4 per cent of the population in Scotland in 1993, compared to 12 per cent in England, had private health insurance cover.

Education

The Scottish education system continues to offer denominational schooling and adopts a broad-based curriculum in the senior years of secondary schooling where candidates normally study five subjects to 'higher level'. This approach is also reflected in the university system where honours degrees are normally of four years' duration rather than three years in England. Approaching 50 per cent of young Scots entered higher education in 1996–97 (Scottish Office *Scottish Office* 1998c).

Governance

Scotland was a separate nation state until the union of the Scottish and English parliaments in 1707. This union was not intended to effect a complete assimilation of the two countries, provision having been made for continuance of the different established churches and the legal system (Himsworth and Munro 1999, p.viii). Himsworth and Munro (1999) argue this allowed the preservation of different identities within

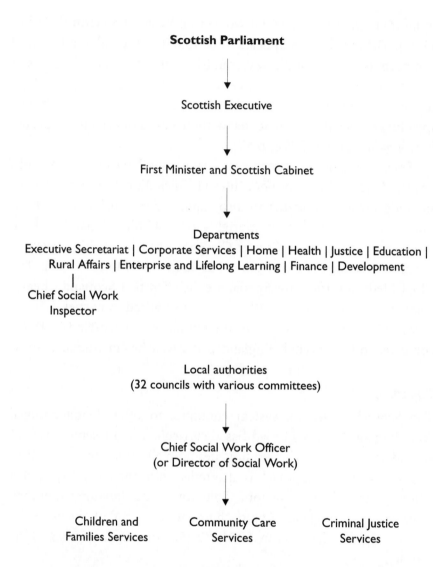

Figure 5.1 Simplified diagram of the governance of Scotland

a unitary British state. McCrone (1996) describes Scotland as a 'state-less nation' with similarities to Quebec and Catalonia. He argues that these three regions have in common the presence of coherent civil societies that are not independent states but have varying degrees of political autonomy (McCrone 1996, p.46).

There is also a long history of administrative devolution from 1885 when the Scottish Office (now the Scottish Executive) was created as a department of government (Himsworth and Munro 1999, p.viii) with its minister (the Secretary of State for Scotland) responsible for law, order and education. Himsworth and Munro (1999) argue that over the last one hundred years, the importance of the Scottish Office grew to the point where it had responsibility for most functions of UK government in Scotland (excepting, for example, defence, foreign policy and social security). This devolution has paved the way for the creation of the modern Scottish Executive following the Scotland Act 1998 and the inception of the Scottish Parliament.

THE SCOTTISH PARLIAMENT

The Scotland Act 1998 set up the processes for the election of members to the Scottish Parliament, the creation of a Scottish administration, and ministerial functions. The Act also defines the legislative powers that are devolved to the Scottish Parliament. These include, among others, social work and health services, education and training, housing, law and order. Other issues are reserved to the UK Parliament[2] including social security, foreign policy and defence. The UK Parliament retains the power to make legislation in the devolved areas although it is not expected to do so without the consent of the Scottish Parliament.

The Scottish Parliament was elected on 6 May 1999 and was invested with its statutory powers on 1 July 1999. There are 129 members of the Scottish Parliament (MSPs) and a Scottish Executive headed by the First Minister and a team of 10 ministers, 10 deputy ministers, and the Lord Advocate and the Solicitor General. There is no solution yet to what has come to be known as the 'West Lothian' question,[3] namely the consequences of devolution for the UK Parliament. The varying development of devolved arrangements in the UK (i.e., the creation of the Welsh Assembly and Assembly for Northern Ireland) suggests that the Scotland Act 1998 has not created a unilateral system of devolution but an asymmetry in the constitutional arrangements of the governance of the UK (Himsworth and Munro 1999, p. xvii).

LOCAL AUTHORITIES

Major local government reorganisation[4] was undertaken in Scotland in 1996, influencing the pattern and delivery of social work services. There are 32 local authorities that vary widely in terms of geographical size and population. Highland Council encompasses a large rural area of 2,578,000 hectares and a population of 200,000 people (Scottish Office 1995b, see English 1998, Table 1.2). This contrasts with Clackmannanshire, with a population of less than 50,000 and a land area of 16,000 hectares (Scottish Office 1995b, see English 1998, Table 1.2).

The new legislation[5] removed the need for local councils to have a social work committee and a director of social work, although all the new authorities must have a chief social work officer. Some local authorities have combined housing and social work departments and others are choosing to organise services around particular client groups, for example children and families, by putting together education and social work services. Expenditure in 1995/96 by local authorities in Scotland was dominated by education (39%) and social work (16%) (English 1998, p.15). However, further reorganisation is expected following the McIntosh Commission Report (1999), which addresses the relationship between local government and the Scottish Parliament following devolution.

Social work

The architecture of social work services in Scotland was first outlined in the White Paper *Social Work and the Community* (Scottish Office 1966) and enacted by the Social Work (Scotland) Act 1968. The Kilbrandon Report (1964) and the report of the McBoyle Committee (1963) informed the proposals, although Kilbrandon's recommendations to create social education departments was rejected in favour of introducing social work departments. These came to have wide-ranging responsibilities to provide services to children, families, older people, people with mental health problems, with disability, and offenders. These paralleled developments in England and Wales following the Seebohm Committee's Report (1968), which also highlighted the inadequacies of existing statutory services and argued for greater co-ordination of provision.

In Scotland, different solutions were arrived at in relation to probation and other services for adult offenders. Whereas in England and Wales a separate probation service was retained, Scotland opted to locate criminal justice social work within local authorities (an arrangement which still continues). Direct funding from central government has been made available to local authorities for criminal justice social work since 1990. A grant to enable local authorities to provide community-based services for people leaving long-stay hospitals was introduced in 1991 (Mental Illness Specific Grant). These services have been provided mainly by the voluntary sector.

Since the formation of the Scottish Executive, policy responsibility for different aspects of social work services is being handled within the Justice Department (Criminal Justice Social Work Services), the Health Department (Community Care), and the Department of Education (Services for Children and Families). The Social Work Services Inspectorate (SWSI) is formally part of the Department of Education but its staff work closely with administrative staff across all the departments concerned with social work services, in some cases working alongside them. The changes are intended to facilitate 'joined up government' and to improve cross-disciplinary planning and co-ordination. For example, responsibility for social work policy development for children and families is now located within the Department of Education. A new young people's group has been created, creating the possibility of linking social work and education services for children.

Local authority social work services remain a substantial source of employment in Scotland, with just under 50,000 individuals in post at October 1998 (Scottish Executive 1999b, p.4). This included 20,038 full-time staff and 27,691 part-time, making a whole time equivalent of 35,197 (Scottish Executive 1999b, Table 5.3). The proportion of professionally qualified social workers is comparatively small (around 6000 in 1998). Social care is also provided by a broad range of voluntary agencies. The entire voluntary sector in Scotland has an annual income of £2bn and employs over 51,000 people, not including the co-ordination of voluntary unpaid work (Smith 1997). Local authorities remain one of the key funders in this sector, which provides a wide range of caring services including residential and day care for community care groups, domiciliary services, respite care, advocacy and advice projects.

Recent developments in law and social policy

The Scottish Parliament is developing a legislative agenda that includes issues ranging from land reform to modernising social work services. Twenty-five Acts have been introduced since the inception of the Parliament. One of these concerns the rights and protection of adults who lack capacity for whatever reason (Adults with Incapacity (Scotland) Act 2000). This Act follows many of the recommendations of the Scottish Law Commission's Report on Incapable Adults (1995), which found that the present law was failing to meet the welfare (including medical needs) and financial needs of adults with incapacity. The intention behind the law is to reflect the following principles: anything done under the new law should be of benefit to the adult; account is to be taken of the adult's wishes and those of the nearest relative, primary carer or guardian if appointed; and, most importantly, to be the least restrictive of the adult's freedom while still achieving the desired purpose (Scottish Executive 1999a).

Further improvements to current mental health legislation are expected. A review of the Mental Health (Scotland) Act 1984 is being undertaken by the Millan Committee (chaired by Bruce Millan, a former Secretary of State for Scotland) focusing particularly on issues relating to the rights of patients, their families and carers, and the public interest. A separate committee, chaired by a high court judge (Lord MacLean), has recommended a new sentence for high-risk offenders that would remain in force for the offender's entire life – Order for Lifelong Restriction.

The Royal Commission on Long Term Care of the Elderly (Sutherland Report 1999) addresses the fields of social security and pensions. These matters are reserved to the Westminster Parliament. However, other areas of policy relating to social work, health and housing are devolved to the Scottish Parliament. Any adoption of the Royal Commission's recommendations will require liaison between the two parliaments. Scotland's First Minister indicated the costs of personal care for the elderly in long-term care would be met (see the Community Care and Health (Scotland) Bill currently before the Scottish Parliament).[6]

The Scottish Executive Justice Department issued a consultation document, *Parents and Children*, to review family law. One of the most prominent issues was the status of unmarried fathers and the extent to which they should be given parental responsibilities and rights. The Scottish Executive proposes that unmarried fathers who jointly register the birth with the mother should be automatically entitled to parental responsibilities and rights.

The need for change in the field of domestic violence is also recognised. Consideration is being given to extend matrimonial interdicts with a power of arrest to divorced partners and former co-habitants. Current Scottish legislation does not address the problem of domestic violence in the context of same-sex couples (only spouses and co-habiting heterosexual couples and their children are offered protection under the Matrimonial Homes (Family Protection) (Scotland) Act 1981). Norrie (1999) identifies the need to extend the law to protect any person who lives in the same household as a violent person, thus addressing the family arrangements of same-sex couples.

Modernising social work

The White Paper *Aiming for Excellence: Modernising Social Work Services in Scotland* was presented to the Westminster Parliament in March 1999. The then Secretary of State for Scotland saw the creation of the Scottish Parliament as a unique opportunity to shape the future of social work services in Scotland (Scottish Office 1999, p.5). There are two main proposals: first, to create a new body (the Scottish Social Service Council) for registering social services workforce and setting out codes of conduct and standards. The 'Council' is expected to recognise courses leading to certain qualifications, to co-operate with related bodies within the UK and to promote international learning within social services (para 6.6). The second proposal is to create a Scottish

Commission for the Regulation of Care. The Commission would act as the independent regulator of the majority of social work services for adults and children. It is expected be an independent statutory body with the power to act in its own right, accountable to the Scottish administration and ultimately to the Scottish Parliament. A bill to take forward these proposals was presented to the Scottish Parliament in December 2000 (see Regulation of Care (Scotland) Act, 2001).

Social work in the criminal justice system

Prosecution against crime in Scotland is through a system of public prosecution (private prosecutions are possible but extremely rare). The Crown Office headed by the Lord Advocate has the ultimate control over prosecution, policy and practice in Scotland although decisions about prosecution for less serious crimes are delegated to the Procurators Fiscal Service (a regional service located in each Sheriffdom[7] in Scotland). Procurators Fiscal decide whether to prosecute, the charges to be laid, the type of procedure to be used, and the level of court in which an accused is to be tried. There is no provision for an accused to claim a right to a jury trial, as is currently the case in England, although juries are used in cases that are more serious. Three possible verdicts are available to Scottish criminal courts: guilty, not guilty, or the charge is not proven which has the same effect as an acquittal.

There are three levels of criminal court in Scotland, the district court, which deals with minor offences, the sheriff court,[8] which can deal with more serious cases, and the high court whose sentencing power is unlimited. The House of Lords does not hear criminal appeals from Scottish courts. These are heard by the appellate jurisdiction of the High Court of Justiciary, which sits in Edinburgh.

Social workers in Scotland contribute to the criminal justice system primarily in the provision of reports to the courts and the supervision of offenders; they also provide social work services within prisons and after-care services. Probation was first established in Britain by the Probation of First Offenders Act 1887 and was further extended by the Probation of Offenders Act 1907. It was not until 1949 that specific legislation for Scotland was introduced (Criminal Justice (Scotland) Act

1949). This Act saw the development of local authority committees including magistrates, justices of the peace and sheriffs. The probation officer's role was extended to include assisting, advising and befriending offenders (Mays 1997). This led to major expansion in the scope and size of probation services in the 1950s and 1960s. These developments were soon overshadowed by the broader reforms advanced by the Kilbrandon Committee (1964) and the White Paper *Social Work and the Community* (Scottish Office 1966). Their recommendations were enacted in the Social Work (Scotland) Act 1968, integrating probation within local authority social work departments. In contrast, England and Wales retained an autonomous probation and after-care service. This integration of 'probation-type' services within mainstream social services appears to be unusual in the field of criminal justice (Moore and Whyte 1998).

Following the 1968 Act concerns arose whether criminal justice social work was being given a low priority in the generic social work departments. While community service orders had been introduced, probation developments remained limited (Moore and Whyte 1998). The government, partly in response to these criticisms, made provision for the full funding of certain core criminal justice services provided by local authorities.[9] These include, *inter alia*, community service by offenders, probation and other supervision of offenders, parole and early release. Moore and Whyte (1998) argue that local authorities became the agent of central government, being held accountable for these services through fiscal, inspection and planning mechanisms.

At the same time national objectives and service standards were developed and continue to be updated (Social Work Services Group 1991). These objectives include the reduction of custodial sentences; the promotion of a broad range of community-based social work disposals; the provision of services for prisoners and their families in preparation for release from custody, and resettlement in the community (Moore and Whyte 1998 p.12).

Many local authorities have developed specialist criminal justice teams to improve the delivery of service, while remaining part of the local authority social work service. The Government issued a consultation document (*Community Sentencing – The Tough Option* 1998) exploring community based sentences and how these could be developed to create safer communities. The review also examined options for restructuring of criminal justice social work services. A new structure involving greater co-operation between councils in the provision of services is to be in place by September 2001. There will be 11 mainland groups plus the Islands Councils.

New legislation has considerably increased the role of social workers in supervision of more serious offenders. For example, the 1998 Crime and Disorder Act introduced provision for 'extended sentences' for sexual or violent offenders, allowing for longer periods of post-release supervision.

Scotland has a high prison population (110 per 100,000) and was ranked third highest of 18 major Western European countries in 1995 (Prison Reform Trust 1997). This compares unfavourably to England and Wales where the same study found a prison population of 99 per 100,000. Changes in parole and early release following the recommendations of the Kincraig Report (1988) have also extended social work supervision for offenders released from custody.

Research findings

Following the introduction of national objectives and standards, a programme of research was initiated by the then Scottish Office including, for example, studies of social work practice in relation to throughcare (McIvor and Barry 1998a) and the provision of social work reports to the Parole Board (McAra 1998a). The national standards required social workers to shift their emphasis away from a traditional expertise in welfare to becoming experts on offending, with the key aim of reducing offending behaviour. McAra (1998a) found that social workers provided insufficient information on the risk of re-offending in their reports. McIvor and Barry (1998a)[10] discovered that both practitioners and managers viewed throughcare practice as the least developed area, with limited communication and joint planning between prison and the community-based social workers. They observed the majority of work, conducted on a one-to-one basis by the supervising social worker, focused on practical issues such as accommodation, financial matters and employment. There was some evidence of improvement in the social circumstances of ex-prisoners following the period of community-based throughcare.

Studying probation, national standards were seen to provide a useful framework which had shifted the emphasis of supervision from a solely welfare focus to also directly addressing the probationer's offending (McIvor and Barry 1998b).[11] Paterson and Tombs (1998) in their overview of the programme of research argued, however, that the progress found in the study of probation practice was not fully echoed across all the studies.

As in other jurisdictions, concerns about sex offenders have been to the fore in Scotland, particularly following a highly publicised case where a sex offender under social work supervision was convicted following the death of a child. The McManus Report (McManus 1997) investigating the supervision arrangements found liaison between police and social workers was inadequate and that there was a lack of suitable supervised accommodation in the community. There was also a failure to see the offender frequently enough. McManus (1997) observed that this type of case marked a departure from traditional social work supervision in the community. Supervision was imposed without the consent of the offender where there was a high risk of reoffending after a period of imprisonment.

A review of the arrangements for the supervision of sex offenders in the community was undertaken by the Social Work Services Inspectorate (SWSI) (Scottish Office 1997). The SWSI report considered the arrangements for monitoring introduced by the Sex Offenders Act 1997. The report focused on the importance of risk assessment and how supervision might be strengthened. Included among the report's seven recommendations were proposals to review the skill-mix of staff in criminal justice social work services with the aim of involving a broader range of professional disciplines in personal change programmes; to consider the use of unqualified staff in undertaking supervision tasks under a case worker; and to examine whether a specialist residential facility should be established.

The past five years have seen a growing interest in women who offend. In 1998 the then Scottish Office published a major report reviewing community disposals and the use of custody for women offenders in Scotland (Scottish Office 1998e). This report arose out of concern over an unprecedented number of suicides in the women's prison at HMPI Cornton Vale between 1995 and 1997 – nine suicides in all. Many of these suicides involved women prisoners on remand. An earlier study of Cornton Vale (Loucks 1996) found among the women a high use of drugs, and to a lesser extent alcohol, misuse, as well as high levels of sexual abuse in childhood. The problem of suicide and the use of drugs is apparently more pronounced in the Scottish women's prison than in England and Wales (Scottish Office 1998e). The vulnerability of women offenders, especially those in custody in Scotland, is made apparent in the findings of both these reports.

Women Offenders – A Safer Way (Scottish Office 1998) recommended that all local authorities should review arrangements for women who offend and that, by the year 2000, young women under 18 years of age should not be held in prison.

These developments, along with a continuing commitment towards the development of community-based sentencing as a means of reducing or holding down the prison population, remain a central aspect of criminal justice social work services in Scotland.

Children's services

The major child care legislation in Scotland is the Children (Scotland) Act 1995, which brings together private and public family and child law into one statute. This is not, however, a complete codification of the law; the Adoption (Scotland) Act 1978, for example, continues to provide the legal basis for adoption. Prior to the 1995 Act, a series of reports influenced the development of policy and law in Scotland.

The inquiry conducted by Lord Clyde (Scottish Office 1991) into the removal of children from Orkney under pre-1995 legislative measures led to the introduction of a new emergency child protection order as part of the Children (Scotland) Act 1995. This order requires the initial removal of a child to be authorised by a sheriff and the grounds are more rigorous. Since the Clyde Report, the social work department has made considerable progress towards rebuilding public confidence and to reforming their procedures for child protection, although there remains a lack of investment in support services for families (SWSI 1996).

Despite similarities in child welfare policy within the UK, differences remain in the legal and organisational arrangements for children and families services. There is a well-established tradition in Scotland of charitable and voluntary organisations providing child care services (Hill *et al.* 1991). Historically, greater emphasis has been placed on non-institutional care with a significant use of 'boarding-out' of children with foster parents or guardians (Hill *et al.* 1991).

LOOKED-AFTER CHILDREN

The 1995 Act introduced the concept of 'looked-after' children[12] with Scottish local authorities having legal responsibility for around 11,000 children. The majority remain at home subject to supervision under the 1995 Act with approximately 4500 looked after in residential or foster care (Scottish Office Home Department 1999). Local authorities are required to have care plans for individual children and to participate in the Looking After Children Programme. This programme, first developed by the Department of Health for England and Wales, provides a set of age-related forms to gather information about a child's current health, development and educational status, including future needs. Scotland has had an extensive pilot scheme aimed at adapting the materials to the Scottish context. The Looking After Children forms have now been amended for use in Scotland and meet the requirements of the Children (Scotland) Act 1995 (Scottish Office 1999).

The development of foster care has been a key policy aim of the Scottish Office.[13] Triseliotis *et al.* (1999), in a study of foster care and foster carers in Scotland, counted 2231 carers at the end of March 1997. These carers provided for 2708 children, which represented for the first time in over thirty years an increase in the number of children fostered in Scotland. Difficulties in providing placements were identified especially for black and Asian children, children with disabilities and more generally for older children. The study explored the reasons why carers stopped fostering, identifying the operation of the services themselves and difficulties arising from the child's behaviour or that of the birth parents. Other factors included changes in the personal circumstances of the foster carers such as retirement, illness or moving house.

Residential accommodation remains a significant resource for looked-after children in Scotland. There has been a decline of 26 per cent in the number of children accommodated since 1988 from 2300 to 1700 in 1998 (Scottish Executive Education Department 1999). Boys were over-represented in residential accommodation constituting between 60 per cent to 65 per cent of the population. Placement patterns suggest an even divide between those children who remain in short-term care (for less than six months, two-fifths) and those in longer-term care (for one year or more, two-fifths). Children in care are mainly aged between 11 and 15 years, a pattern that has remained constant between 1988 and 1998 (Scottish Executive Education Department 1999). Since 1993 admissions to secure accommodation have seen an increase in the number of girls admitted, with figures at 31 March 1998 showing 30 per cent of residents were girls compared with 13 per cent at 31 March 1993. Just over three-quarters (77%) of children were resident for less than six months (at 31 March 1998) with 3 per cent remaining for one year or more (Scottish Executive Education Department 1999).

In 1992 a strategic overview was completed of residential child care services, including the quality of daily life of young people in residential care (SWSI 1992 – the Skinner Report). Sixty-six recommendations resulted, ranging from admission policies, guidance to ensure the quality of day-to-day living, training needs and systems for addressing complaints against staff, especially where suspicions of sexual and physical abuse pertained. The status of some of these recommendations remains unclear, although a programme to centralise and to streamline training for residential child care is being developed.

The importance of these recommendations has been reflected in the recent inquiry into the abuse and neglect of children in care in Edinburgh (Marshall *et al.* 1999). The inquiry was set up following the conviction of two former residential care workers for offences against children in their care. Some of the recommendations of the inquiry are very similar to those in the Skinner Report, including the need to employ fully qualified professional staff in residential child care.

The *Children's Safeguards Review* (SWSI 1997b) reported on the arrangements for protecting children who are cared for away from home in Scotland. This review recommended that every child without immediate access to a parent should have a befriender or guardian appointed. It also recommended that all young people leaving a unit should have the opportunity of an interview to comment on their experience and any concerns arising from it. The review is unambiguous in the need to improve the training and education of residential child care staff.

As a consequence of the review a Children's Services Development Fund has been established with an extra £37 million over three years. The purpose of the fund is to secure an expansion of foster care services; advocacy services for children looked after by local authorities; and an expansion of family centres especially for families with very young children (Scottish Office 1999, para 4.10).

CHILDREN'S HEARINGS

In Scotland, there is no separate juvenile court. The children's hearings tribunal system, established in 1971,[14] integrates under one forum juvenile offenders and children in need of care and protection. Decision making emphasises 'needs' rather than 'deeds'. Children who commit very serious crimes may be dealt with in the adult court system, although they can be referred to the children's hearings for disposal.

The children's hearings system is highly distinctive (McGhee, Waterhouse and Whyte 1996), remaining largely unchanged since its inception. While in England and Wales there has been major legislative change (Crime and Disorder Act 1998) aimed to reduce youth offending, no corresponding legal initiatives have been taken in Scotland. A Scottish review of youth crime may lead to a greater investment in preventive services (Hogg 1999).

Anyone can refer a child to the reporter to the children's hearings, who is the official with the decision-making powers at this early stage in the process. After investigating the circumstances she or he will decide whether a child requires to be referred to a children's hearing. To do this one of the grounds of referral set out in section 52(2) of the Children (Scotland) Act 1995 must be in place as well as the possible need for compulsory measures of supervision. Grounds include, for example, that the child has committed an offence, or that there has been a lack of parental care of the child.

A children's hearing is not a court but a tribunal of three lay volunteers who meet with the child and his/her family. Social workers also prepare a social background report in advance and attend. The reporter is present for the purposes of providing legal advice to the lay panel but does not take part in the decision making. The aim is to work in partnership with parents and to find solutions that reflect the child's best interests. The hearing may decide to discharge the referral, or they may place the child under the supervision of the local authority, which could also involve the child living away from home. There is provision for the child and/or parents to challenge the legal grounds of referral in the sheriff court. If the grounds are not upheld at court the case is discharged. There is also provision to appeal the decision of a hearing.

The patterns of referral to reporters have changed since the early 1980s. Martin, Fox and Murray (1981) found a system that was mainly focused on offence referrals. Recent statistics show an increase in children referred on non-offence grounds. There is now a broadly even distribution between children referred on offence grounds and non-offence grounds (Scottish Office 1997b).

Until recently, the research by Martin *et al.* (1981) was the largest empirical study of the hearings system. In 1994, the then Scottish Office commissioned two studies focusing on decision making (Hallett *et al.* 1998) and on the children referred (Waterhouse *et al.* 2000). A review of the international context for child welfare decision making was also undertaken (Hallett and Hazel 1998). Hallett *et al.* (1998) interviewed a range of professionals and panel members, finding widespread support for the children's hearings system and the principles on which it is based. The main disquiet concerned the lack of adequate resources to provide preventive and support services within the community for children and their families. Professionals perceived the system was best suited to children in need of care and protection and less suitable for persistent offenders. Despite the principle of participation, children and families, although normally present, were found to contribute only briefly to the discussions.

Waterhouse *et al.* (2000), in their study of outcomes for a cohort of over a thousand children referred, found that the children were growing up in circumstances of social and economic disadvantage. State benefit was found to be the main source of income for over half of the children's families and lone parent households were common. The main outcome for children referred to a hearing was the imposition of a supervision requirement. A small group of parents and young people were interviewed, the majority considering the system fair and that their views were listened to. They, like the professionals in the study by Hallett *et al.* (1998), concluded that the system promised more in support than was ever delivered in practice.

ADOPTION

Adoption applications in Scotland have fallen steadily over the last ten years from 800 in 1988 to under 500 in 1998 (Social Work Services Group 1999). The average ages of the children were just under seven years, with 5 per cent of applications made for children less than one year old. Around half of all adoptions are by step-parents and this has been a consistent pattern in most years. In the last three years 90 per cent to 95 per cent of these adoptions involved a birth mother and a step-father.

Post-adoption support remains an important resource for adoptive families beyond the initial adjustment period. This was specifically recognised in the Children (Scotland) Act 1995 which amended adoption law to include counselling and other assistance be made available to adopters and adoptees (Cleland 1995). McGhee (1995) evaluated a post-adoption consultancy service set up by the Scottish Centre of the British Agencies for Adoption and Fostering. She found that families who approached the service were experiencing a range of problems related to the adoption of their child and valued the reassurance and support the consultancy was able to provide.

Community care

The Social Work (Scotland) Act 1968 saw the creation of social work departments throughout Scotland, placing a general duty on local authorities to promote social welfare.[15] The intention of the 1968 Act was to bring together a range of welfare agencies, which dealt with children, adults, offenders and older people into one organisational framework. The NHS and Community Care Act 1990 amended the 1968 Act by inserting new sections that set out the legal basis for community care in Scotland.

Community care has become increasingly dominant in social work services. Over 70 per cent of Scottish social work departments' total budget is spent on supporting community care services for the elderly and people with learning disabilities and mental health difficulties (English 1998). As in the rest of the UK, services for these groups had a history of neglect, explained in part through the stigma associated with policies of institutionalisation. The balance of care in Scotland has always favoured institutional rather than community care, relying on public-sector provision over voluntary or private provision (Titterton 1990).

There has been a rise in nursing home places from 5000 in 1987 to almost 20,000 in 1995, with an associated decrease in NHS long-stay beds for the very old by some 2000 over a similar time period (English 1998), and a steady increase in day centre places for older people and in the number of recipients of home help services (English 1998). Despite the transfer of some resources from hospital- to community-based care, it is clear that some older people have simply moved from hospital to residential or nursing care funded to a certain level by the local authority. These changes have served to increase the burden of cost of residential care to the individual and led to many debates regarding the divide between health and social care. The recent report of the Royal Commission on Long Term Care[16] has suggested that nursing care should be free but that a charge should be made for accommodation.

While the numbers of hospital beds for people with learning disabilities have fallen by about 1000 in 1996 (Scottish Office 1998d), this is matched by an almost identical increase in the numbers admitted to residential care homes. Care homes have become smaller, with over 70 per cent accommodating ten residents or fewer. Day centre attendance of people with learning disabilities has changed little since 1990. These patterns suggest that community care and the closure of large hospitals in Scotland have proceeded at a slower pace compared to England. The rapid closure of institutions in England has brought a greater demand for community services for those with acute needs. In Scotland, the 1990 Act has resulted in modest changes in patterns of care with a continuing use of institutional care for the frail elderly and people with learning disabilities.

The 1990 Act set out the duty on local authorities to create community care plans. This led to detailed guidance from the then Scottish Office who strongly encouraged councils and health boards to enter into planning agreements and joint plans (MacKay 1997). The varied planning cycles of these different services have created real problems in practice (MacKay 1997). In England and Wales joint planning between health and social service departments is obligatory.

In Scotland, Stalker *et al.* (1994) found that the majority of health boards and local authorities had produced protocols in relation to hospital discharge arrangements but very few of these were collaboratively produced. A study of discharges of frail elderly patients in the West of Scotland found that none had received a comprehensive assessment by a social worker prior to discharge (Fitzpatrick 1995b). Moreover, significant numbers waited up to three weeks before seeing a professional following discharge.

Mental health

In 1990 the then Scottish Office introduced a specific grant (Mental Illness Specific Grant) to increase the development of community-based services for people with mental illness. Key aims were to reduce admissions to hospital and to support people on discharge. Continuing this development, the Scottish Office (1997a) issued a circular setting out a comprehensive framework for mental health services in Scotland. The purpose was to 'assist staff in health, social work and housing agencies, including Scottish Homes, to develop a joint approach to the planning, commissioning and provision of integrated mental health services' (Scottish Office 1997b, p.4). The framework focused on the needs of people with severe and/or enduring mental health problems (including those with dementia) as a first priority.

Other policy initiatives to assist this process included a mental health development fund to support general practitioners, NHS trusts, local authorities, and other statutory and voluntary agencies to develop community-focused services for people with mental health problems. Some initial funding to create the Scottish Development Centre for Mental Health Services was also allocated by the then Scottish Office. The role of the centre is to provide assistance, advice and support to agencies in the field as well as offering training to front-line staff. Close collaboration with key agencies, service users and carers is primary to the work of the centre.

In contrast, the Accounts Commission for Scotland (1999) observed that too many resources remain committed to institutional care. They found that 78 per cent of NHS spending on specialist adult mental health services went on hospital in-patient beds. Variations throughout Scotland, unrelated to geographical location, were noted. For example, Highland spent 91 per cent on institutions compared to 71 per cent in the Scottish Borders. This continuing pattern of expenditure on institutional care was seen to be a by-product of continuing difficulties in communication between health and social work services. One factor appears to be uncertainty between agencies about the means for identifying and reinvesting income released by long-stay bed closures.

As outlined earlier a review of mental health law in Scotland is underway. The Mental Welfare Commission for Scotland has the statutory duty to protect persons who, by reason of mental disorder, may be incapable of adequately protecting themselves or their interests. This includes reviewing compulsory detentions in hospital.

The role of the mental health officer[17] (MHO) is being examined. MHOs almost invariably make the application for detention[18] in hospital and must consent to the application. Ulas *et al.* (1994, p.90) found that MHOs saw their legal role in assessing the mental state of an individual as ambiguous, although some MHOs felt more confident in challenging the appropriateness of a decision. There was a tension between acting as an advocate for the individual and a guardian of public safety. The latter is very much to the fore in the light of the number of inquiries that have found that individuals appear not to have received appropriate services, often with tragic outcomes. The study also drew attention to the lack of alternatives to detention in hospital and of means for supporting people on discharge (Myers 1999, p.116).

The original ideal of matching services to individual need requires continuing development against a reality of limited resources, escalating need and professional disputes over agency responsibilities. Aspects of these broad factors continue to be identified in research findings (Cameron and Freeman 1996), reports of formal inspections (SWSI 1998) and public inquiries (Ritchie *et al.* 1994 re. Christopher Clunis). Improvements are urgently needed to develop coherent local planning and strategies across professional boundaries; to free up resources to support community care reforms; and to develop imaginative community supports which allow service users real choice and a say in the future development of services (Cameron and Freeman 1996).

Major educational developments in social work

The Central Council for Education and Training in Social Work (CCETSW) has had responsibility throughout the UK for promoting and regulating social work education and awarding professional qualifications in social work. CCETSW is being divested of these functions. In Scotland, these will be transferred to the Scottish Social Services Council (Scottish Office 1999). This new body is expected to recognise courses leading to qualifications in social work and to provide for the registration of social services personnel. The relationship between the different councils in the UK is not yet clear, although the White Paper for Scotland (Scottish Office 1999a) proposes co-operation with related bodies at home and abroad.

Debates in Scotland concern the possible introduction of an all-graduate profession; a rationalisation of training into centres of excellence; and specialisation in the undergraduate curriculum. The current reforms create opportunities to advance the educational standards of the social work profession, bringing them more in line with other disciplines.

Conclusion

The creation of the Scottish Parliament, with its devolved responsibilities, raises a major question of how far policy and services in Scotland will come to vary from the rest of the UK. There are already signs of growing divergence in law and in practice. Many of the wider social and economic trends affecting the UK are found in Scotland. Poverty remains a major social problem.

Two fundamental issues affect service provision in all areas of social work: the adequacy of resources and multidisciplinary working. These factors raise important concerns about the future direction of social work and its role in Scottish society. Scotland faces a challenge to overcome deficits in the economic and social circumstances of its population. It remains to be seen whether the new parliamentary agenda for change and the contribution of social work services can make a difference for all people, young and old, living in Scotland.

Notes

1   The ratio of divorces to marriage.
2   Often referred to as the Westminster Parliament reflecting its site in London.
3   Named after the MP for West Lothian, Tam Dalyell, who first raised the question.
4   The Local Government (Scotland) Act 1994.
5   Op cit.
6   The Scottish Executive made an official response to the Royal Commission on Long Term Care in October 2000. See the Community Care and Health (Scotland) Bill.

7   Scotland is divided up into sheriffdoms and then further into sheriff court districts. A sheriff is a professional judge. Each sheriffdom has a sheriff principal who has the duty to ensure that the business of the court is carried out in an efficient manner. The sheriff court has both civil and criminal jurisdiction plus some administrative functions.

8   The sheriff court also exercises civil jurisdiction in Scotland. The highest civil court is the Court of Session that sits in Edinburgh. Appeal to the House of Lords in civil cases is possible.

9   See the Law Reform (Miscellaneous Provisions) (Scotland) Act 1990 amending s. 27 Social Work (Scotland) Act 1968.

10 It should be noted the total sample consisted of 60 ex-prisoners who were subjected to a variety of throughcare arrangements and were selected from four local authorities.

11 The sample, drawn from four local authorities, was comparatively small and the distribution of cases was uneven, with two local authorities dominating.

12 Section 17 Children (Scotland) Act 1995.

13 Now the Scottish Executive.

14 The legislative basis for the children's hearings system in Scotland was originally set out in the Social Work (Scotland) Act 1968 but is now found in the Children (Scotland) Act 1995.

15 Section 12 Social Work (Scotland) Act 1968.

16 Op cit.

17 Similar to the approved social worker in England and Wales.

18 The nearest relative may also apply but this is very rare. They may also consent to the detention in urgent situations. Application for compulsory detention is made to the sheriff except in urgent cases.

Chapter 6

Social Work in Wales

Mark Drakeford and Charlotte Williams

Introduction

Professor Dai Smith, sometime historian of the South Wales Miners Federation and later, and stereotypically for Wales, a BBC *apparatchik* uses an aphorism which provides a useful starting-point for this chapter – 'Wales is a singular noun but a plural experience'. As we hope to demonstrate, that experience is not only plural, but also contentious and disputed. One of the dangers in providing an introduction to the Welsh context for social work practice is that of trying to do too much – a digest of history, geography, sociology and political economy, to give but four examples – it succeeds in nothing more than a dumbing-down blandness, a combination of received wisdom and current orthodoxy. Our aim is to provide an account that draws out both the positive advantages which Wales provides as a place where social work can be practised while pointing also to the real challenges and difficulties which fruitful practice has to face and overcome. It is based upon the belief that there are important ways in which social work practice in Wales is different and distinctive and that, if it is to be effective, these differences and distinctions need to be properly integrated into what social workers actually do.

We begin with the simple statement that Wales is a nation and not a region. It is neither a Hobsbawmian nation, created from above by a nineteenth- and twentieth-century intellectual construction of 'nationalism'; nor is it a neo-conservative embodiment of an ancient, unchanging unit of collective life. Rather, it is an active amalgam of both, rooted in a culture, history and language which pre-dates, by many hundreds of years, the mass, industrialised democracy which, in its current form, is barely thirty years old and yet is re-formed daily in the experience of modern times. The creation of the National Assembly, in May 1999, was of course the most striking example of such re-formation at the political, legislative and administrative levels.

Wales now has in place a 60-member Assembly, elected by a form of proportional representation and operating on a fully bilingual basis. The Assembly has neither primary legislative, nor tax raising, powers.

Financially, it has the responsibility for allocating those central government funds that were previously channelled through the Welsh Office. Capable of being calculated in a number of different ways, the sum is set to rise to £11bn in 2003–04.

Legislatively, while the Assembly cannot generate law, it has the responsibility for the application of secondary legislation in the Welsh context. A Westminster trend towards framing principles in primary legislation, while leaving implementation to regulation, produces a secondary legislative programme for the Assembly of more than 400 pieces in each year.

Structurally, the Assembly deals with its business by an amalgam of Westminster and local government models. Nine assembly ministers form a cabinet, responsible for development and implementation in all major policy areas. The work of the ministers is scrutinised by parallel committees, constituted according to the strength of the political parties within the Assembly. Committees also possess a policy-generation capacity.

Politically, the results of the first election produced a hung Assembly, with Labour forming a minority administration. Contrary to initial expectations, Plaid Cymru, rather than the Conservative Party, formed the main opposition, having won 16 seats to the 28 held by Labour. Minority administration continued until October 2000. It proved an unhappy experience for the ruling party, with the three opposition groups combining to defeat the administration at crucial intervals, including the defeat – and subsequent resignation – of the first First Minister, Alun Michael, in February 2000. Eighteen months into the Assembly's first term, worn down by the daily grind of doing deals on each and every issue, Labour entered into a coalition, or partnership government as it was called, with the Liberal Democrats.

Administratively, the social services and health portfolios were grouped together as the responsibility of one assembly minister, and its concomitant committee.

In terms of its demography, Wales is a place where just under three million people live, two-thirds of whom are to be found in the urban south-east. The population of Wales has grown in every decade since 1945 but overall figures disguise substantial phenomena of out-migration, in which individuals born in Wales leave to earn a living elsewhere, and in-migration, in which individuals – often of retirement age – move to live within its borders. The result is a population in which the proportion of people aged 65 and over is expected to increase by almost 13 per cent between now and 2011, while the number of children in the population is expected to fall by the same figure. In the words of the Welsh Office publication from which these figures are taken (Welsh Office 1996, p.2), 'this changing population structure will have far-reaching implications for education, employment, health care and the social services'.

The demographic make-up of Wales makes the effective delivery of health and social care an urgent priority for the National Assembly. While the population of Wales has grown gradually over the past twenty years, the proportion of the population below retirement age has declined as the number of older people has grown. Wales now has the lowest proportion of 16 to 44 year-olds of any part of the United Kingdom and by far the highest proportion of people of pensionable age. Over 17 per cent of the population is aged 65 and over. As a result, Wales has a very high dependency ratio of people of pensionable age as a percentage of the working population aged 16 to 64. This dependency ratio is one which has almost doubled since 1950 (Welsh Office 1995). These figures make the care of people in later life a matter of real urgency for policy makers. Other factors of a demographic nature add to the social welfare policy framework. Wales has the highest proportion of teenage pregnancies anywhere in Europe. It has a legacy of health problems from heavy industries, which means, for example, that admission rates to hospital are 18 per cent higher in Wales than in England while GP consultations are almost one-fifth higher (TUC Cymru 1999).

Demographic factors form part of a more general calculation that determines the funding of public services in Wales. Known as the Barnett Formula – named after its author, the then Chief Minister to the Treasury, Joel Barnett – this attempts to calculate the cost of providing an equivalent level of services in Scotland, Wales and Northern Ireland to that in England. Factors taken into account in addition to demography include such diverse factors as road lengths, recorded crimes and the numbers of substandard dwellings. The result, for Wales, is per capita spending 9 per cent higher than expenditure in England (House of Commons 1998). In the context of devolution, of course, such formulas come under particular scrutiny. The budget of the Welsh Assembly is almost exactly the same as the shortfall between monies raised in Wales through all forms of taxation and money spent through all forms of public expenditure. Demands for additional funding for services face the response not only that this is taxpayers' money but also that very many of the taxpayers concerned live rather far away, and have no say over how the funds so raised are to be expended.

In many other countries of the UK, religion is a factor that interacts significantly with the delivery of public services. Religious affiliation in Wales traditionally has been characterised by political as well as spiritual dimensions. During the nineteenth century, in particular, the established Church in Wales was known as the Tory Party at prayer, while radical Liberalism was closely associated with chapel-going and the Welsh language. The disestablishment of the Church immediately after the First World War and the supplanting of the Liberal Party by Labour in Wales happened at the same time. With both events, and the general decline in religious observance in which Wales has shared, came the effective end of the connection between public policy formation and private faith. While Wales continues to produce an unusually high number of ministers of religion who are active in politics, the public significance of religious affiliation is almost entirely at an end.

Issues for Social Work in Contemporary Wales

Context

In April 1996, local government reorganisation in Wales created 22 new unitary authorities replacing the eight old authorities. For all authorities this meant reorganisation of social services. For the most part this has involved a reduction in the capacity to provide specialist services and a dilution in expertise at managerial level as social services departments were subsumed under joint directorates with education, housing or both.

It is currently estimated that there are 50,000 people working in social work and social care within Wales (Jones 1999) and some 58,000 Welsh health service employees (Osmond 1998). Figures for 1994 suggested about 17,000 of social work/care employees were working within the local authority sector (CIPFA 1997).

Revenue and capital expenditure on social services in the period 1997–98 totalled £540.8m and £8109m respectively but with considerable variability in spending by individual local authorities across Wales. In counties such as Pembroke, for example, 15 per cent of its total revenue budget was allocated to social services whereas Wrexham spent 22.5 per cent. In the same period, in some counties such as Flintshire and Torfaen, there was no capital expenditure while Swansea and Newport spent over £1m on infrastructure projects within the social services. In 1995/6 on average almost 40,000 people per week were in receipt of some social service from local authorities alone, at a total net expenditure for Wales of £436,892,00 (Welsh Office 1998). It remains widely perceived however that this level of human and material resources is inadequate to meet demand.

In almost all areas of the social services, a mixture of statutory and independent-sector provision is to be found in meeting the needs of client groups. However, there is some evidence to suggest that private- and voluntary-sector provision is underdeveloped in many authorities, giving rise to considerable territorial inequalities. The major impact of local government reorganisation has been to produce a plethora of often small-scale organisations in which co-ordination and the achievement of equity has been elusive.

Against this general background, this chapter now goes on to consider, in some more detail, a series of characteristics of Wales which are particularly relevant to social work. These are: language, poverty, rurality and 'race'. A following section then looks at prospects for social work practice in Wales, reviewing some recent research evidence and considering the likely impact of the Assembly for Wales upon future developments.

Language

We begin with language because, if a shortlist were to be drawn up of claims upon which Welsh nationhood could rest, language would be high upon it. Such a claim would be highly contentious because of its easy elision into a suggestion that, 'to be Welsh, in any meaningful way, a person must speak, or at least understand Welsh' (Aitchison and Carter 1994, p.3). Despite such an unambiguous contention, research (see, for example Roberts 1994) suggests that, in reality, language policy plays a deeply ambivalent part in Welsh identity. Non Welsh speakers retain both an affection and regard for it, combined with hostility and suspicion at any suggestion that their own monolingualism might qualify their sense of Welshness or rebound to their disadvantage.

Our position is this: Welsh *is* the first language of half a million people. It is in daily use in all parts of the country, with more speakers in the urban south than the rural north and west where the proportion of speakers is highest. It is also a language of the young, rather than the old, with the highest proportion of fluent Welsh speakers (32 per cent) to be found among the under 16-year-olds. Such bilingualism places Wales in the mainstream of European experience (see Davies 1994). Almost every state in Europe is at least bilingual, in the sense of having more than one indigenous language as well as languages spoken by migrants from other places. The issues that arise in the design and delivery of social welfare services in such contexts, therefore, are part of the daily fabric of civic life across the whole continent. Moreover, despite its 'minority' status, Welsh is a language which, on the last occasion upon which such a question was asked, in the census of 1981, is the only means of communication for over 20,000 people. Most significantly, for this chapter, monolingual Welsh speakers are most often very young children, the elderly and individuals with learning disabilities – in other words, among groups most likely to be in need of social welfare services.

The formal relationship of such services, in a bilingual context, has been shaped by a changing legal landscape. A series of Acts of Parliament now embody obligations placed upon agencies to provide services in a linguistically sensitive manner. The 1989 Children Act, for example, contains a requirement that due consideration be paid to 'race, religion, language and culture' when making decisions about services for young people. The Mental Health Act of 1983 and Section 95 of the 1991 Criminal Justice Act contain analogous obligations in their own spheres. More broadly, the 1993 Welsh Language Act, widely regarded as the single most significant piece of legislation of its kind, has brought about a legal requirement for all public bodies (including local authorities) to produce language plans which have to be approved by the statutory Welsh Language Board.

The resulting principle that service users, wherever they may be in Wales, have a right to receive that service in the language of their choice embodies, as a consequence, not only essential civil and political rights but, in the social welfare arena, is a fundamental of worthwhile practice.

Poverty

Poverty is, without rival, the defining characteristic of those citizens with whom social workers are in contact and the overwhelming truth of that appalling fact is felt even more powerfully in Wales than any other part of Britain. As Becker (1997) makes clear, 90 per cent of social work clients live in deep and enduring poverty, and it is the search for help with that poverty – both directly and in terms of the wider impact which it produces in their lives – which brings individuals and families to the doors of social welfare agencies.

The Welsh economy is essentially a tale of two parallel universes. In the one, inward investment, high productivity and advanced technology make Wales a candidate for joining the motor regions of the European Union (Morgan and Morgan 1998). In the other, 'the picture

that emerges is one in which low skill, low paid employment dominates, and in which unemployment and economic inactivity continue to
be a serious problem' (Welsh Office 1997, p.5). A few figures must
illustrate this wider picture. Gross domestic product in Wales is only 83
per cent of the UK average, largely because the proportion of the population which is economically inactive, at 25.6 per cent, is higher than
the UK average of 22.6 per cent (Welsh Office 1997, p.3). Average
earnings in Wales have fallen from 98 per cent of the British figure in
1979 to 89 per cent in 1996/97. The result is that personal income and
personal disposable income in Wales is the lowest of any area in Britain
for which figures are collated – 85 per cent of the UK figure – and that a
significantly higher proportion of weekly household income is derived
from social security payments than over the United Kingdom as a
whole.

Over Wales as a whole the parallel universes referred to above have
spatial and social, as well as economic, characteristics (see McKendrick
1995 for a detailed analysis of poverty by geography in Wales). In the
words of the Welsh Office (1997, p.5), 'Inward investment has not
helped all parts of Wales equally'. Development has been concentrated
in the areas most attractive to inward investors; the eastern sections of
the A55 and M4 corridors, and the Newtown Welshpool area. By
contrast, the industrially decimated areas of South Wales include parts
such as the Cynon valley, which emerged, in an European Union survey
based on local authority boundaries, as the poorest area in the whole of
the Union, other than one rurally underdeveloped part of Portugal.

The city of Cardiff provides a vivid illustration of the social consequences of this geographic reification. Analysis of the 1981 census
returns (see Jenkins 1994) reveals a city containing a number of the
most and least advantaged local government wards in Wales, but
grouped around a solid core of middle-ground localities which exhibit
neither extremes of wealth nor poverty. The 1991 census revealed a
very different picture. Now six of the ten most prosperous wards of the
610 in Wales were to be found in Cardiff, as were six of the wards with
the greatest concentration of difficulty and disadvantage. All but two of
the 40 wards in Cardiff appear in the ranking of the 50 most or least

prosperous areas. In other words, within a decade, that solid core of 1981 had dispersed, heading either for the prosperous Thatcherite uplands or sinking to the economic badlands where social workers ply their trade.

Contemporary social welfare policies combine with this picture to create direct impacts upon the social work task. The high proportion of economically inactive people in Wales contains 'high reported rates of long-term sickness, concentrated in deprived industrial areas, notably the south Wales Valleys' (Welsh Office 1997, p.3). Two consequences follow: the first lies in the demands for community care services which long-term sickness generates; the second is to be found in the impact produced by the increasing suggestion that the long-term sick include a significant number of 'malingerers' for whom the benefit system has to be made less accessible. In a population which is already characterised by penury, and in which social security payments make up a vital proportion of national income, these policy changes are very significant. In the words of Anne Clwyd, as she prepared to vote against the Labour Government's cuts in lone parent benefits, 'What would my right hon. Friend say to people in my constituency where there are 1500 lone parents and 200 jobs advertised in the job centre?' (Hansard, 10 December 1997).

The most visible symbol of the extent to which poverty dominates the Welsh experience, however, is to be found in the agreement, by the European Union in March 1999, of Objective One status for the whole of West Wales and the Valleys. Hailed at the time as a triumph for the negotiating skills of the Blair administration (Welsh Office 1999), it was only possible because a convincing case had been made that, over such a wide area, gross domestic product was less than 75 per cent of the Union average. The release of Objective One funding, over the next five years, provides the only significant additional sources of funding – £1.3bn – likely to be available to the National Assembly, and the single most important opportunity to tackle the poverty gap both within Wales and between Wales and other parts of Europe.

Rurality

Mapping out something that is distinctly rural in terms of community, lifestyle and culture in Wales may be more difficult than determining its specifically geographical characteristics or indeed the associated markers of poverty and deprivation. Concepts such as 'community spirit', solidarity, reciprocity, harmony and continuity so often associated with the Welsh rural idyll in many respects may be more imagined than real as this potential is continually undermined by the relentless march of modernisation, movement and change. Large parts of Wales can, however, in a strictly geographical sense, be classified as rural with several concomitant factors.

During the 1970s a glut of academic research highlighted the nature and patterning of deprivation in rural as opposed to urban areas (Winrow and Priestley 1976) and some research focused specifically on the provision of social services in rural areas (Grant 1978). Similarly, a plethora of sociological research emanating principally from Wales explored the nature of community in such areas. Day (1998) goes as far as to argue that much of what is British rural sociology might be said to have originated in Wales.

An area of repeated concern has to be the association of poverty and deprivation with rurality. In the 1980s McLaughlin's (1985) study of deprivation in rural England, for the Department of the Environment, documented powerfully the association of poverty with rurality irrespective of widely differing circumstances. In 1997 Cloke, Goodwin and Milbourne, with funding from the Welsh Office, replicated this study in comparably diverse environments within Wales. Between 1990 and 1994 four areas of rural Wales, Devil's Bridge, Tanat Valley, Teifi Valley and Betws y Coed, were surveyed with over 1000 households responding to questions on issues such as housing, employment, transport, community and health. The Cloke *et al.* (1997) study largely corroborates the evidence that emerged in the English study. A picture of a submerged and underprivileged minority with deprived mobility, lacking in access to key services and resources and with significantly low cash incomes. Between 36 per cent and 44 per cent of households surveyed had gross salaries for the main wage earner of less than £8000 per annum. Poverty levels were significant, with 30 per cent of the households in Betws y Coed, 29.7 per cent in Tanat Valley, 26.4 per cent in Teifi Valley and 25.1 per cent in Devil's Bridge defined as being on the margins of poverty.

As the Objective One debate, outlined above, would indicate, therefore, a significant minority of households in rural Wales had income levels that severely restricted opportunity. These households were mostly characterised by having elderly residents or young people who were either unemployed or on low income. The study highlights how individuals within these circumstances carefully conspire to conceal the impact of this poverty. The study also highlights communities drained of their talented youth and experiencing in-migration on such a large scale that the language and culture of Wales are inevitably and necessarily threatened. This pattern of in-migration, coupled with depopulation of those who leave the area, meant that two-thirds of the people who had lived in the survey areas for up to 15 years had no close relatives to act as a support network (Cloke, Goodwin and Milbourne 1997).

This manifestation of poverty and deprivation is a major challenge facing social services departments in Wales which are often trying to maintain standards of provision within shrinking budgets. Jackie Tonge, previously Director of Education and Leisure in the north London Borough of Haringey and now Chief Executive of Powys, spoke of the challenge of poverty in rural Wales:

> Powys is geographically huge, but the population of 125,000 is half the size of Haringey and my budget of £120 million is what I had to run education and leisure services before. It might not be high on the poverty indicators like Haringey but it is a low wage economy. (*Guardian* 21 January 1998)

There is some evidence also that voluntary sector activity is constrained in Wales. For example, it has been noted that domestic violence in rural areas receives less attention and therefore less funding in national agendas (Charles 1995). In addition, the scarcity of independent sector provision in some service areas leads to a lack of choice for the user.

Household and mobility deprivation also pose particular challenges for the delivery of social services (Cloke *et al.* 1997). While Wenger's

(1995) longitudinal study of older people in rural North Wales found that in comparison with their age peers in more urban areas they received relatively no lower a level of domiciliary services, there were clear differences in the way these were accessed and she noted poorer levels of health and higher levels of impairment among the rural dwellers. Practice accounts attest to the patterning of household and mobility deprivation. Some areas that are less than five miles outside of town centres display the challenges of rurality because of the poor transport networks. People experience deep isolation and consequent depression, as they are unable to socialise, get regular access to shops and facilities or easily attend medical appointments. In many areas of Wales natural meeting-points for the community such as schools, chapels, post offices and community centres have gone and social network patterns that can provide a high degree of protection have been disrupted.

It is too often the case that authorities cannot justify the provision of transport to these areas because numbers are small or the routes for the transport that is provided are so long that for many the upheaval of 'waiting with your coat on for hours for the social services transport' becomes a factor in non take-up of services.

The recruitment of staff such as home carers from within small communities also has its problems. The scarcity of available carers, and in particular those with a command of the Welsh language, produces difficulties in terms of the quality of care giving. In addition, there are problems with sustaining commitment, parochiality, gossip and confidentiality. An adult placement scheme, which had been run for many years in the urban areas of Liverpool, experienced a particular array of problems when imported to rural North Wales. Problems of matching and availability, suspicion of 'strangers', and issues in relation to the Welsh language and culture served to make the implementation of 'house share' and 'adult placement' schemes more complex. One worker reported 'even between the valleys the culture is so very different and people have a natural suspicion of outsiders'.

However, within these environments workers have responded innovatively developing day care in local pubs and hotels, promoting volunteer transport schemes, using existing institutions to expand to reach new needs, providing mobile services and developing partnerships with independent sector providers.

Antiracism and Wales

Racism is a feature of every European country and concern has grown over its more recent escalation right across Europe. There is nothing to suggest empirically or anecdotally that Wales is an exception (Williams 1995). Incidents of street racism and the presence of racial discrimination in housing, social services, health and employment are part and parcel of Welsh life as elsewhere.

However, it is now increasingly recognised that there is not one racism but many racisms and that the manifestations of racism not only vary across time and place but are in some ways a reflection of the particular histories and culture of a country. A noticeable and specific feature of dialogues on 'race' and racism in Wales is an apparent widespread neglect and denial of the issues in contrast, for example, with England where 'race' has been raised as a highly politicised issue since the early 1960s. This characteristic has been documented in the other Celtic countries, Ireland and Scotland (Miles and Dunlop 1987; McVeigh 1992). This complacency has many and complex causes noted elsewhere (Williams 1995) not least a pervasive belief in the idea of Wales as a tolerant nation. What is of interest here, however, is the way in which such ideas shape the social work task and antiracist strategies within that. What social workers most frequently experience in their work with and within helping agencies in Wales is a denial of the need to address issues of racism and the needs of black and ethnic minority groups on the basis of the fact that 'there are few or none of them living here' and the notion that 'there is no problem here'.

The first of these elements leads to a tendency to equate issues of racism solely with the presence of people from such minority groups and, as a consequence, to agencies playing the numbers game – few in numbers therefore no need to provide services. It does, however, have some grounding in relation to the particular demographic distribution of black and ethnic minority peoples in Wales. Over half of the 41,000 people who registered as being from black and ethnic minority backgrounds at the last census live in or around Cardiff in South Wales. The other half are scattered in isolated pockets right across Wales with very few areas displaying significant concentrations. In some of the new unitary authorities of Wales with populations in excess of 90,000 there are fewer than 700 people from black and ethnic minority groups. In other areas, vast square mileage leads to extremes of physical isolation. It is easier, therefore, for these people from ethnic minority groups to become largely 'invisible'. While it would be wrong to suggest that the Cardiff caucus are well serviced and supported by the social work services, it is increasingly apparent that a key concern in Wales is the manifestations of racism in what have been called 'predominantly white areas' and the constellation of factors which produce 'rural racism'.

Some attention has been given in the literature to the position of black and ethnic minorities in more rural environments (Jay 1992; Agyeman 1993). The highly invisible/visible axis has been noted; that is, highly 'invisible' in terms of services and support and highly 'visible' in terms of street racisms, harassment and abuse. Among the individuals themselves the experience is of extreme isolation, lack of networks of support and redress, ignorance of and therefore poor take-up of services. When services are provided they are often insensitive and inappropriate to their needs. Often individuals and families will not complain or demand services for fear of becoming more conspicuous and subject to labelling, and confidentiality is a key concern (Williams 1998). In parts of Wales there are no formal agencies of redress geared to these concerns such as Race Equality Councils or outposts of the Commission for Racial Equality. Many communities in Wales prove little open to the challenges of multiculturality and social closure is rife. This has important implications for identity building in Wales. Many young people from black and ethnic minority groups, born or brought up in Wales, are making claim to their Welsh identity and to the recognition of their place in contemporary Wales.

This picture means that social workers have to be creative and innovative in meeting these challenges. Their contribution is vital in challenging the picture of neglect and ignorance, in developing appropriate service delivery and in fostering the embryo of a black Welsh identity. Responses that include cross-border collaboration and multiagency fora are proving central in addressing gaps and shortfalls in provision. The stimulation of networks such as Mewn Cymru, an organisation geared towards the needs of ethnic minority women throughout Wales, and support for voluntary organisations such as Barnardos Multicultural Centre, Multicultural Crossroads and a black women's refuge based in Cardiff are all promising developments. Overall, however, the black voluntary sector in Wales is very weak in comparison with other parts of the United Kingdom.

Gradually a recognition of the failure to respond to the needs of Wales's black population is dawning. The patterns of neglect and complacency fostered by beliefs that 'there is no problem here' are being challenged. However, there is still a long way to go. The norm is for unitary authorities and voluntary agencies not to be conducting ethnic monitoring exercises, not to be undertaking staff training and not to be developing democratic processes that ensure the involvement of these minority communities (Williams 1998). Symbolically, the National Assembly elections failed to produce a single black member of the new body.

Indeed, the important developments in respect of the promotion of the Welsh language ushered in with the Welsh Language Act 1993 and devolution in Wales forms an interesting intersection with issues of 'race'. In the past, the aims of antiracism and the activities to promote the Welsh language have not always travelled comfortably together. Accusations around language ring-fencing of jobs have been countered in Wales by the Commission for Racial Equality developing an accord with the Welsh Language Board to protect against potential discrimination in employment. Some concerns have also been raised in respect of ring-fencing in certain service delivery areas. While this is not empirically established, without explicit strategic planning and targeting of services for ethnic minorities it is clear that these sensitive negotiations and priority setting will continue to be left for front-line practitioners to negotiate.

Social work in Wales today

Social work services in Wales, as in the rest of Great Britain, continue to be vulnerable both to changes in the wider social policy environment and to the endemic pursuit of the fashionable. Thus, it is not always possible to be confident that progressive developments will become rooted as sustainable strategies within the service delivery frame. Practitioners in Wales have been subject to rapid and extensive policy-driven change in the last few years, produced not only by the NHS and Community Care Act 1990, implemented in 1993, the Carers (Recognition and Services) Act 1995 and the Community Care (Direct Payments) Act but also as Local Government Reorganisation. In this turbulent transitional period, many well-established initiatives particular to Wales and principles of good practice offering the potential to substantively underpin the new reforms are fast being sabotaged. Such features are clearly evident in the core social work tasks of community care and child welfare, to which this chapter now turns.

Community care

Three developments in Wales are of particular significance to an understanding of the new arrangements for assessment and care management. The All Wales Strategy for the development of Services for Mentally Handicapped People (Welsh Office 1983) provided a context in which monies were ring-fenced over a period of ten years to be spent on creative approaches to individual planning. Individual planning expressed through multidisciplinary team-working practices in each locality and key worker models aimed to provide a vehicle for the development of accessible, locally based services and the co-ordination of interdisciplinary and inter-agency work at the front line. Such locality planning also made possible the transmission of information about service deficiencies.

Many of the successes and benefits of the All Wales Strategy were manifest in its early years (Felce *et al.* 1998) but there were also many tried and tested lessons for the development of the care management framework to come (Grant 1994). What became clear was that good individual planning was very time consuming, did not wholeheartedly involve service users, fell far short of providing individual needs assessment for all and indicated serious problems with developing strategic planning based on a system so wholly reliant on individual planning (Felce *et al*. 1998). The success of care management seemed to point to resource sufficiency, a mixture of traditional and new services and their compatibility, good purchaser/provider agreements but not necessarily a split between them, local community resources and a participatory approach to working which embraced the civil rights of the users and their families (Grant 1994). An important legacy of the Strategy was a body of practitioners well established in multidisciplinary working and individual planning.

In relation to services for older people, again a series of initiatives within Wales enabled a testing of ideas central to the community care reforms. In 1985 the Welsh Office consultation document, *A Good Old Age* laid the ground from which emerged a scheme to finance a variety of projects aimed at demonstrating good practice and balancing cost effectiveness against quality of care. The universalist orientation of this initiative differed from the Strategy, emphasising collaboration in the co-ordination of local services between health, housing and the independent sector. In its emphasis on extending consumer choice, the initiative highlighted a particular role for the voluntary sector. Again, many of these early projects provided important lessons about packages of care and flexible service provision across the service sectors (Robinson 1994, Parry Jones *et al*. 1998).

The third key Welsh Office initiative, *Mental Illness Services, a Strategy for Wales* (Welsh Office 1989) provided crucial lessons on individual needs assessment, care packaging, joint planning and the development of integrated, co-ordinated and accessible local services. The focus of service delivery was the Community Mental Health Team (CMHT) and considerable effort was put into the development of such teams in each locality, leading to patterns of new services, and service infrastructures. The evidence suggests many of those resettled from large long-stay institutions enjoyed improved quality of life (Crosby and Barry 1995) although concerns remained about inclusion into the community (Forrester-Jones and Grant 1997). Nevertheless, a structure of service delivery had been established that provided a good precursor to the new community care framework.

These Welsh policy initiatives created a context in which considerable experience of needs-led assessment, care packaging, interdisciplinary and interagency working and priority setting had been established with obvious transferability to the new legislative frame. In theory, therefore, many of the lessons for the successful implementation of the NHS and Community Care Act should already have been learned. In addition, a number of demonstration projects in a range of processes and skill development needed for the appropriate implementation of the new Act were funded by the Welsh Office (Parry Jones *et al.* 1998).

What is evident from a major study currently in its second phase of reporting is that despite these pioneering developments, social work services in Wales have appeared unable to benefit from the ground gained. The *All Wales Assessment and Care Management Study* (Parry Jones *et al.* 1998) is one of the first empirical studies of front-line care management practice in the UK. As such, it provides an important indication to other areas of the UK of the implementation of the new reforms and their impact on workers. In 1995 over 500 care manager practitioners from across Wales responded, and in the follow up study of 1997 nearly 200 practitioners from selected areas of Wales completed questionnaires.

The study enquired into the views and experiences of care managers of their roles and responsibilities, on developing needs-led services and on their levels of stress and job satisfaction. The findings indicate practitioners struggling to reconcile the needs/resources conundrum within a context of ever-shrinking budgets, increased workloads and onerous administrative responsibilities. Almost half the respondents reported a decrease in the quality of service they were able to provide, many attested to the loss of client contact, and the majority of practitioners reported increased stress levels and a drop in job satisfaction since April 1993. There seemed to be little evidence that practitioners had benefited from local government reorganisation, with improved accountability and control and more localised decision making reported by only a few. The study notes that the social care market in Wales remains seriously underdeveloped. The degree of budget decentralisation to promote flexible care planning has not been operationalised by most Welsh local authorities (Parry Jones *et al.* 1998). More than any other factor, local government reorganisation appeared to be associated with budget cuts and reduced community resources. Under these circumstances many practitioners reported that maintaining the needs-led approach was almost impossible, that there was little scope for them to draw on their professional skills and, as a consequence, many expressed disillusionment and demoralisation (Parry Jones 1998).

Despite clear forewarnings from major initiatives in Wales suggesting the value of different care management models, most authorities appeared to have adopted a purely administrative model characterised by large case loads and too much paperwork with deskilled workers forced into unimaginative ways of working with an emphasis on formal service delivery and a diminution of client contact and participation. Such a rigid adherence to the single administrative case management model produces an unduly tight separation between assessment and purchasing, mitigating against the more empathetic dimensions of professional work (Parry Jones *et al.* 1998). The more rewarding aspects of practitioner/provider roles therefore seem to have been eroded, as do many of the service quality indicators established by the All Wales Strategy.

In terms of administrative and organisational structures, a pattern exists in Wales where in certain specialisms, such as learning disability and mental health, some continuity from the All Wales strategies seems to have been achieved. There exist therefore discrepancies not only in service delivery approaches between localities but also within localities based on specialism. However, the recent history of multidisciplinary working within mental health and learning disability fields does continue to influence front-line care management practice.

Child welfare

In Wales, statutory services child care teams cover the broad spectrum of work involved in child welfare, including child protection services and work with teenagers in trouble, offering both protection and family support to children and young people in their own homes, in foster homes and through family centres. The major national child care charities such as NCH, Barnardos and NSPCC are operative within Wales although their coverage across the country is patchy. A continuing debate in Wales is the extent to which local authority reorganisation has exacerbated problems of co-ordination and collaboration between the major agencies and this is of particular concern in work with children and families.

In March 1997, there were 1016 children on the child protection registers in Wales (Digest of Welsh Statistics 1998). A pressing issue for child welfare in Wales is concern to readdress the balance between prevention and protection. By far the greater amount of social work time is spent in working with the smaller number of families where abuse is alleged or proven. Arguments abound for greater efforts being channelled towards easier and earlier access to services, flexible responses, provision of services to children in their own homes and interdepartmental initiatives that look holistically at services to children and families – that is, more preventive work (Butler *et al.* 1998). A tri-national study (Colton 1999) found that in Wales stigma was a major part of the experience of service users and service providers in child welfare. Statutory child welfare services and compulsory service were experienced as stigmatising by users and viewed negatively by social workers themselves. This issue will have to be addressed if preventive aims are to be achieved.

The independent Waterhouse Inquiry (2000) into the abuse of children in residential homes in North Wales reported on the 15 February 2000. This was the most recent in a number of scandals that have marred child care in Wales. The report confirmed the picture of poor-quality public care and the failure of the system to protect vulnerable children separated from their families. This report, together with the ongoing investigations of child abuse in children's homes in South Wales and in other parts of the UK, provided the impetus to continue to raise standards of substitute care. The Labour administration at the National Assembly was already committed, by its manifesto, to the early establishment of a Children's Commissioner in Wales (Labour Party

1999). This appointment was duly made in December 2000, and the office of the Commissioner was established with a budget of £750,000 in order to support its work each year.

The White Paper *'Social Services – Building for the Future'* (Welsh Office/Department of Health 1998) announced the reform of social services, which fell to the new Assembly in Wales to take forward. The reforms included the establishment of a Care Council for Wales/Cyngor Gofal Cymru, a Commission for Care Standards in Wales and, significantly, a new quality of care programme for children, *Gwarchod.* It was hoped that these measures would ensure safe environments and higher standards of care in residential homes for children and in care provided in their own homes. The arrangements also look towards strengthening children's advocacy and complaints procedures as well as the establishment of a Children's Commissioner. These developments were welcomed across Wales but concerns were also expressed that the White Paper did not address the serious shortage of resources in Welsh social services departments and these measures appeared, during the first two years of the Assembly's existence, to have to be carried forward with no substantial new money being made available. In the aftermath of the Comprehensive Spending Review of July 2000, however, all parts of the Welsh budget experienced significant increases, with social services' spending set to rise by 8.5 per cent in 2000/01 (National Assembly for Wales 2000).

Language and culture are salient issues in the development and delivery of child welfare services in Wales. The Children Act 1989 has made it incumbent on local authorities to consider the linguistic needs of children receiving services and this duty is enhanced by the provisions of the Welsh Language Act 1993. The work of Colton *et al.* (1995) found that the linguistic needs of Welsh-speaking children are better attended to in areas where there is a high number of Welsh speakers in the general population.

Within Wales, substitute family placement that reflects a 'racial', linguistic and religious match remains a challenge, as elsewhere in the UK. The placement of Welsh-speaking children within Welsh-speaking substitute families remains difficult to achieve, but the support of legislation ensures that it remains on the agenda of local authorities.

Future developments

This section now turns to a consideration of the prospects for future social work development in Wales. It begins with a brief discussion of the political and administrative context within which policy and practice has been developed before going on to look in more detail at the changes which, over the longer term, the Welsh Assembly might bring about. The section ends with some consideration of the prospects for a socially inclusive approach to social work which these developments might encompass.

The bald and central fact of Welsh politics and administration is its domination by parties of an other-than right-wing or Conservative character. Fewer than three out of ten voters in Welsh constituencies have supported the Conservative Party in any of the past five General Elections, culminating in the 1997 election with that left-wing nirvana, a Tory-free Wales. Until the elections of May and June 1999, at least, the same pattern had been repeated in local and European elections in Wales.

Administratively, the map of Wales has been radically redrawn during the 1980s and 1990s. At the same time, the notion of a 'democratic deficit' in Welsh political life became established as a truism among commentators, academics and politicians (see, for example, Morgan and Roberts 1993; Jones 1994). The Conservative Government, lacking a presence on the political ground in Wales, successively transferred powers away from locally elected bodies to the great quangocracy, which was to become one of its major administrative legacies. By the 1990s, figures released by Ron Davies, then Shadow Minister of State for Wales, suggested that 110 such bodies existed in Wales, responsible for £2.3bn of public expenditure each year (Davies 1994). Local government reorganisation compounded this position, involving a fall of 35.5 per cent in the number of elected councillors to a position below the estimated number of 1400 quango appointees in Wales (Osmond 1994). Labour's solution to the 'democratic deficit' was the foundation of the National Assembly which, as well as taking over the Welsh Office, assumed responsibility for oversight of the quangos in Wales. These include, for example, the major housing quango, Tai Cymru, which was early identified as a candidate for direct transfer to the Assembly's control.

In positive terms, what does the Assembly mean for social services and social workers? In the space available here, we are able only to sketch in some of the immediate and most significant issues that form part of the Assembly's early agenda in this area.

As noted above, the impact of LGR, in social services terms, has been to produce a plethora of often small-scale organisations in which co-ordination remains problematic and in which the variation in size of authority makes the achievement of equity elusive. Equity – the notion that any citizen should be able to rely upon a similar standard and range of core services regardless of, for example, income or geography – has been a traditional aim of social policy, albeit one which was shifted sharply lower down the policy priority order during the Conservative years. With the long-established political affiliation patterns of the Welsh electorate reflected in the election of Assembly members – who are overwhelmingly drawn from left-of-centre parties – the demands of equity are likely to command a more important place in its policy for-mulation. As the strategic authority for social service development in Wales, therefore, the impact of LGR provides a set of policy challenges which demand remedial attention and action, and which continue to be at least more urgent than the arguably more important development of new approaches.

The fragmentation caused by local government reorganisation meets a number of other existing policy thrusts which add to the sense of instability that is endemic to social service delivery in Wales. The Conservative agenda for public services in general placed a major emphasis upon the introduction of privatisation and marketisation into the social as well as the economic sphere of government. The extent to which it was successful in having such approaches adopted in local areas depended, to a large extent, upon the political character of local government. In Wales, the wholesale transfer of buildings, staff and services from the public to the independent sector simply did not take place in a way which was characteristic of, for example, local authorities in the south of England. Rather, Welsh councils were more likely to adopt policies of active opposition to sale of assets or loss of function and exhibit at least passive opposition to the marketisation of services through Compulsory Competitive Tendering, provider/purchaser splits and development of internal quasi-markets (see Butler *et al.* 1998).

Any administration that has almost twenty years at its disposal, however, is bound to make substantial inroads against local sources of opposition. The Assembly has therefore inherited a social services pattern in which diversity (to use a term favoured by its supporters) is more firmly embedded in patterns of provision than the political instincts of many members might find palatable. Even those who find the claims of diversity and choice convincing face the instability which such fragmented patterns have undoubtedly engendered in the day-to-day operation of social services departments.

In addition to these general policy trends, there are a number of other immediate issues that the Assembly has inherited in the social work arena and which have found an early place upon its agenda. Two must suffice here, as an illustration of possible developments ahead. The first revolves around the twin political problems of scandal and risk management. The report of the independent inquiry into the abuse of children in North Wales made early demands for the Assembly's attention, both before it has had an opportunity to develop reliable working patterns and before its politicians have been able to gain confidence in their new capacities. The care and protection of vulnerable children will always be matters of acute public concern and a sensible and sensitive response to revelations and proposals contained in Waterhouse remains one of the challenges against which the performance of the Assembly will be judged.

A second dimension, the youth justice aspect of social services in Wales, is one which may yet have implications for the development of the institution itself far beyond the social services sphere. The difference between youth justice and almost all other social service responsibilities lies in the extent to which the discharge of youth justice respon-sibilities will depend upon relations with other public bodies and gov-ernment departments which lie outside the direct authority of the Assembly. While other social service dimensions require co-ordination and co-operation between different professional groups and services – education, in the case of children, health services in relation to older people, for example – these areas fall within the Assembly ambit. The major players in youth justice, by contrast, almost all lie outside that direct sphere of influence. The Lord Chancellor's department will retain control of the Crown Prosecution department and the judiciary. The police and probation services are set to remain independent and relatively autonomous organisations. In both cases there is little distinc-tive which can be added about their operation in Wales. The probation service, for example, remains firmly under the wing of the Home Office and, under the most recent reform proposals (Home Office 1998), has seen local ties weakened even further. Some genuine efforts have been made – for example through the North Wales probation service and the probation officers' union, NAPO – to develop the Welsh-specific dimensions of criminal justice practice. Generally speaking, however, probation remains dominated by the conservative and Anglo-centric character of the Home Office, whatever party happens to be in govern-ment.

In youth justice, the Assembly has thus taken on a policy area which is contentious in itself, highly politicised in character and where its scope for decisive or distinctive action will be heavily circumscribed by the actions of other organisations over which it has no control. It is in this sense that the area might develop a significance over and above the salience of youth justice issues themselves. The whole question of powers and responsibilities has been among the most contentious in the establishment of the Assembly. It would be naive to expect that these issues will not continue to be developmental, in the sense that an oper-ating Assembly is bound to give rise to new information and new views in relation to the practical organisation of its powers and functions. The partnership Government between Labour and the Liberal Democrats of October 2000 contained a specific commitment to a formal review of the Assembly's powers and method of election, to report in the year following the next Assembly elections in 2003 (National Assembly for Wales 2000a). Youth justice, combining substantial contention and insubstantial powers in equal measure, might well provide a testing bed for some of the most acute of these questions.

If these are among the challenges which face the Assembly, does evidence exist which might suggest that the Assembly provides any real prospect of a social policy and a social welfare practice which will be sensitive to the particular needs, circumstances and preferences of the population of Wales? Our argument begins from an understanding of the character of Welsh political life as one that includes a rooted and continuing commitment to collective means of meeting individual needs. It also retains a practical and ideological determination that meeting these needs requires the active involvement of the state, rather than a reliance on an opportunistic and crude individualism. Welsh political culture, in our view, continues to be organised around the Richard Titmuss – rather than the Norman Tebbitt – test of extending the boundaries of this consensual community to incorporate a commitment to caring for strangers (see Drakeford 1995 for a more extended account of this argument in the Welsh context).

A positive belief in the moral and practical obligations to care for strangers is, of course, one of the sustaining forces which underpins the provision of social work services. A community which seeks positively to extend the chains of interdependence and support to those for whom such links have otherwise been broken places social work far closer to the heart of what it believes should be provided than the derision and dislike which so often appears to be the fate of English counterparts. There is hard evidence for this contention to be found in the practical actions of Welsh local authorities. A Rowntree study in the early 1990s found that, despite the democratic deficit, a distinctive pattern of local government practice in Wales still survived. If there was one single factor that the authors identified as symbolic of this difference, it was the distinctively high priority afforded by councils in Wales to spending on the social services (Boyne *et al.* 1991). The Audit Commission, reporting early in 1995, reached the same conclusions. In terms of total expenditure per head of the population, Welsh counties occupied seven of the eight top places in the list of 47 non-metropolitan councils in England and Wales. In social services expenditure this pattern was repeated and reinforced. In terms, for example, of assistance given to older people both to live in their own homes and to be supported in residential accommodation, Welsh authorities dominated the lists of those councils offering best assistance, occupying six of the top 11, and five of the top nine places respectively.

Social inclusion

Much of the debate about social welfare services in a Welsh context, as set out in the previous section, might be summarised as revolving around questions of social inclusion and exclusion. The general case we have advanced is one that suggests that, potentially at least, the political and administrative character of Wales might lead to a renewed emphasis upon policies which seek to extend the boundaries of inclusion, rather than the deliberate exclusion of individuals who fail to meet the behavioural preferences of governments.

Yet, a cautionary note must be sounded in all this. The very term 'social inclusion' is in danger of dilution to the point where it will join or supplant 'community' as a 'spray-on' term, attached to an otherwise questionable concept, in order to deodorize it of unpleasant or problematic connotations. Only a little investigation is required to establish the fact that inclusion is far from the hallmark of many policies pursued by the same government responsible for the establishment of the social exclusion unit. New Labour, in some of its dimensions at least, has a distinctly social authoritarian approach to policy. The Crime and Disorder Act 1998, for example, contains the Anti-Social Behaviour Order which will allow for the imprisonment of individuals who transgress behavioural requirements in essentially social areas such as housing tenancies. The Minister of State for Education informed teacher union conferences in Easter 1998 that the state will be 'hard as nails' with parents who fail to measure up to new responsibilities to be placed upon them. Within weeks of taking office, New Labour's first minister responsible for mental health services announced new powers for the compulsory treatment of the mentally ill and a moratorium upon the closure of mental institutions.

These developments expose a certain contradiction within the social exclusion debate, for they suggest that there are significant elements within the population to whom the inclusionary embrace is not to be extended. From a social services perspective such a contradiction would be particularly significant, for social welfare work so often involves engagement with just such groups and individuals – the troublesome, as well as the troubled. At the very least, inclusion, in these circumstances, is not an unambiguous policy goal which can be unproblematically pursued. In the Welsh context, as our earlier argument has suggested, we anticipate a more generous and less authoritarian emphasis within the social policy making of the National Assembly. Social welfare workers have a significant part to play in generating the effort to make the difference that may be possible, and so valuable, here.

Social work education

Finally, and briefly, we explore how some of the themes discussed in this chapter might find their way into the education of social workers in Wales. If social work is to make the most of whatever opportunities, however limited, which might emerge for a more inclusive development and delivery of services, then that inclusivity will have to be predicated upon a sensitivity to the linguistic and cultural context within which workers practice and users live their lives (Drakeford and Lynn 1999). Preparation for such a practice will require programmes which are rigorous and challenging in their investigation of cultural and linguistic differences and which extend that rigour to include those other social divisions, such as poverty and rurality, which so profoundly influence the lives and prospects of social work clients.

Education itself, of course, provides a link between the individual and the social that can both include and exclude, which can help liberate or subjugate the individual. In our experience, the focus upon difficult and challenging material which obliges individuals to consider their own values and experiences is bound to give rise to powerful emotional as well as intellectual reactions and to generate conflict as well as agreement. Tenacity and a willingness to succeed slowly are part of a strategy which aims to shape a social work that has at its core a determination to prioritise the interests of the powerless rather than the powerful. It is because, as we hope this chapter has demonstrated, Wales provides a context both where problems are in evidence, yet where the soil for a worthwhile solution might still prove to be fruitful, that we think these efforts are so worth making.

Chapter 7

Guernsey
Social Work on a Small Island

John Wolfe

The islands, covering an area of approximately 3000 square miles, that lie in the stretch of sea between England and France have been described in many different ways: 'The Aegean of the Channel' or 'Rich crumbs from a French table' are just some of the terms that have been used to denote this group of islands now known as the Channel Islands. Victor Hugo once described the Channel Islands as 'fragments of Europe dropped by France and picked up by England'. This group of islands, which now seems very 'British' in culture, still maintains the flavour of its French antecedents (remnants of the historical 'tug of war' between France and England). At some point in the past, the Channel Islands were one entity for administration and government. However, more recently in their history, these islands were divided into two bailiwicks[1], Jersey and Guernsey. Both of these bailiwicks have remained, to the present time, independent states except for the conduct of foreign policy and defence – these responsibilities rest formally with the Crown (the House of Windsor) but are in practice are acquitted by the UK Government at Westminster. This chapter concentrates upon the bailiwick of Guernsey (which includes the islands of Guernsey, Alderney, Sark, Herm, Jethou and Brecqhou), providing an overview of social work policy and practice within this group of islands.

The Islands in the Bailiwick

Guernsey

Guernsey has a population of approximately 59,000, with an area of approximately 24 square miles. This makes Guernsey one of the more densely populated parts of the British Isles. Guernsey is perhaps most well known as a holiday island and for the industries of tomato and flower growing. Due to the mild climate (snow is a rarity), horticulture has always been a substantial contributor to the economy of the island. Other economic sectors include manufacturing, non-financial services, tourism and, to a lesser extent, sea fishing. However, in recent years the finance industry has become the largest contributor to the island's wealth. At the last count, there were 76 established banks on the island. The island derives significant benefits from its status as an offshore finance centre. In 1998, the island's finance sector generated approximately 33 per cent of Guernsey's gross domestic product. Guernsey GDP enables the island to finance its infrastructure, health and social services without recourse to public-sector borrowing. As if to underline Guernsey's independent financial status the island also mints and prints its own money.

English is the main language, although there is a patois, which is Norman French and can still be heard spoken within some of the quieter parishes. In recent years there has been an influx of people from Portugal and the Philippines and a substantial number of people from Yugoslavia. This has introduced a hitherto unknown factor within the island – the potential for visible racism and discrimination.

Guernsey became an island following the last ice age (some XX, 000 years ago). The earliest recordings of human settlements date to 7000 BC. The island is covered with the remains of Dolmens and Menhirs. Romans, Vikings and others visited and used the islands as trading posts. Guernsey has seen the French and the English come and go. The island has changed allegiance many times and even acted as the base for privateers in the seventeenth century.

While the First World War had very little direct impact on the island, which was not invaded, as in other parts of the British Empire large numbers of men were never to return home. By comparison, the

Second World War had a large and undeniable impact on all the people of Guernsey. From 1940 to 1945, the German forces (a total of 35,000 troops surrendered to the British when the islands were retaken) occupied the islands. More than 5000 children, accompanied by teachers and many mothers, went to England prior to the invasion by the Germans. Some of these children lived in foster homes, either placed singly or in a group of two or three, some stayed with their mothers and others had a group-living experience within children's homes. Anecdotal stories are variable recalling the quality of care that the children received, ranging from in some instances from extreme cruelty bordering upon slavery to compassion and high-quality care. Some adults now recount how returning to Guernsey meant leaving those they saw as and felt to be their parents. The impact of the Second World War on the culture of the island can never be underestimated. Post war, a large number of children, young people and families who had experience of life outside the islands returned, each bringing a new view of the world and, more importantly, a new framework through which to evaluate and contribute to an island culture which had changed forever.

Sark

Sark is in effect two islands, with a total length of five kilometres and width of two kilometres and is totally traffic free, apart from tractors and horse-drawn vehicles. Since its liberation following the Second World War, Sark has shown that however archaic the framework of its government (feudal), it possesses a form of autonomous rule on a widely representative basis which is totally unique within Europe. Its legislature is known as the Chief Pleas, and is presided over by the Seneschal. The Chief Pleas must defer in matters of dispute to the Royal Court and in extreme situations to the Privy Council. Sark has autonomy from the rest of the bailiwick of Guernsey, let alone the United Kingdom! While many services, such as police and health, are provided from Guernsey, committees such as the Children Board (social services) have no statutory obligations or rights regarding the island of Sark. The island boasts one of the smallest prisons in existence, which is rarely used – perhaps not surprisingly with a population of 550.

Herm

Until shortly after the Second World War the small island of Herm was leased to various individuals by the British Government. However, following liberation it became the property of the bailiwick of Guernsey. Since that time it has become home to a very small community of people and is more noted by others as a holiday destination or destination for a boating trip for the day. It has a small primary school, but all other services are provided by Guernsey.

Alderney

Alderney is the northern most Channel Island with a population of approximately 2200. It lies some 14 kilometres from France, as opposed to 30 kilometres from Guernsey. The island encapsulates the idea of a quiet, steady pace of life. On 1 January 1949 Alderney came under the authority of Guernsey, whose government assumed financial and administrative responsibility for police, education, the maintenance of the airport, immigration, main roads and sewers, social services, health services and water supplies. In return, Alderney adopted Guernsey's rates of taxation, the proceeds of which accrued to the States of Guernsey.

During the Second World War Alderney was completely depopulated by the German forces and inhabited by slave labour and the German army and navy. Culturally the island has therefore had to re-establish itself in the postwar years There are a number of Italians and small numbers of other nationalities; nonetheless the population is principally made up of people who have chosen to resettle on the island from the United Kingdom and other parts of the bailiwick of Guernsey. It has a unique and distinct culture which, while hard to define, resembles the culture that might be expected of an isolated village with tremendous self-pride.

The social and political context within the bailiwick of Guernsey

Social services are delivered within the political framework of the bailiwick. Politically, Guernsey is quite independent from the United Kingdom and by Royal Charter administers its own affairs as a Crown dependency. The civic head of Guernsey is known as the bailiff and is appointed by the Crown – the Crown's representative in the bailiwick being the lieutenant governor. Both act in liaison with the island's government. The government is structured around a parliament consisting of the legislature and assembly known as the States of Deliberation, which are grounded more on French law than English. There are no formally organised political parties and the deputies (MPs) who meet in the States of Deliberation are there as individuals from their respective parishes. There are 45 deputies. In addition, each of the ten parishes within the island is represented by douzeniers (parish councillors). In the past, the island was largely governed through the douzaines using a system reminiscent of Poor Law. Indeed the term Procureur of the Poor is still existent and active as an alternative means from which people draw money when in dire circumstances.

It is important to note that the States of Deliberation are the mechanism for making the law, which is subsequently subject to royal assent through the Privy Council. This means that important pieces of legislation current within the UK are not enforceable within the bailiwick of Guernsey. However, Guernsey has subscribed to the principles and wherever possible has worked within the spirit of the UK Children Act 1989 – the bailiwick need not have done so, as the bailiwick of Guernsey has its own range of legislation and particular legislation governing and controlling the actions, responsibilities and requirements laid upon departments dealing with children and young people.

Benefit system

The benefit system in Guernsey is somewhat different from that of the UK. There is no equivalent to Housing Benefit or Working Families Tax Credit. There are currently 1750 claimants (up to an income maximum of £190 in 2000) of Supplementary Benefit per week (a means-tested statutory welfare benefit paid to families or individuals – loosely equivalent to UK Income Support) with approximately 150 adults, dependants and 675 child dependants. There are approximately 9000 people over the age of 65 resident in Guernsey, of whom approximately 90 per cent are in receipt of Guernsey Old Age pension. It is the current policy of the Guernsey Social Security Authority to increase pensions above RPI (retail price index). With effect from January 2000 the full rate of pension for a single person is £101.25 per week and £163 for a couple.

Housing issues

In Guernsey, the demand for housing is significant, with pressure resulting from population growth and changing demographic and social trends. As the population has grown, restrictions have been introduced to govern the accessibility of the property market in the island. (A controlled system, operating both and open and closed markets exists; in practice there is one market for locally qualified residents and another for incoming residents, this difference being largely reflected in the value of property and hence the cost of property to locally qualified residents as opposed to incomers.) The current local house price index shows that the average house price for 1999 was £160,624, with those on the open market being substantially more. The 1998 Policy and Resource Planning Report identified the need for a minimum of 250 additional units of accommodation per year to alleviate the current pressure on the local housing market.

The average private-sector rent paid by a sample of 150 claimants of Supplementary Benefit, surveyed by the Social Security Authority in 1998, was £71.53 per week. In the majority of cases this represented over 50 per cent of weekly income. This does not of course reflect the average rent paid overall, which is considerably more. The Housing Authority provides approximately 2100 public-sector units of accommodation. Rents are set below those in the private sector. The Housing Authority is not mandated to provide for homeless persons or single people. There are no people sleeping rough. However, there is real concern over young people who move from one person's floor to another and are considered vulnerable.

Health care

There is no equivalent in Guernsey to the National Health Service, as found in the UK. Local residents are responsible for meeting the costs of primary health care, GPs, chiropodists, physiotherapists, opticians, dentists, etc. Charges are also made for the ambulance service and prescription drugs. Local residents also pay for medical treatment in the Princess Elizabeth Hospital (the island's main hospital), Accident and Emergency Department, where medical cover is provided by GPs who are in private practice. (If a child is admitted then the services of the hospital are free but there are charges for the GPs' services, including attendance at the hospital.) Secondary health care, including in-patient physiotherapy and hospital accommodation, is generally provided free of charge to residents under a contributory health insurance scheme. The Guernsey Social Security Authority runs a means-tested medical expenses assistance scheme (MEAS) providing grants towards primary care medical bills.

Universal health services for children (from birth to school age) are delivered by health visitors, and dental treatment is provided throughout a child's school career. The Board of Health offers a child and adolescent mental health service and child development service, which are situated at Bell House. For children with learning disabilities (in 1999, there were 48 such children) a range of services is provided to help these children lead as full a life as possible. Thirty-three of the children used The Croft (Respite Home) for respite care for varying amounts of time.

Employment issues

The working population in Guernsey, employed or self-employed, is approximately 30,500. Guernsey presently enjoys full employment (unemployment is 0.3 per cent of the island's current workforce). As a consequence of this low level of unemployment, there is a labour shortage, both skilled and unskilled. These shortages can only be met by importing staff on essential or short-term licences. At 31 March 1999, 948 skilled/professional people held housing licences (which give the person the right to live on the island for a specified period), issued because they were in a capacity considered essential to the community. The majority of such licences are issued for up to a five-year period, but can be issued for up to 15 years (at which stage the holder gains full residential qualifications). There is no minimum wage legislation in Guernsey.

Non-local workers fill many seasonal posts in the horticulture and tourist industries, most typically on short-term licences for between nine months to three years. Again, at 31 March 1999, 1147 such licences were in force. Short-term licence holders typically occupy staff quarters or lodgings. The majority of seasonal workers come from Madeira. While their contribution has been deemed necessary by businesses, there is a long-term cost to the island in terms of the need for additional infrastructure as working adults are joined by other family members.

Social work

There are, within the Guernsey Board of Health, Education Council, Children Board (social services) and a range of voluntary agencies, social work services comparable to those found in most areas of the UK. However, the delivery of these services – in both structure and impact – is somewhat different from the rest of the British Isles. But delivery of some services can be both efficient and more accessible than in some of the large bureaucratic systems found elsewhere in the British Isles. The mandate of the Board of Health is to:

- advise the States on matters relating to the mental, physical and social well being of the people of Guernsey and Alderney, including: health education; promoting, protecting and improving environmental and public health; preventing or diagnosing and treating illness, disease and disability; caring for the sick, old, infirm and those with disabilities

- develop, present to the States for approval and implement policies on the above matters for the provision of services, introduction of legislation and other appropriate measures which contribute to the achievement of strategic and corporate objectives

- exercise the powers and duties conferred on it by extant legislation

- be accountable to the States for the management and safeguarding of public funds and other resources entrusted to it.

The first social worker formally employed by the Board of Health was appointed 23 years ago. Since that time the Board of Health's social work resource has grown to include seven qualified social workers and three social work assistants with administrative backup. These social workers are concerned with issues relating to older people, adult mental health, child and adolescent psychiatric social work and general medical social work. While there is a general service available in these areas of practice, there are others that cannot be accommodated within the island setting. There is, for instance, no therapeutic community, no facility such as that provided by the Richmond Fellowship and no specific day care or residential facilities for adolescents. Some young people suffering from mental health or behavioural problems are placed off the island. In some cases, this can be a placement of choice and have real benefits given the distance from some of the environmental problems.

Practitioners have commented that they believe the benefits of working in the island community are that they have time to become more deeply involved in their particular cases, and also that their general availability to the client group is fundamentally more accessible. On a personal level, social workers, living within the community, have little chance of anonymity. This can be a negative feature if not addressed and handled appropriately.

The following sections provide a more detailed account of one service provider to the community, that of the States of Guernsey Children Board whose nearest comparator would be a social services department or a form of the children's department found before 1971 in England (pre-Seebohm and local government changes of the early 1970s).

States of Guernsey Children Board

The Children Board commenced its duties on the 1 January 1929 in accordance with the provision of the order in council 'Loi ayant rapport a L'Asile des Enfants' (registered on the Records of the Island on the 24 November 1928). At that time the Children Board had responsibility for registering all those children under 20 years of age who were in the care of the St Peter Port Parish Poor Law Board, the Country Hospital Board, the St Sampsons Parish Poor Law Board and the St Martins Parish Poor Law Board.

The Children Board's role, as defined in the order in Council of 1928, was to establish a children's home. Consequently, during the years between 1929 and 1938, the Children Board was active in both developing the law and securing a property. The most significant development occurred in 1937 with the passing of the 'Protection of Children and Young Persons Law'. The effect of this was that 'duties of granting permission to persons to undertake the maintenance of children for reward and visiting such children had passed from the Parish Poor Law Boards to the Children Board on the 1 January 1938' (Children Board Minutes 10 January 1938). The Children Board held its first meeting in January 1938 as it was then required to oversee the development and running of the children's home. This home was established on the previous Greenfields site (now Le Carrefour and Perruque House) and was known as the 'Castel Home'. In March 1938 there were a total of 136 children in care. The breakdown was as shown in Table 7.1.

Table 7.1 Number of children for whom the Children Board were responsible in March 1938

	Boys	Girls	Total
In the children's home	43	56	99
Town hospital	0	0	0
Country hospital	8	14	22
Sanatorium	0	2	2
Homes in England	4	6	10
In service	1	1	2
Boarded out	0	1	1
Totals	56	80	136

The following month there were 104 children in the home and the number was to stay at about a hundred for several years. The consequent evacuation of 5000 children, plus adults, from Guernsey was inclusive of children who were in the state's children's home.

However, by 1947 these figures had changed (Table 7.2). This situation remained much the same throughout the 1940s, but in the early 1950s discussion started concerning a house called 'Swissville', previously known as 'Hirzelbourne'. In 1953, Swissville was purchased by the States and opened as a 'nursery'. By 1955 it was established, and it was noted in the Children Board minutes that 'the Nursery was working very satisfactorily, but it was felt that the walls and ceiling in the milk room should be cleaned down to prevent paint flakes falling in the children's food' (Minutes of States of Guernsey Children Board 1955). At that time, not only were the board members involved in deciding upon the detailed administration of the 'Castel Home' and 'Swissville Nursery' but also they were responsible for the admission of children into care. During this period there were still strong overtones of the Poor Law and domestic involvement in what would soon be recognised as professional decision making.

Table 7.2 Number of children for whom the Children Board were responsible in March 1947

	Boys	Girls	Total
In the children's home	34	13	47
Boarded out	1	1	2
In private homes	4	6	10
In service	2	1	3

In the early 1960s, discussion commenced concerning the development of 'more homes' in which 'foster parents' could be installed with a number of children. Hence, in the late 1960s and early 1970s the Children Board establishing five 'family group homes' run by house parents and relief house parents. The Board was also by this time an adoption agency and in the mid 1960s the need for a children's officer was discussed, as the work outside the children's home and nursery was increasing. Therefore, in January 1964, the Children Board confirmed that the States Establishment Committee had approved that a child care officer or children's officer be appointed on a part-time basis for 18 hours per week. At this same time, the first advertisements were seen for foster parents, now known as foster carers.

In addition during this period, attention was being given to the development of the Children Act. This resulted in the Children and Young Persons (Guernsey) Law 1967. The Children's Officer of that time noted that 'if the Children Act comes into force – there will be a sudden increase in the work and responsibility of the Children's Officer which might be more than one person can carry out'. This turned out to be a very perceptive statement, particularly with the benefit of hindsight – today there is an establishment of over a hundred staff, a sizeable proportion of whom are qualified individuals.

The Children Board's priorities throughout the 1970s were principally baby adoption, some fostering and the management of Swissville and Greenfields as well as the emerging family group homes.

During this period, through the appointment of child care officers (now known as social workers) the number of staff not working in one of the 'homes' increased, and by the early 1980s the basis for the current child protection and families team had been established. It was at this time that a shelter was also agreed by the States to offer emergency accommodation for women with small children who were subject to domestic violence or at a point of crisis because of homelessness.

The beginning of the 1980s saw a department which had many inadequacies (despite some dedicated and highly caring staff), poor levels of accountability, low standards with regard to child care in some areas and, regrettably, a high-profile child protection case resulting in the near death and consequent paraplegia for a child. The one positive outcome concerning this period and the episode in question was the decisive way in which the politicians and civil servants of the time acted to bring about real change within the services provided by the States of Guernsey Children Board.

It was in 1982 that the first Department of Health and Social Security review was held and another followed this in 1984. The following year, there was a further review undertaken by Peat Marwick Management Consultants. The reports had many areas in common. The key themes were:

- the development of preventative work
- the need for written policies and careful planning
- the development of a strong management team
- the development of professional staff
- further development of fostering and specialised fostering
- consideration of the reduction of the residential units and reallocation of resources
- development of a family centre
- development of the adolescent residential unit
- improvement of inter-agency working and establishment a group specifically to consider child protection issues

- improving staff training and inter-agency training
- defining the tasks of staff.

The reports set a clear agenda for the Children Board that was essentially about modernising the department.

Through the latter part of the 1980s the Children Board considered and implemented many of the recommendations of the review and the basis for the current organisation was clearly established. During this period of time a significant factor began to emerge that was to place child protection agencies under increased pressure. This was the identification of, and subsequent widening awareness of, sexual abuse, with the resultant need for investigative and therapeutic services.

Much of the early 1990s provided a period of stabilisation and consolidation for the huge changes that had taken place in the 1980s. In 1993, the Children Board adopted the following statement of purpose:

> The Children Board exists to promote the welfare of children and young people in partnership with families and other agencies, and to provide a service within a legal framework which will protect them.

However, by 1995, new initiatives were taken when the new senior management team spent considerable time formulating a new five-year plan for the Children Board. This team recognised by that future plans need not be shackled to developments in either the UK or elsewhere in Europe with regard to work with children and families. Moreover, here was a unique opportunity to strive for a service tailor made for the islands. After extensive consultation with external agencies, including police, probation, Board of Health and judiciary, and internal discussions with staff at all levels (manual, qualified, unqualified, residential workers and managers), a five-year-plan was produced. This plan reflected a desire for a truly preventative service, with the primary aim of providing a supportive service to clients while maintaining the role of the agency responsible for child protection work.

May 1996 saw the inception of the new structure for the Children Board, illustrated in Figure 7.1.

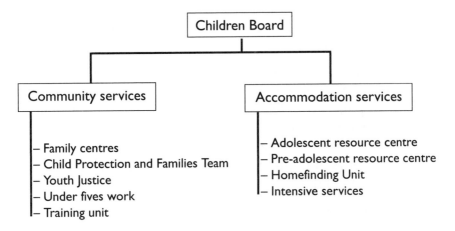

Figure 7.1 Organisation of the Children Board After May 1996

Inherent in this restructuring of the department were the normal problems associated with change. There were also a number of strategic and corporate objectives that made this a difficult exercise.

- A flatter organisation was needed. There would be no room in future for 'armchair managers' – uncomfortable for some who had striven to move into management roles and now found themselves re-cast as practitioner managers who would be centrally engaged in direct work with clients. This enhanced the service; both for clients and other staff members by bringing the managers' skills back to active use. (Social work is sadly littered with those whose objective has been either to leave residential roots or basic practice!)

- Unqualified staff were to be given sufficient training and opportunities to be involved in work that had become the specialised domain of those with a CQSW or DipSW. Many people who had given considerable years of service and had gathered skills which had been enhanced both through training and practice were not being given the opportunity to use these skills to their full capacity. The means of achieving these goals for staff within the family centres, residential and resource centres in a preventative role. (The numbers of locally trained CQSW or DipSW staff has increased in the last three years to some 44.44 per cent of the workforce)

- Family centre projects, both static neighbourhood facilities and a roving playbus, were seen as crucial developments. A joint project with the local housing department resulted in a family centre project which was quickly overwhelmed with people from the community wishing to be involved – resonances of forms of social work advocated in the Barclay report (1982).

- Youth justice needed a radical overhaul. Coinciding with the 1998 Crime and Disorder Act and moves within the UK towards 'caution plus' and 'restorative conferencing', the newly formed team were able to have a considerable impact on the establishment of new ways of working within the bailiwick of Guernsey, with the result that Guernsey was at the forefront of changes desired in the UK.

Such changes incorporated were not achieved without some birth pains. However, as the cycle of planning begins again Guernsey will be refining what is already a credible service, and will no doubt be the envy of many local authorities.

The current structure, policies and practice for the States of Guernsey Children Board

The Children Board has responsibility for children in need: it is mandated to undertake preventative work[2]. In 2001 the board was working with approximately 250 children and young people at any one time. Although the Children Board is the lead agency for children in need, their needs will often be complex, requiring a range of services provided by more than one agency. At a strategic level, close liaison is necessary to ensure that a comprehensive range of services is developed locally. For example, collaborative working with parents and other agencies such as schools and education services, health services, the police and probation services and the voluntary sector has been crucial for the full range of needs of the individual child to be met.

One of the aims of the Children Board is to safeguard children who are at risk of significant harm through reducing risk by enabling the child to live in a safe family environment. This involves targeted work with children, young people and families and the development of a range of wide family support services in Guernsey. Those agencies involved with children and families generally and service users have identified the need for a wider range of services that families can access easily to receive help and advice to prevent crises within families developing. Families are sometimes reluctant to be referred to what they perceive as formal states services. They are requesting services that can be easily accessed where they can drop in for advice and support without the need to go through any referral process. Agencies are developing initiatives to address this need. The Children Board is further developing its Family Centre Programme with the aim of establishing centres in the community where parents can drop in and receive advice and support. In addition, to meet the needs of older young people further youth workers have recently been appointed, and the health visiting service offers groups on parenting. The Children Board is also running a pilot project called The 15+ Housing Project in conjunction with a local voluntary agency, Youth Concern, and NCH Action for Children.

Child protection

The Children and Young Persons (Guernsey) Law 1967, and the subsequent extension of the legislation to Alderney, has placed a duty on the Children Board to investigate situations where children are suspected of being at risk of significant harm within the bailiwick. Other agencies, such as the police, also have statutory responsibilities to investigate any crimes relating to the ill-treatment or abuse of children. (The NSPCC has no statutory role in Guernsey – unlike the UK).

All referrals for an investigation where there is concern that a child may have been or is at risk of being abused are made to either the Children Board Child Protection and Families Team or the Guernsey police. The Children Board and Guernsey police have joint procedures which relate to the investigation of possible abuse of children. These procedures have been developed in accordance with the Department of Health (UK) procedures found in 'Working Together', and good practice guidance contained in the 'Memorandum of Good Practice for Interviewing Children' (Department of Health 1992). Part of any initial enquiry involves information gathering from other agencies that are involved with a child and a paediatrician undertakes any necessary medical examination of the child. Depending upon the outcome of the investigation and enquiries, a child protection case conference may be called to consider the placement of a child on the register (see table 7.3 for a comparison of Guernsey and UK). This is in line with the Guernsey Child Protection Committee's Guidelines, which give clear criteria for registration. Other agencies, including health professionals, probation service, education service, NSPCC, playgroups, day nurseries and the voluntary sector all contribute to the identification and notification of child protection concerns.

The placement of a child's name on the Child Protection Register is by way of an initial child protection case conference which is organised to share information, analyse risk and recommend responsibility for action. Conferences are attended by family members and by professionals from all the agencies that are in contact with the child and family (for example, police, health visitor, teacher, GP, probation officer and social worker).

Table 7.3 Comparison of the registration data of Guernsey and UK		
	Guernsey	UK (average)
Numbers on the register per 10,000 population aged 0–17 years	32 (1995)	32 (1994)
Registrations per 10,000 population	23 (1995)	27 (1994/95)
De-registrations per 10,000 population	35 (1995)	27 (1994/5)
Initial child protection case conferences per 10,000 population 0 –17 years	23 (1995)	43 (1994)

Source: Children Board Annual Report: 1996

While family conferencing as such has not been used in Guernsey, the current system of child protection conferences has a high expectation of attendance by individuals, as was mentioned earlier.

One of the benefits of working in a small community is the potential for an enhanced level of responsibility. Provided sufficient attention is given to networking between the agencies and within parts of the primary agency itself, responses towards co-operation are likely to be high compared to many places. For example, the police and social workers receive joint training locally under the joint investigation procedures and the interviewing procedures. Despite the advantages of developing networks in a small community, it must also be recognised that sensitivity and political awareness are of considerable importance in a small community.

There are several current child protection issues that the Board is considering:

- *Criteria for registration.* Of the children registered in 1997, almost 50 per cent were registered under the 'Category of grave concern' – a category no longer used in the UK. The continued use of this criterion for registration in Guernsey is currently under review.

- *Thresholds.* Debates on Guernsey mirror those in the UK, concerning thresholds for invoking formal child protection procedures, the need to consider child protection issues within children's wider needs, and for services for vulnerable children who are in need yet for whom a full Child Protection Investigation Registration is inappropriate. Following publication of 'Messages from Research' (Department of Health 1995) there have been workshops in Guernsey to consider these issues:

- *Support services.* An ongoing concern, which has been highlighted by the Guernsey Child Protection Committee, is the need to develop further resources for the victims of abuse. The therapeutic resources that can be needed by a child and their family are extensive, and some children and their families will need support over a period of time. This can place a drain on the resources that are available.

'Looked after' children in Guernsey

The States of Guernsey Children Board and the Board of Health (for children with learning disabilities and children with mental health problems) are the lead agencies for children who are looked after in Guernsey. Reasons why children or young people may become looked after are complex. In Guernsey, the majority of children who are looked after by the Children Board are placed in families, either foster families or with members of their extended family. In some circumstances it may be more appropriate to place the child for a short to medium term in a resource centre that offers residential accommodation. It is recognised that it is important to retain the local contact with family and schools as this facilitates the rehabilitation or leaving care process. It is necessary in some exceptional circumstances to place children off the island, but this will only be appropriate when the local resources do not meet the need. This may be because of the child's disability, educational needs, social behaviour or a combination of these difficulties (see below).

The Children Board follows the key principles of the Children Act 1989 in the UK – recognising that it is generally best for children and young people to be within their own families and that it is the Children Board's responsibility to encourage and enable family members to undertake their responsibilities without resort to legal proceedings.

Children in the care of the States of Guernsey Children Board will have been accommodated through several main routes:

- *Voluntary care.* By agreement with the parent (without resort to court proceedings) who, for a range of reasons, temporary or for the longer term, is unable to provide adequate care.

- *Place of Safety Order.* Under this temporary order (28 days), a child can be looked after by the States of Guernsey; the child is removed to alternative accommodation or retained there for protection from significant harm (as in the UK pre-Children Act 1989).

- *Fit Person Order (Care Order).* This order gives parental responsibility to the States of Guernsey Children Board, although the parents retain certain parental rights. Whenever possible, parents must also be allowed reasonable contact with a child and be involved in decision making. The Court should only make a Fit Person Order if it is satisfied that the Order will positively improve the child's welfare, for example in serious cases of harm or neglect.

- *Secure Accommodation Order.* An order made by the Court when a child or young person needs to be placed in secure accommodation to prevent self-harm or harm to others. (This Guernsey legislation is taken from the Children Act 1989).

- *Remands to the Children Board.* A young person may be remanded by the Juvenile Court through criminal proceedings to the States of Guernsey Children Board.

As is evident from the different routes through which children become looked after by the States of Guernsey, they are not often of a homogenous group but have particular needs requiring a range of care environments. While being looked after, children and young people may be placed with relatives, friends, an approved foster carer or in a resource centre with a residential component. A care plan will identify the primary goal for the child or young person. Where possible, the goal will be to return them to their birth family as soon as it is appropriate to do so. Where this is not possible, an alternative long-term care plan (permanency) is formulated with an adoptive or long-term foster family.

Partnership with the family, the child and the key professionals is established at the outset from the assessment of need to the development of a care plan and an agreement about the respective responsibilities and expectations of the family and the agencies involved. This care plan is regularly reviewed with the child and family on a multi-agency basis. The care plan identifies the reasons for the child being looked after, the child's needs including physical and mental health, educational, cultural and social needs, appropriate and specific services to meet these needs, the long-term goal for the child which may be rehabilitation back to their family following a short-term placement, a period of respite or long-term or permanent alternative care. In providing care placements for children, one of the aims is to ensure continuity of links with their families and school. One of the challenges facing

Guernsey is the diseconomy of scale and, as a consequence, agencies have developed services that are multifunctional.

At the age of 16 to 18, having been prepared for independent living, young people move to their own accommodation with support from the Children Board. This service can provide a smooth transition from being looked after by the Children Board to independence.

Over the years there has been a significant reduction in the number of children in residential care and an increase in the number of children in foster care. Overall, the number of children accommodated by the Children Board has decreased as preventative services have made an impact on the family situation. Children and young people who are accommodated within Guernsey can be placed in a range of needs-led resources.

- *Foster care.* Over 75 placements; also encompasses a number of supported lodgings for a number of young people.

- *Garden Hill Resource Centre.* For six pre-adolescent children plus two emergency beds.

- *Le Carrefour Resource Centre.* Provides six places plus two emergency beds for adolescents and provides outreach and support for families.

- *Independent living resources.* Property has been rented from private property owners who have had 'granny wings' available.

- *Secure accommodation.* A two-bedded setting which was a conversion from a domestic dwelling on a residential site (governed by legislation directly drawn from the UK Children Act 1989).

- *Intensive services.* A bungalow whose purpose is to accommodate a young person in a setting where they can make sense of immediate chaos without the need for secure accommodation.

The quality of the provision affects the way that resources are used; for example, following a complete upgrade of Le Carrefour, the young people using the Resource Centre have raised their expectations and indeed their respect for the Centre. In addition, the effectiveness of any of these resources is dependent upon the network of support services provided by a range of agencies to both the child and the carer. Close operational links are promoted between social workers, teachers, health visitors, resource centres, GPs and carers, and the range of specialist support services that have been developed in Guernsey. However, for any of the above to work effectively together and create a dynamic for change, insistence on clear planning for the child or young person is one of the essential features. These issues are constantly addressed in meetings, which feed on creative tension.

Off-island placements

There is a need for a minority of young people to use the equivalent of out-of-area placements, known locally as 'off-island placements' which can be widely diverse both in terms of the resource being used in the UK and the geographical location. The placement of children and young people in off-island placements is not a recent phenomenon. In the 1960s, 1970s and 1980s young people were leaving the island either on criminal charges to Borstals, youth detention centres and other establishments with a more therapeutic outlook, sometimes involving a range of differing disciplines. During the 1980s there was a period when it was fashionable to use observation and assessment centres, which some saw as providing a curative approach.

Before 1987 a number of working parties had considered issues concerning provision on-and off-island for children and young people with behavioural and other problems. In 1987, the States approved the development of a community home with education (CHE) on island. However, due to changing attitudes within the Departments involved and also recommendations from Her Majesty's Inspectorate of Schools, this was never established. Hence, four places were reserved at Le Chene School in Jersey (a strictly behavioural model of placement run within an educational setting). To some extent, this filled the vacuum. In 1997, the use of Le Chene School was withdrawn by the States of Jersey due to the number of placements needed within the Island of Jersey itself. Also, representatives of the Education Council Guernsey and the States of Guernsey Children Board who had concerns regarding the type of placement provided at Le Chene and the outcomes which were evident over the previous three to four years.

Meanwhile, in 1992, a study group from the Education Council and Children Board was formed to consider off-island placements and surrounding issues. The group concluded:

> Interagency liaison and co-operation is maintained at a high level in an attempt to resolve and improve the services offered through the various professional agencies.

and

> It is the study group's view that although this will benefit a number of children and young people this will not necessarily obviate the need to make a small number of United Kingdom/Jersey placements each year. (Children and Education Council, 1992)

This study group went on to make a number of recommendations concerning issues that to be addressed in the future (such as the creation of a Young Justice System – in 1993 the Child and Adolescent Service was formally established). During 1997 States of Guernsey Children Board took a strategic decision to search for individual tailor-made placements for young people – wherever located – to provide a greater probability of positive outcomes for the young person. While there is a range of placements on Guernsey to meet these needs it is still necessary sometimes to use off-island placements (financially supported in their off-island placements on a tripartite, shared and individual basis by the departments). Resources within the Island of Guernsey for young people exhibiting extremely difficult or violent behaviour are limited because the only provider of accommodation and resources has been the Children Board.

There are many differing philosophical and practical issues concerning off-island placements. There are, within all departments involved, staff who have a practical longitudinal view concerning the benefits and disadvantages of using off-island placements. While the Children Board would not subscribe to the view that past methods of using off-island placements provided maximum benefit to the children and young people concerned, it believes it is possible to demonstrate more than marginal benefits for a number of young people during the period that the development of new-type placements has been used. Children Board staff are of the view that were it possible to provide a larger number of resources within Guernsey it would be of benefit. However, a truly pragmatic look at this approach to developing services within Guernsey would appear to be costly both in terms of direct costs and of other features such as increased licence holders needing to be employed – with consequent wider implications for Guernsey.

Conclusion

This account concerning an extremely complex and diverse organisation suffers from brevity. Much has happened within the development of the Child Protection and Families Team concerning both support and preventative work alongside the statutory child protection obligations awarded to this team. Likewise the Homefinding Team which, in its attempts to match positive developments within the United Kingdom concerning placements and so on, has in many instances been at the forefront of good practice. Similarly, there have undoubtedly been positive responses to the various reports coming out of the UK, such as the reports by Utting (1997), Waterhouse (1997) among others. Great strides have been made to implement real safeguards for children and young people within the system.

A cautionary observation is that such a setting must be protected against those who would bring zealous enthusiasm with bright tales of utopian plans. To give undue weighting to these messages can be dangerous – distracting from agreed goals and plans for the future. The last four and a half years have seen far less credence given to utopian knee-jerk reactions. This is not to say that Guernsey is not prepared to learn from others and listen for anything that will be of benefit to the service provided. The joint forces of community politics personified, dedicated local staff at all tiers of the structure of the organisation, the new and exciting ideas of staff on short-term contracts combined with those of the longer-term participants and the inherent desire of

Guernsey to do well by its inhabitants will in the end continue to improve the services provided to children and families.

Guernsey and Alderney (to some extent) have been described as rural communities with inner-city problems, these include high levels of alcoholism, suicide, violence to women and other social ills that effect the individual child or adult are all present. Indeed this island of sun and sand and for some, great wealth, has much the same challenges for those who seek to care, challenge and change.

Notes

1   A bailiwick is the district under the jurisdiction of a 'bailie' or bailiff.
2   In accordance with the States Resolution in Billet d'Etat XLVI of 25 April 1974.

Chapter 8

Social Work in the British Isles
Continuities and Differentiations

Malcolm Payne and Steven M. Shardlow

Introduction: the 'national' and social work in the British Isles

Our starting-point in this book lies in images of the 'national' in the UK. We have organised accounts of social services and social work in the British Isles according to national boundaries. The point of doing so, at this historical moment of the beginning of the twenty-first century, is that a change is taking place in the relationships between the nations within the geographical entity of the British Isles. A major devolution of administrative powers to nations within the UK will inevitably alter perceptions of the importance of national divisions within the UK, and will probably alter perceptions of relationships between the UK and its constituent nations and other nations in the British Isles and beyond. The pattern of social services in the UK will alter because of this devolution; changes in relationships between the social services within the UK nations will occur; there will probably be an impact on the pattern of services in their relationships with the other nations in the British Isles and beyond. Likewise, the development of cross-border institutions bridging the Republic of Ireland and Northern Ireland – a constituent country within the UK – is likely over time to affect the development of social work and social care in ways that are difficult to anticipate. The accounts of social services in this book indicate that what is being differentiated is the organisation and administration of social services within the British Isles.

This change in the 'national' may be important; we argue that it will be so. However, a change in the 'national' does not necessarily imply a change in the local; a change within the UK or any part of it does not necessarily lead to change in other nations. A change in organisation and administration does not necessarily lead to a change in the images with which we started this book. A change may lead to divergence, but this may not necessarily be so. There are already divergences between the nations. Change may bring convergence. The Council of the Isles, for example, set up as part of the Northern Ireland peace process, is designed to offer opportunities for connections and interrelationships between the devolved nations and the Irish Republic. There are regular meetings between the governments of the Crown Dependencies, the Channel Islands and the Isle of Man. Both of these linking arrangements may bring convergence rather than difference. Much will be maintained, even though there is change. National boundaries and administrative arrangements within countries and between will not alter. What is maintained may be important; we argue that it will be so. The accounts of social services in this book indicate that what is maintained is the nature and role of social work within the services. Thus, while the administration and delivery of social services is diverging, social work, an international profession conceived on a far broader canvas than these isles, helps to maintain continuity between the countries.

The separate countries contained within the British Isles are part of the European Union.[1] Hence, the governments and assemblies of the British Isles may be subject to increasing pressure to develop common approaches and standards that harmonise with other countries of the Union. Such influences exist already, for example the Kent (1997) report into child care provision in Scotland canvassed, as one of its recommendations, the development of a profession of social pedagogy – drawing upon European models for the provision of social care. Over the next ten years the relations of the countries, the evolution of the constitutional, economic and social relationships of the countries within the British Isles to other countries in the European Union, may have a significant impact on forms and practices of social care. The interplay of two contrasting trends: first, greater regionalisation and the development of devolved forms of government with in the British Isles; second, a closer integration at the European level may be expected to generate considerable tensions. Similarly, at the broader international level, nation states are assumed to be subject to global forces in the economic, political and social sphere. Drawing on the work of Giddens, Adams (2000) comments: 'The term "globalisation" is now generally applied when referring to those processes of transformation that rapidly impact upon each location, sector, aspect and problem across and within Nation States' (p.1).

Although the term 'globalisation' is still imprecisely defined and employed in both academic and popular discourse, in an incautious way it has value in that it refers to a set of processes that require greater investigation and exploration. The impact of these processes upon social work with in the British Isles is likely to be of considerable importance in the future. Opinion varies as to the desirability of the impact of globalisation. For example, Dominelli (1999) is pessimistic, particularly in relation to the UK, believing that the application of market principles to social work has been disastrous in that these principles have severely damaged the ability of the profession to help service users. On the other hand, Midgley (2001) is more optimistic, offering the possibility that the forces of globalisation may help to construct a global agenda for social reform.

In this final chapter we identify some issues in the relationships between the nations that will be crucial in making for change and sustaining similarities and differences, both in general and in social welfare. This is important because difference often brings in its wake inequality and inequality leads, as night follows evening, to social processes of oppression and exclusion. This is not new: the history of relationships between countries in the British Isles is a record of oppression and exclusion, and it is to such social processes that social work seeks to respond. Our argument has four points. First, we argue that new relationships between nations develop in the context of past and existing relationships. Second, we suggest that the social services have been, in some respects, important elements in the history of those relationships, even though they are administered at a local level. Third, we propose that social welfare in the British Isles will maintain many similarities, even in the face of national changes, because of the coherence offered by the profession of social work. Fourth, we believe that many diversities in the British Isles, not just national diversity, contribute to our life and to social welfare, and that national changes draw attention to the value of these diversities. One of the crucial linking aspects of social work in our view has been its commitment to social justice and inclusion through anti-oppressive and anti-discriminatory practice.

On the first point, the perception, implementation and implications of nationhood change over time. The perception and implementation of nationhood is partly a legal and administrative issue: treaties between governments and legislation within nations create boundaries. Within those boundaries different governments, laws and conventions hold sway. Often those boundaries are established because of cultural and social differences, but often there are also continuities. Part of the implementation of nationhood lies, therefore, not in the legal and administrative but in social and cultural implications. As time progresses, cultural and social differences between neighbouring nations may develop more strongly, as in Ireland as the separation between North and South has progressed during this century. However, as in this example, it does not usually create an impermeable boundary. Television and other modern communications create connections wherever we are, for example. The administrative and legal differentiation created by the strengthening of the 'national' is emphasised in the development of the social services, because these derive from government, policy and law. The profession of social work is allied more directly with the social and cultural continuities among the countries, and thus has a greater capacity than the social services to contribute to maintenance of relationships among the services.

Administrative and cultural divisions potentially affect social welfare even within the small compass of the British Isles. The strikingly different accounts produced by the authors on the different countries suggest that this is a legitimate and useful way of exploring differ-ences in social work around the British Isles. Thus, on our second point, national differences in the delivery of social welfare within the British Isles are clearly evident and must therefore play their part in creating the differences in nationhood. That this is so is surprising, since the UK is often considered a centralised and unitary state. It dominates the islands in population and in political and social power. Until the late twentieth century, the exceptions to this have seemed insignificant. There were separate legal and administrative systems in Northern Ireland and Scotland, minor devolutions of power to Wales, national independence for the crown dependencies and Ireland was an inde-pendent state. Compared to the apparently overwhelming legal and administrative power vested in the UK Parliament and the large popu-lation of England compared with the others, these distinctions seemed minor. Even the changes in powers achieved through devolution in the UK, and through the peace process in Northern Ireland, seem minor compared with the overwhelming importance of the Westminster Par-liament. Part of the purpose of this book is to understand how the dif-ferences in the social services between the countries of the British Isles are created by and create the national identity of those countries, and how continuities in social work may maintain links as part of the cultural relationships between the countries.

That these differences are surprising – or at least, if they have often been unconsidered – must be because we have been accustomed to seeing the similarities within the British Isles as more important or more significant than the differences. Similarities may indeed still be more important than differences, but these changes at the end of the twentieth century suggest that we should look at and evaluate again similarities and differences between the main national groups. There-fore, the remainder of this chapter focuses on our third and fourth points: what these similarities and diversities will mean for social work within the British Isles as it develops during the twenty-first century. Will it be able to maintain its continuity across national divides?

Similarities and differences in the British Isles: origins

Identifying issues about similarities and difference raise the question: differences from and similarities to what? The answer must be England. Both the identities of particular nations and of the whole British Isles derive from relationships with England, the country with the largest land area, the largest population and the closest to the European mainland, which the geographical and political statements in Chapter 1 show to be a crucial relationship. Table 8.1 sets out brief accounts of important political interactions. In history, there was a pressure towards unions between the other countries and England, together with sometimes violent resistance to and movement away from those unions.

Table 8.1 A history of oppression and resistance in England's relationships with other parts of the British Isles

Date	Country	Event	Effect
1284	Wales	Statute of Rhuddlan	Legal influence on Wales
1493	Ireland	Poynings' Law (abolished, 1921)	Irish Parliament could only convene with permission of the English monarch; limited Irish legal rights
1503	Scotland	Marriage of James IV of Scotland to Mary Tudor of England	Led to union of the Scottish and English thrones
1536–43	Wales	Act of Union	Control of Wales by the Tudor monarchs (Henry VIII's reign)
1541	Ireland	Act of Lordly Title	Ireland (an independent lordship) becomes a puppet kingdom
1603	Scotland	Death of Queen Elizabeth I	Accession to the English throne of King James VI of Scotland (James I of England)

1702–14	Scotland	Reign of Queen Anne	Anne had no heir, and from 1703 the Scottish Parliament passed measures indicating a willingness to end the union of crowns
1707	Scotland	Act of Union	Safeguarding the existing union of crowns by removing the Scottish Parliament
1713–46	Scotland	Jacobite unrest	Attempt to dissolve the Act of Union defeated (1713); two invasions of England; Scots defeat at Culloden (1746) led to repression of language and culture
1720 *et seq.*	Ireland	Legislative control of Ireland	British Parliament given the right to legislate for Ireland (1720); later, voting limited to Protestants; penal laws excluded Roman Catholics from public service
1792	Scotland	*Bliadhna nan Caorach* (Year of the Sheep)	Height of land clearances where Scots peasants were evicted in favour of sheep farms
1792	Ireland	Grattan's Parliament (more parliamentary independence; period of appeasement)	Followed agitation influenced by the American War of Independence (Ireland was seen as similar to the American colonies) and the French Revolution
1795	Ireland	Orange Order	Protestant social movement founded
1798	Ireland	Nationalist uprising	Led by Wolfe Tone, of the Society of United Irishmen, and supported by French troops; death toll of 30,000; ended appeasement policy
1800	Ireland	Act of Union	Removal of Irish Parliament

1800–29	Ireland, Scotland	Struggle for Catholic emancipation	Campaign (led by O'Connell) for removal of legal limitations on Catholics, opposed by Georges III and IV and the House of Lords; Act finally passed 1829
1820	Scotland	Uprising to end the Union	85 leaders executed for high treason; beginnings of radical, separatist movement
1839	Wales	Newport Chartist uprising; Rebecca riots	Chartist petition for working-class political rights rejected; led to uprising; many killed, leaders transported; riots against road taxes during agricultural slump
1840	Ireland	National Association for the Repeal of the Union	Formed by O'Connell to campaign for Irish Home Rule (allied to Catholicism)
1843	Scotland	Disruption (split) of Church of Scotland	Move towards state responsibility for care
1845–51	Ireland	Potato famine; fall of Peel over Irish Coercion Bill	Decline of Irish population due to famine and emigration; decline of Irish language
1845	Scotland	Poor Law Amendment (Scotland) Act	Created Board of Supervision
1848	Ireland	Irish tricolour flag introduced	Used by 'Young Irelanders', a breakaway from O'Connell aiming to unite Catholic and Protestant
1858	Ireland	Irish Republican Brotherhood	Founded from the Fenian movement; militant policies, supported from abroad because of emigration
1867–8	Ireland	Fenian uprisings	Serious nationalist uprisings
1867	Scotland	Board of Supervision extended	Public health responsibilities delegated

1879	Ireland	Land League	Direct action campaign against bad landlords (using boycott)
1880–1920	Ireland	Campaign for home role	Home Rule Party, led by Parnell and Butt supported by Liberals (Gladstone); Bills defeated in 1886 and 1893
1888	Scotland	Goschen formula established	Gave Scotland 13.75% of comparable expenditures in England and Wales in Education; came to be applied to other expenditures
1885	Ireland	Irish Loyal and Patriotic Union (Unionist Party)	Formed to maintain the Union
1885	Scotland	Secretary for Scotland Act	Limited department based in London established
1905	Ireland	Sinn Féin (Ourselves)	Formed to seek, by constitutional means, total separation of Britain and Ireland
1912–13	Ireland	Ulster Volunteer Force	Formed after military-style demonstrations by Unionists; armed mainly from Germany
1913	Ireland	Irish Citizen Army	Formed after a strike/lock-out forcibly put down by police; brought labour and nationalist movements closer together
1914	Ireland	Home Rule Bill passed	UVF prepared for militant conflict
1915	Wales	Miners' strikes, uniquely in Wales	Perception of workers' exploitation by (English) profiteering owners, supported by government, during 1914–18 war
1916	Ireland	Dublin uprising (Easter Monday)	Unsuccessful attempt to establish independent republic; put down by military force; many killed; leaders executed and became martyrs

1919	Ireland	Sinn Féin MPs establish Irish Parliament (*Dáil Éireann*); Anglo-Irish War of Independence	Irish Republication Army formed; 'Black and Tans' (undisciplined and ruthless ex-soldiers) recruited by English
1920–1	Ireland	Government of Ireland Act; Anglo–Irish Treaty (1921)	Independence of Ireland; division of Ireland
1926	Scotland	Scottish Secretary of State appointed	Associated with further delegation of powers before and after
1926	Scotland, Wales	Miners' strikes led to general strikes and civil disorder	Particularly important in Welsh and Scottish coalfields
1929	Scotland	Local government reorganisation	Specialised local bodies replaced by general local councils
1939	Scotland	Gilmour Report	Scottish Office created
1940–4	Channel Islands	Occupied by German forces	
1948	Ireland	Declaration of Republic of Ireland	Complete separation from English administration
1951	Wales	First Minister for Welsh Affairs	Beginnings of recognition of Wales as a political entity
1955	Wales	Cardiff recognised as capital	Followed by other national administrative developments
1964	Wales	First Secretary of State for Wales	The first Welsh Secretary threatened resignation unless the Welsh Office was given powers
1966	Wales	*Plaid Cymru* (Party of Wales) gains first MP	Collapse of empire and decline of heavy industry led to high unemployment
1967	Wales	Welsh Language Act	Move towards equal validity for the Welsh language, following demonstrations organised by the second Welsh Language Society

1978	Scotland	Barnett formula established	Goschen formula outdated by population decline; Scotland gained 11.11% and Wales11.76% of England expenditures
1979	Scotland, Wales	Referendums on devolution to a Scottish parliament and Welsh assembly	Failure led to initial disarray, especially in Scotland where a majority voted for devolution but, not quite the required majority of the population
1979–80	Wales	More than 30 English holiday homes set on fire	
1979–82	Wales	Thatcher Government reneged on an election pledge to create a Welsh fourth TV channel	Following campaign of civil disobedience; threat of further civil disobedience and hunger strike led Government to renounce opposition
1985–7	Scotland, Wales	Miners' strikes	Scotland and Wales affected by mine closures
1997	Scotland, Wales	Following referendums, Scottish Parliament re-established; Welsh Assembly established	

Source: Davies (1993); English, 1998; Kinealy (1999); Wolfe (Chapter 7)

At least four elements arise in these relationships between England and other countries within the British Isles. The first element is relationships with the continent of Europe. Second, Celtic identity and its consequences for relationships among and with the countries of the British Isles is an important factor. Third, dominance and sometimes oppression by England of the other countries is an element in relationships between the countries. Finally, the historical role of the United Kingdom as a colonialist nation needs to be considered. In the next sections we briefly examine each of these factors in turn.

Relationships with the Continent of Europe

Relationships with the Continent of Europe, both historically and in present-day politics, create a background for national relationships in the British Isles (Kinealy 1999). Various tribes from the Continent first populated the islands. The northern parts of the British Isles, and particularly the Isle of Man, still bear the identity of the Viking invasions of the first millennium after Christ. The Channel Islands demonstrate the close relationships with France and the French language that derive from the invasion and close relationships between France and England in the early part of the second millennium. England has had enmities for many centuries with the Roman Catholic countries of Europe, and connections through its royal family with the Protestant northern countries of Europe, sometimes more widely. The history and culture of Scotland was tied up with France, particularly during the Jacobite conflicts of the eighteenth century. During the Napoleonic wars, France invaded the United Kingdom through Ireland and Wales. Both Protestant and Roman Catholic interests in Ireland were armed from Germany in the first two decades of the twentieth century as part of their demand for and resistance to home rule.

In the twentieth century, European wars have been followed by what has become the European Union. This has been an attempt to integrate the conflicts of interest among European nations into a framework of negotiation and co-operation and reduce the possibilities of war intervening in economic and social progress. However, northern nations in Europe have been less certain of their participation. The Nordic nations, Britain and Ireland joined later than the central and southern European nations, and sharing or giving up sovereignty, for example by giving up control of customs, immigration and currency, has proved difficult for the UK, although less so for Ireland. Increasingly, regions within England and nations within the UK see the possibility of relationships with Europe directly, rather than through political institutions in London. It is possible, therefore, that devolution of some powers to the UK nations will lead over the long-term to more extensive administrative contacts and political relationships directly with European Union institutions.

Social work arose alongside the development of state responsibility for the populations of a country. Its character varies in different parts of the world (Payne 1996). In Europe, however, an important characteristic of social welfare is the creation, after the war of 1939–45, of welfare states. Social work in Europe in the last part of the twentieth century is always part of welfare states. This is not so true of the more individualistic forms of social work typical of the United States of America, the ambiguous role of state welfare in developing countries such as those on the Pacific Rim, and the focus on social development in third world countries such as those in Africa. An important aspect of social work's identity in the British Isles is the particular form of welfare state in which it is practised. We can see the importance of this differentiating factor in the British Isles by examining the conflict about the idea of a 'welfare state' in Ireland, where the very idea was opposed by the Catholic Church (Chapter 3) or the lesser role played by welfare in the more limited provision of the Channel Islands (Chapter 7). European social work, therefore, has the potential, along with other social and cultural aspect of life, to be a linking factor among the countries of the British Isles.

Celtic and other ethnic identities

Celtic identity in Ireland, Scotland and Wales is an aspect that distinguishes these countries from England (Pittock 1999). There is a history of racism against the Celtic nations which is related to the perception of the centre for the periphery (the 'Celtic fringe'), the urban cosmopolitan for the rural and the rich for the poor. This kind of racism is described in Chapter 1, where the example is given of Shaw's review of a play deriving from the Isle of Man.

The existence of distinct ethnic identities in the 'fringe' has permitted England's identity to stand out as coherent, so that its more homogeneous culture and more centralised administration and politics can seem more unitary than those of the Celtic nations. However, this conceals localised administrations and a variety of cultures that exist within England's boundaries. For example, there is at least one Celtic identity within it, in Cornwall. As the twentieth century progressed, dislocation, war, technological advance, particularly in communications, and globalisation all stimulated migrations and cultural influences, which have had opposite influences. Every apparently homogeneous nation includes people from many different ethnic backgrounds and there seem to be tendencies to harmonise and homogenise cultures, with some becoming dominant. We sometimes think this of American culture internationally and English culture in the British Isles. Yet, these same movements in peoples and technologies also permit resistance and the maintenance of identifiable cultures, as more television channels permitted the Welsh to fight for a channel in their own language.

Possessing the cultural heritage of the Celtic languages offers cultural and social strengths that may not exist for more cosmopolitan cultures, such as those of the English. Equally, the awareness of more diversity within England may alter attitudes towards national diversities among the countries in the British Isles. Recognising ethnic diversity within England, resulting from migrations from new Commonwealth countries in the late twentieth century, may increase the recognition and change the valuation of national differences between England and the Celtic nations.

Such cultural differences, however, while relevant for government and administration, do not have the same impact on social work, whose creation is at a more international and European level. There is the potential for similar social work with a Celtic and England identity, and this is perhaps one of the origins of social work's role in creating continuities among the countries, as social and cultural continuities in general offer the opportunity for maintaining rather than differentiating the 'national'.

Britain as a colonialist power

Britain's role from the sixteenth to the twentieth centuries as a colonialist power is a crucial aspect of English identity, which has been called 'British' identity. This has had several consequences for the relationships among the nations. First, the wealth and power deriving from the colonies was an important factor in cementing some of the unions in the

UK. The Scottish Parliament agreed to union in January 1701 at least partly to enable its merchants to gain access to growing colonial markets. It was a factor in the influence brought to bear for Irish union. It was important for Welsh industrial growth in the nineteenth century, based on coal and steel. Equally, the loss of empire and the industrial might associated with it led to economic and social difficulties in Northern Irish, Welsh and Scottish industrial areas and strengthened nationalist movements in the late twentieth century, which led to devolution of power from Westminster (Davies 1993; Colley 1994; Kinealy 1999).

Second, the Celtic nations provided a substantial labour force to maintain the empire. The growing empire required a large army and population by Europeans. It therefore offered opportunities for emigration to oppressed populations in the Celtic areas. The Celtic areas provided a disproportionate number of emigrants throughout the nineteenth century, partly because of persecution by the English. They also provided a higher proportion of members of the armed forces, for example in the war of 1914–18 (Kinealy 1999), although initially they, particularly the Welsh, had been resistant to serving in support of the English state as it came to dominate the raising of armies in the eighteenth century (Colley 1994, p.311–2).

These first two points draw attention to the ambiguous inheritance of colonialism: its benefits and its part in the history of oppression. The experience of empire also stimulates the perception that in some respects the relationship between England and the other nations of the British Isles is, at least partly, colonial. England gained and maintained dominance in government and culture, by force of arms and by economic, religious and cultural oppression. Perceptions of the peoples of the other nations have sometimes been racist, as we saw in Chapter 1; the view of a master race for its inferiors. This may be important to social work because welfare has often been associated with administrative systems that in other respects are means of exploitation. Alternatively, where oppressed peoples require help, or particular social conditions affect their lives adversely, social work may have a role to ameliorate or combat the ill-effects of disadvantage. Again, therefore, there is some potential for social work to offer continuity in the face of the differentiation of the 'national'.

England as oppressor

England is the dominant nation in many of its relationships with the other nations. It has a larger land area, is more populous and is closer to the European mainland than the other countries. Much of the time it has also been richer, although there have been rich resources in the other countries. The information in Table 8.1 demonstrates clearly that there is a history of conquest and domination of political and social institutions, together with concomitant resistance. At times, oppression and resistance has been by force of arms, at others by cultural and economic influence or separation.

An important aspect of the oppression and resistance has been related to religion. England's Protestant identity has distinguished it from other nations in the islands. The continuing conflict with Roman Catholic European powers placed England at risk from its Roman Catholic oppressed peoples, as invasions from Europe through Ireland and Wales have shown. The forms of Protestantism dominant even in different parts of the UK vary considerably. In England, the Anglican Church is an established church, so that it is entwined with the state. In Wales, a particular form of socialist Methodism is important, while in Scotland the Presbyterian Church is the most influential. In Northern Ireland, militant sects of Protestant Churches are closely involved in political interaction. Throughout Ireland, the influence of the Roman Catholic Church is crucial in the formation of political and social life.

Social work's position within the British Isles

How can we understand the position of social work within this set of cultural relationships in the British Isles? Social work emerged from aspects of these societies that are closely connected to many of these elements of oppression and resistance.

The first two points refer to how the social services are organised. First, early social work was closely connected to religious organisations and commitment, so the importance of religion as an element of oppressive and resistant relationships placed social work as part of the oppression and resistance. Social work is still associated with religious organisations, particularly in Ireland, where the influence of the Catholic Church, although waning, continues. However, many voluntary organisations throughout the British Isles have religious connections. Moreover, in the UK voluntary organisations often have connections with the Crown, through patronage and support, and the Crown is associated in England with the established Church of England. Local charities are supported through fundraising by honorary figures, such as the mayors of towns, many of whom have charitable funds, or sheriffs and lords lieutenant of counties, who are also representatives of the Crown.

Second, social work in the last half of the twentieth century was increasingly part of the administrative, legal and government institutions which had earlier been, and to some extent were still being, used for oppression, and to express resistance, separation and difference.

This first group of points suggests, therefore, that social work emerged from just those social elements in the relationships between England and the other countries of the British Isles that were oppressive. How, then, may we regard it as potentially a factor in maintaining continuity among the countries? We suggest that this is because it operates particularly in aspects of the social environment that are particularly crucial in the other countries. Thus, though social work may be mainly an English creation, it offers much to the other countries.

This may be seen in the second group of points on oppression and resistance.

The second group of three points deals with social work's position in its wider social environment. The third point is that social work deals primarily with the poor. This has significance, which draws from national identities, because England has been the richest of the countries. The poverty of Ireland, the different view of poverty in Scotland and stresses of social change arising from the late twentieth-century collapse of mining in Scotland and Wales are all relevant to perceptions of the social burdens experienced by particular countries.

Fourth, social work arose alongside the development of Britain's industrial and colonial pre-eminence, indeed is a product of that development. The rise of industrial and colonial power created the pressure for union, for example in the wish of Scots merchants to gain access to colonial markets through union. It also created the character of the social environment in which social work developed, for example in the industrialisation of South Wales, which is still far more dependent on manufacturing than the rest of Britain. The decline of industry and colonial power has equally had major differential social effects on the countries of the British Isles. Moreover, this has cultural and national consequences. Table 8.1 shows how important working-class movements, such as Chartism, Rebecca, the National Strike of 1926 and the miners strikes of the 1980s, have specific national resonances for Wales and perhaps Scotland, as well as their personal and cultural importance for working-class communities.

Fifth, as part of its development, social work is associated with the state. During social work's emergence, the state has become more important in social relations generally. Social work developed initially in both the state, as part of the poor laws, and within the civil society, particularly through the work of the churches and voluntary organisations. Different countries arrive at varying balances between the role of the state and civil society, balances which change through political and social movements. We have already noted how social work's development in connection with the welfare state, and how the voluntary sector element of civil society are associated with other powerful institutions within the state.

Oppression and resistance as a background

Social work, referring to the profession and activity, and social welfare, referring to the ideology and system of help with social problems, are intimately bound up with the history of oppressive relations between England and other countries. Welfare is an element in the social control by England of the other nations. The English culture of welfare and English policies have historically been imposed, sometimes inappropriately, on the other nations in the British Isles. However, social work is also a personal service, which needs to be particularly responsive to local conditions and aspirations. Social welfare is a motivational, aspirational element of any culture, often associated historically with religious ideology. It often motivates people to respond to others' needs. Help and support in adversity are often important factors in community solidarity and historically and to some extent still, such solidarity is often associated with religion.

Social work often represents a tension, therefore. There is a contradiction between its interpersonal and community objectives and support and its liability to be involved in oppressive institutions. These contradictions are widely experienced in social work as a tension for the aware practitioner and as an ambivalence in the creation of policy. The tension provides an opportunity: to intervene where oppression acts upon individuals and to seek to empower them to overcome it. The tension is also an inhibition to practice: an obstruction to trust and participation. This book identifies what Chapter 4 calls the 'national question' in relation to Northern Ireland as potentially one that affects social workers throughout the British Isles.

This also has its impact on policy making. In the UK, the English Department of Health is a dominant policy maker for standards and services within which social work is placed. Yet other nations have had their typical approaches to practice. This has always been so. For example, Hunter and Wistow (1987), in a pioneering study, examined the development of community care policy before the changes adopted through the National Health Service and Community Care Act 1990. They found that there were significant differences in the arrangements in each country. The Welsh Office had succeeded in developing joint policy making more comprehensively than the English department. The Scottish Office presided over a system that was more strongly institutionalised than either of the other countries, and had had difficulty in changing this tendency. The English department had had difficulty in making progress with joint planning and development. Many of these features persist today, after substantial policy development, as the various chapters in the book show.

Are there, therefore, myriads of little 'social works' in different policy environments with nothing that connects them together? From our language and behaviour, it seems not, because we talk everywhere about 'social work', and we assume that social workers are doing more or less the same thing. International organisations of social workers are prepared to accept under their banner activities such as social development and social pedagogy, which have political, philosophical and theoretical differences but are identifiably related sorts of activity. There are varying boundaries to what people call social work in different nations: for example, 'youth and community work', a separate profession in the UK, would be seen as part of social work in Germany or the USA.

This conception of the variation of social work connects to ideas about the nature of postmodern societies and globalisation. As globalised culture makes connections between what seemed distant and allows some cultures to dominate others, we suggested above that it also permitted greater differentiation and response to the local. This creates many opportunities for and pressures towards variation as well as pressures for homogeneity. Social work is no exception to these trends. Social workers face the tension between the local and personally responsive as against the national and policy driven. An example is the modernisation agenda of the new Labour Government in the UK from 1997. This demands responsiveness to local and individual needs but at the same time compliance with national (English) political policies. Social work's role may be defined differently, even in related and similar contexts. One example is the role of probation in relation to social work. In Scotland, social work departments include probation. In England, Northern Ireland, Ireland and Wales social services departments are separate from the probation service. In Ireland, the probation service is about probation and welfare. In England and Wales, but not in Scotland, the UK Government wants to see probation work as separate from social work, and has withdrawn its qualifying training from social work. However, the professional trend towards focusing on offending behaviour that lies behind this administrative change is reflected in Irish thinking, too (Chapter 3). Here we see, therefore, that the pressure for differentiation lies in service organisation and policy, while the pressure for continuities to be maintained in professional thinking, research and knowledge.

This example draws attention to some of the reasons for exploring comparative developments in some detail. English politicians constructed an administrative division between social work and probation in training and in organisation. They did so to emphasise a change in practice direction, calling upon the same knowledge foundation and professional trend that is apparent in Ireland. Does the lack of such an administrative change in Ireland demonstrate weaknesses in the English administrative decision or weaknesses in the definition and management of social work in Ireland? Will the differences between Scotland and England lead to poorer and better social work and probation in one or the other country?

The English decision responds to a particular political situation, in which the political judgement was that public confidence was declining in community responses to criminal behaviour. The answer to this was to emphasise a change in professional thinking and practice by making an administrative change. In a different political context, Ireland, this was unnecessary. Similarly, Chapter 5 shows that, in Scotland, there is greater continuing acceptance of the 1960s idea, lost in England and Wales, that criminal behaviour and social deprivation are closely associated, at least in young people. This led to retention of the children's hearings, which make connections between youth crime and youth deprivation. The imperative to return to a separation of probation is not so powerful. Lying behind this continuity appears to be a greater public concern about social deprivation and a more significant shared experience of it in Scotland than in England.

From this example, therefore, we may draw some of the aspects of difference that may be relevant:

- administrative decisions and divisions
- political and public attitudes and experiences
- cultural and social expectations and experience
- professional thinking

- knowledge and research.

Each of these has both a present and a history, both conditioned by the historical relationship between England and the other countries. The present is created by the history but, of course, maintenance and change represent a present that may be reacting against the history, a development upon it or an innovation. For example, currently Irish social work education has its own governing body, whereas until the 1990s it looked to the UK organisation, CCETSW. This development is an innovation, and permits future innovation that moves away from UK practices. The withdrawal from CCETSW was partly stimulated by changes in CCETSW and the British Government, which sought to focus expenditure on the national role and develop partnerships between educational institutions and agencies, which was hard to administer across national boundaries. The Irish development, therefore, was not a reaction against CCETSW so much as a change in thinking in the UK.

Without close attention to the historical movements it is hard to say which of these aspects of difference formed changes and traditions. For example, administrative decisions may both form and be formed by political and public attitudes. Professional thinking may develop from knowledge and research or it may come from changes in the demands presented at social agencies, from changing public and political attitudes. Alternatively, administrative demands such as local government reorganisation may bring social services along in their wake. It has been argued, for example, that the extensive reorganisations in Scotland and Wales, possibly politically motivated, have had significant impact on the social services, which are more muted in England (Winchester 2000).

The following sections examine something of what we can learn from the accounts in this book about the impact of each of these different areas of difference on our understanding of social work in the British Isles. As in the discussion so far, we begin with administrative, legal and policy issues, which lead towards differentiation according to the 'national' and move towards more social, cultural and professional, where continuity seems more significant and differentiation, are less relevant.

Administrative decisions and divisions

The introduction to this chapter emphasises that there will be complexity in the relationships between different forms of the social services in different countries in the British Isles. We can identify national boundaries, and to some extent the social services respond to the legal and administrative differences created by those boundaries.

Historically, one of the aspects of domination by England of other parts of the islands was the imposition of English legal and administrative systems on indigenous systems (Kinealy 1999). Davies (1993, pp.88 *et seq.*) argues that the traditional Welsh legal system, based on the law of Hywel, was a folk law rather than a state law. It was concerned to reconcile disputes between different kinship groups, and gave considerable rights to women. However, the Statute of Rhuddlan (1284) sought to replace this with a less merciful English law. This focused on punishment by the state for transgressions against the state's – that is, the king's – interests. In contrast to the position in Wales, the Scots managed to retain an independent legal system. Moreover, because Wales was not united before it was conquered, it was only in recent centuries that its identity as a nation with a geographical location was established; national identity resided for many in language. Davies (1993, p.168) argues that this meant that Scots resistance to English control could reside in its separate legal system. In Wales, this was not possible, so resistance developed an emphasis on the language as an important basis of cultural separation. He also argues (Davies 1993, p.169) that the cost of conquering Wales forced King Edward to reduce his efforts in Scotland, and to strengthen the beginnings of the international capitalist system, by relying on loans from Italian bankers.

Changes in ownership, inheritance and the judicial system were among the first Anglicisations of Wales after the Act of Union in 1536. Scotland retained much of its separate legal system after the union of the crowns in 1603 and the Act of Union in 1707. Ireland had a separate parliament, with latterly considerable independent powers which were removed in the Act of Union in 1800. In the nineteenth century, welfare was an important factor in imposing English administrative systems. In the sixteenth century England and Wales were the first countries anywhere to provide for state involvement in poor relief. The new Poor Law, introduced in the 1830s, was also used as the administrative vehicle for other welfare developments (Kinealy 1999, pp.69–70). In Wales, as in some mainly northern English regions, it was vociferously opposed, and some Welsh Poor Law Guardians resisted administrative imposition from London by speaking in Welsh. In Ireland, a less draconian system, based on traditional models of assistance, was proposed, but the English system was introduced with even harsher elements, the first state intervention in poor relief. The strictures of the system were enhanced because there was perceived to be a more serious problem of poverty in rural areas, which had to be controlled, and prejudice led to the belief that the Irish were lazy and feckless and would prefer to depend on the state rather than work (Kinealy 1999, p.71). On the other hand, the separate Scottish legal system produced a delayed and less harsh poor law system than in England and Wales. Again, prejudice played its part, because the Scots, although considered to have more poverty than England, were thought more provident (Kinealy 1999; Levitt 1988; Levitt 1989).

Social work, being an interpersonal and community endeavour, is often administered at lower levels of formal structures. One consequence of this is a greater administrative variety than in high-level policy, such as foreign affairs. Social work does not require administrative or professional consistency, whereas foreign affairs increasingly require co-operation across continents to create sufficient power to achieve outcomes. The chapters show that the UK has substantially devolved legislation from Westminster, except in Wales. Even in Wales different administrative arrangements to implement the legislation are in place. Legal differences in the UK make for important distinctions in the context within which social work is practised. Northern Ireland and Scotland have their own different legislation on mental health and child care, on probation and the court system. There have also been differences in the law on homosexual behaviour. Often the systems come back into line at some point, but at times there has been considerable variation. The crown dependencies and Ireland have legal requirements for social work practice that are similar to those in the UK, but differences reflect separate development at different times.

Not only the legal but also the administrative systems vary. Social services departments in Ireland and Northern Ireland are part of an administrative structure of health or health and social services boards. In Great Britain, social services are separate from the health service administratively at the time of writing, although there are proposals for increasing connections and there are many links. The variations in probation have been discussed above. The pattern of public authorities also varies. In South Wales, there are many small unitary authorities; these are less predominant in England. Scotland has experienced a substantial local government reorganisation. While these changes have placed democratic control of social work closer to the communities in which it operates, it makes specialised services more complex to provide.

There is continuity in the difference. As Waterhouse and McGhee (Chapter 5) show and we have exemplified in this chapter, Scottish law and administrative practices has been continuously separate and different, based on the historical movements and inhibitions explored in the first part of this chapter. For Scotland, that continuous difference has been important in maintaining the national characteristics of its welfare system. For other countries, other factors have been more important in maintaining difference and creating change.

Political and public attitudes and experiences

Considering the administrative and legal basis of social work, therefore, exhibits a tension between the national and the local. This is also reflected in political and public attitudes towards it. Political and social conflict have always been an aspect of the relationship between England and the other countries in the British Isles. However, in social work cross-national links exist despite these conflicts. Moreover, professional and social issues, as for example in child care, are often shared. However, national political policy making may still be crucial in forming how social work responds to issues that it faces. Social work is one of the areas of social action where official and civil society overlap and influence or conflict with one another.

Table 8.1 shows that considerable tensions have always existed in the relationship between England and the other countries, spilling over into armed resistance and civil disobedience. It is salutary that, as late as 1979, the Thatcher Government had to be dissuaded from reneging on the pledge to provide a Welsh-language television channel by threat of hunger strike and civil disobedience. However, political change does not necessarily mean change in the social services, as in the continuation of links between the UK and Irish National Societies for Prevention of Cruelty to Children until 1956, long after the Republic's independence from the UK in 1922. Links also continued in social work education, validated by the UK Central Council until the formation of the National Social Work Qualification Board (NSWQB) in the 1997.

One aspect of social work that has been significant in political discourse in recent years has been child care. Child abuse and child sex abuse have been a characteristic concern of the late twentieth century. Ferguson and Powell (Chapter 3) argue that it has been an indicator of the movement away from traditional social structures and values, epitomised by the 'paedophile priest'. They suggest that it marks the rejection of Catholic hegemonic control, that is, powerful control of social structures and values through presenting ideologies as though they were natural and unquestionable.

In England, a series of child abuse scandals has pressed changes in attitudes towards child protection. The Cleveland inquiry (1988) marked the rise of concerns about child sexual abuse. Throughout, there have been concerns about the role of adoption and foster care. To the difficulties of institutional care for children in the first half of the century, foster care and family group homes of the 1950s and 1960s were the answer. These seemed less viable as orphans, deprived and neglected children became less significant at a time when young offenders needed more controlling care. The resultant specialist residential care and institutional care in community home schools of the 1970s were found to be unnecessary in the 1980s or, in the most recent scandals of the 1990s, abusive. The offenders seem to need more secure accommodation, and adoption and fostering are being promoted as an alternative for less disturbed young people. In Wales, the recent Waterhouse Report (1997) on a long-running child abuse scandal has raised concerns about residential care even in communities where there is apparently less extreme social deprivation and potentially more community support for deprived children.

What these histories suggest is a fundamental difficulty with care of children through relatively impersonal organisations with considerable social authority. The picture in the Channel Islands (Chapter 7) is of a more agreed form of practice more related to a smaller and more homogeneous community. What this may say about social work is that there is a value in its politics being local rather than national.

Campbell and McColgan (Chapter 4) note that the principal political discourse in Northern Ireland remains the 'national' question, but this is so dominant that forming a Northern Irish 'social work' is not a significant mission, whereas it is clear that, in the Republic, national identity has become accepted, even though change in civil society is rapid. To some extent, in both Scotland and Wales, the debate about devolution has accentuated the issue of nationalism, so that forming a national identity engages with forming a national social work. The Scots' pride in the distinctive and liberal 'reporter' system for child care hearings is a clear element in the cultural identity of Scotland, as opposed to England. The importance of the devolution decision varies. In Scotland, there is a history of considerable devolution and a different system. This is much less clear in Wales, tied to England administratively for far longer with the Welsh Office, a recent innovation (see Table 8.1). However, Waterhouse and McGhee (Chapter 5) note that the legislation that created the Union of Scotland and England made provision for differences in the legal system and the established Church, in much the same way that Quebec has a different linguistic and administrative heritage in Canada.

Social work in the Channel Islands and the Isle of Man is distinctive but formed by the needs of the population rather than creating a national identity. The identity of the society on these islands appears secure, but is perhaps not concerned with a separate *national* identity, but a separate identity within the UK national framework. England may have a dominating national identity, but this is undeveloped since in many respects it is indistinguishable from that of the UK. Yet the devolution of government in Scotland and Wales, the possibility of return to devolved government in Northern Ireland and the independence of the Republic of Ireland for approaching a century raises the question of decentralising the highly centralised English state. Political society in England in the Thatcherite and Blairite mould seems to rely on corporatist, centralised policy, rather than devolution. The failure of the split Conservative Party under Major, the previous prime minister, and Hague, until June 2001 leader of the opposition, and the importance given to monolithic policy control by new Labour suggests that a continued reliance on centralised policy control is crucial to political identity in England, with its centralised media and constitutional structures. However, devolution to the nations may lead to an alternative form of political identity which resides more in local responsiveness and commitment.

Social work's relationship with political discourse, then, is complex. It is to some extent formed by and influences national political debates, but it may often be seen as a product of more local forces within civil society rather than national political discourse. However, as in child care, international social trends seem to create similar issues for different societies to resolve within their particular political discourses. Thus, social work often responds to cultural and social expectations rather than political debates.

Cultural and social expectations and experience

The civil society of any country, another important factor identified specifically in Chapter 3, is a controversial notion. It may be taken to mean relationships within a society between the individual and family and the state and its organs, it may distinguish the non-official from the official or it may simply refer to the voluntary as opposed to statutory sectors of provision. Some people and some social groups see social care as fundamentally non-official, in that most people assume that it is a function of interpersonal and family relationships and only exceptionally a role of the state or some official body. Yet this is a political and social judgement and modern political discourse, as we have seen, has taken up a concern for the state in most areas of social life, social work included. Another person might say that a fundamental feature of a civilised society should be the way in which people take responsibility for the frail and weak. We might also question what is 'the official'. If the Catholic Church is so important in Ireland, its role might almost be considered official since, in social services and civil society, it dominated the early Irish state.

Another important set of institutions lies in the field of education. This also has been a battleground of attempts at dominance and resistance in the relationships between England and the other countries of the British Isles. In Wales, for example, the maintenance of Welsh-medium education and the importance of the language have been crucial areas of resistance (Davies 1993). Equally, in Scotland schooling is strongly affected by a denominational divide (Chapter 5).

Cultural differences such as these are among the most important aspects of connection and difference among the countries of the British Isles, and the country chapters make it clear that differences in social work emerge partly from such cultural differences. Pittock (1999) shows how Celtic identity is an important aspect of the perceived differences between England and Ireland, Scotland and Wales, which are sometimes referred to as the 'Celtic fringes' of the British Isles. Such phrases assume the centrality of Englishness and the less significant role of the other countries. Cultural artefacts are used to emphasise difference: kilts, bagpipes and whisk(e)y. Books such as the romantic novels of Sir Walter Scott created an ideal of ethnic difference, albeit rather an artificial one in this case. The Celtic cultures have distinctive tribal customs, such as the Highland gatherings (Jarvie 1989), with sports such as hurling or, another example from Wales, poetic and musical *eisteddfodau* (Davies 1993), with culturally distinct ceremonies, music and literature. Even shared sports promote expressions of national rivalry and resistance; an example is the hooliganism around Scotland v. England football matches (Moorhouse 1989).

One of the crucial cultural distinctions in the history of relationships within the British Isles has been religious. More widely in Europe, distinctions may be made between welfare states and within countries according to the influence of the Catholic Church (Hornsby-Smith 1999). Protestantism has been one of the modes of life through which the English have sought to maintain dominance across the British Isles. However, the Church in Wales, Scotland and Ireland never had the influence and importance in local culture that the Anglican Church had in England. In Wales, the importance of Methodism, of a different kind to that influential in parts of England, the Presbyterian Church in Scotland and, above all, the Roman Catholic Church in Ireland. It is not only religious institutions but also the ideologies and priorities that go with them that are important.

Religious division and distinction may seem outdated in England, while in Northern Ireland, as Chapter 4 shows, sectarian conflict is a crucial element in social relations, and in social divisions since Catholics are more often in poverty and out of work. Thus, religion is important in the formation of social problems, while elsewhere it is important in the formation of responses to social issues. Ferguson and Powell (Chapter 3) identify the Catholic Church as a crucial factor in way the social services and social work developed in Ireland. The importance of the family emphasised to a state dominated by Catholicism enforced minimum state intervention in the family and gave the family important, almost inalienable, rights. That social solidarity should be expressed through collective welfare as in Germany (Lorenz 1999), and to some degree in the National Health Service in the UK, accords the family other social priorities.

As Chapters 6 and 4 make clear, the consequence of these religious and social divides is social exclusion. While racism and responses to it are politicised in England, the less cosmopolitan populations of the Celtic countries have led to its relative neglect, except in the relationship with England. It does not arise as an issue in the Channel Islands social services (Chapter 7) and yet its housing policies have emphasised local residents and migration inwards only of richer people. Such policies are likely to lead to social division. Smyth and Campbell (1996) argue that the importance of sectarianism in Northern Ireland should lead to antisectarian training in social work, in the same way that the rising importance of minority ethnic groups in other parts of the UK has led to the development of antiracist and antioppressive practice.

Although the development of social work was and is associated with religious organisation, it is also associated with secularisation and the development of the state as a location of social provision. It was as the role of the Church in social provision receded and the role of the state in many aspects of society developed in the nineteenth century that social work emerged. The more recent development of state social work in Ireland as the role of the Catholic Church receded is another national example of how secularisation is crucial in the development of the social and political role of social work.

It is important, therefore, not to see culture and its impact on social work as immutable and unchanging. As Ferguson and Powell (Chapter 3) show in relation to the Catholic Church in Ireland, the ideological and social thinking of even powerful institutions may be reshaped by powerful social forces. Postmodern culture produced in Ireland a more atomised and individualistic culture, involving both fragmentation and polarisation in policy and political views. Traditional identities have become less important, and diversity and choice, creating a 'lifestyle politics', have become more important. In this way we see general social movements concerned with consumerism, related to commodification, diversity in opinion, in social group and in identification.

Professional thinking

The country chapters identify a range of influences on professional thought deriving from administrative developments, political, social and cultural discourses. Ferguson and Powell (Chapter 3) comment on the loss of a humanist, or perhaps humanitarian, profession and training in the face of managerialism. They also propose that the British Isles are in a late-modern or even postmodern stage. These developments, however, transcend national differences and create links between the countries. The contemporary professional discourse includes issues such as citizenship and social exclusion which, in many respects, are new theorisations about traditional social work values and ideologies in all the countries of the British Isles.

The accounts of social work contained in this book do not emphasise the professional organisation of social work, so that the British and Irish Associations of Social Workers seem to have little impact. It appears, then, that social workers themselves in their representative organisations do not own their profession; its development is in the hands of Government. Yet the 'ownership' of social work contributes to its identity. Ferguson and Powell (Chapter 3) show that in Ireland, for example, the power struggle between Catholic Church and state for control of social work and changes of ideology within the Church formed social work's identity in the latter part of the twentieth century. Similarly, the struggle between official and civil society, discussed above, forms how social work defines and implements its role in any society. It is not only professional or government policy on social care that creates movements in professional thinking. For example, Campbell and McColgan (Chapter 4) show how the Northern Ireland Agreement will push social work towards responding to more deprived communities.

However, the rethinking still responds to the UK government's modernisation agenda, focusing on services that respond to users' requirements within a more flexible system of services created by contract relationships among agencies, rather than monolithic social services departments and health authorities. This system is regulated by external controls through inspection, the proposed Social Care Institute for Excellence, mirroring a similar structure in the health service. Such a devolved approach, using contractual relationships between agencies, is a characteristic of the 'new public management' deriving from managerialist developments in public administration (Clarke and Newman 1997; Payne 2000; Pollitt 1993). This disperses responsibility for service provision, controlling it by contractual relationships and regulatory frameworks, including inspection and performance management through targets and indicators. Dispersal of responsibility and service provision in this way may be associated analytically with the idea of post-industrial, post-Fordist, postmodern trends in society, where centralised, structured accountability fades away in favour of more flexible networks of provision and responsibility is more ambiguous.

Knowledge and research

Social work knowledge derives from at least three sources: from practice experience; from scholarship and research associated with teaching, including that funded expressly for the purpose of developing knowledge by research foundations and funders; and from research informing policy and service development undertaken by agencies and government. However, Broad's (1999) analysis suggests a complex set of relationships by which government, academic bodies and professional organisations seek to influence research and knowledge development. Again, this suggests a postmodern analysis of the development of social work knowledge, from myriad sources in complex relationships.

Research and education seem to be universal, but this is not so. There are a large number of universities and social work courses in England, fewer in the Celtic countries. Research achievement within them is unevenly distributed among the UK nations (Fisher 1999). The Channel Islands and the Isle of Man are relatively isolated. Research is done, and social work is normally taught, in higher education establishments, and none exist in the Channel Islands or the Isle of Man. They are likely to attract less research effort, therefore, and their experience is not likely to influence the knowledge base, since this is mainly created by academics. The organisational system of qualifying and post-qualifying social work courses relies on agencies being in membership of consortia of agencies and higher education institutions. These countries are excluded from that. Indeed, it was the UK Central Council's move towards this structure of course provision that expedited the removal of Irish social work courses from the Central Council's validation role.

However, although there are differences, the contiguity of the countries within the British Isles and the continuing relationship with European influences create demands for links. Campbell and McColgan (Chapter 4) point to how the existence of the Irish National Social Work Qualifications Board complying with European guidelines raised questions about the UK qualification in social work.

Much knowledge development in the UK derives from government and official sources. In the same way that professional organisations remain unmentioned in these accounts of social work, the role of policy, government and law are strong. The UK government sets a strong agenda for research and practice influence (Payne 1998), and this influence is one of the sources of the weakness of professional ownership, discussed above. To some degree, as we have seen, this may be contested by the differing social needs of Northern Ireland, Scotland and Wales, but this has not developed new social works, although there are clearly differences in the tasks that the social services face and some variations in the provision of services.

Conclusion

The accounts of social services and social work in different countries of the British Isles demonstrate that the 'national' is important in the formation of social services, and gainsays the common assumption that the centralised UK state is wholly dominant in the provision of public services. Significant national variations in social services are apparent, deriving from legal and administrative structures. Where, as in Scotland, deriving from the different legal system, these have had historical continuity in the face of English repression, the differentiation has been maintained. Where, as in Wales, the English legal and administrative system has been dominant for longer, variations are less strong, and differences are predominantly cultural in character. Where, as in Ireland, resistance has been strong and important cultural differences, particularly in religion, have existed, and where the secession from the UK has been for a long period, service links have progressively declined and differentiation has asserted itself. These histories suggest that in the future administrative devolution within the UK will lead to significant and widening service differences.

Yet, in relation to the profession of social work, much less differentiation is apparent. In considering criminal justice service provision in England, Ireland and Scotland, we saw that there is a similarity in professional thinking which continues notwithstanding different political and policy reactions. Relationships between services and in professional links have continued, notwithstanding the formation of the Republic of Ireland. Similar professional concerns about child abuse have been shared over the long term.

We have argued in this chapter that the 'national' is strongly affected by administration, policy and the law. The social services are significantly constructed by these factors and are likely to differentiate further in the future. However, we have suggested that social and cultural experiences maintain continuities across legal and administrative boundaries. Because professional practice and knowledge in social work is partly constructed by such cultural and social aspects of life, it is less strongly constructed by the 'national' and more likely to maintain continuities across the national divisions in the British Isles.

National differentiation in the British Isles takes place within the context of a history of oppression by England and resistance from other parts of the Isles. The oppression has been significantly associated with the legal and administrative element of the interactions between the countries. With devolution and national division, it may be that the history of oppression will become a less significant factor in relationships during the decades to come. Although social work is inextricably connected with many experiences of oppression from England, its role has often been beneficial and constructive in important areas of social and cultural life.

We suggest, therefore, that the role of social work and the social services in the relationships among the countries of the British Isles is complex and ambiguous. To social work professionals, we propose that an awareness of the social and cultural contexts of national relationships is an important aspect of understanding how social work and the social services can contribute to appropriate differentiation and the maintaining of valuable links among the countries of the British Isles. To a wider audience, we suggest that considering the experience of the development of social work and the social services within the population of this small group of European islands demonstrates how complex the social relationships among apparently similar nations are, and how difficult it may be to interpret and develop the role of social work internationally.

Note

1   Crown dependencies such as Guernsey are formally outside the Union.

APPENDIX

About the British Isles...

British Isles. Island group in W. Europe, comprising Great Britain, Ireland and adjacent islands.

Webster's New Geographical Dictionary (1972) Springfield MA, G. & G. Merriam, 178

British Isles, group of islands off the western coast of Europe. The group consists of two main islands, Great Britain and Ireland, and numerous smaller islands.

The New Encyclopaedia Britannica (15th edn., 1993) Chicago, The University of Chicago Press; Vol. 2, 530

British Is., archipelago, NW Europe; comprising 2 large is. of Great Britain and Ireland and 5,000 small is., area 315,029 km2.

Cook, C. (ed.) (1998) *Pears Cyclopaedia 1998–99.* (107th edn) London: Penguin.

QUESTION: How many islands are there in the British Isles?

The islands of all sorts and sizes are, in the true sense of the word, innumerable. But considering only those which are 0.2 hectares (half an acre) or more in area and are islands at all states of the tide, the British Isles total about 4,400; of these 210 are inhabited. An additional 6,100 are islands at high tide, consequently not all at the same time. The foregoing figures include respectively about 850, 70 and 1,000 which are in the Republic of Ireland.

Brian Adams (retired hydrographic officer) London SW6.
Whitaker, B. (ed.) (1990) *Notes and Queries* (A *Guardian* book) London: Fourth Estate.

The countries of Europe can be divided into a number of fairly distinct geographical groups.

At the northwest, separated from the mainland by the English Channel and the North Sea, are the *countries of the British Isles*. They include the United Kingdom of Great Britain and Northern Ireland, and the Republic of Ireland. These countries are now entirely separate in a political sense. However, they have been closely associated historically and are still closely linked by trade.

Wheeler, J. H., Kostbade, J. T. and Thomas, R. S. (1975) *Regional Geography of the World* (3rd edn) New York: Holt Rinehart and Winston, 56.

British Isles, archipelago off the north-west coast of the continent of Europe, from which it is divided by the North Sea, the Straits of Dover, and the English Channel. It comprises Great Britain, made up of England, Scotland and Wales; Ireland; the Orkney and Shetland Islands to the north of Scotland; the Isle of Man in the Irish Sea; the Scilly Isles off the coast of Cornwall; and the Isles of Wight and the Channel islands in the English Channel. Total area is about 314,950 km^2. The Isle of Man and the Channel islands enjoy considerable administrative autonomy. Great Britain and Northern Ireland (the United Kingdom) is the political unit that comprises all of the British Isles except the Irish Republic.

Girling, D. A. (ed.)(1978) *Everyman's Encyclopaedia* (6th edn) Vol 2, London: J. M. Dent and Sons, 447.

Britain is part of the United Kingdom of Great Britain and Northern Ireland. The United Kingdom is part of the British Isles... The British Isles are part of mainland Europe and the North Sea and English Channel are shallow and very recent in terms of earth history... Great Britain is a term for the large island (and many smaller ones) which consists of the three 'countries' of England, Scotland and Wales... (Note that the 'Great' in 'Great Britain' is used in the sense of 'large' to distinguish it from 'little Britain' or Brittany in France).

Beddis, R. (1985) *A New Geography of Britain*, Oxford: Oxford University Press, 8–9.

British Isles, two large islands, Great Britain and Ireland, and many adjacent smaller ones rising from the continental shelf of northwestern Europe...

Politically, the British Isles are divided into the United Kingdom of Great Britain and Northern Ireland, a constitutional monarchy with an elected legislature to which the executive is responsible; the republic of Ireland; and the Isle of Man and the Channel islands, which are self-governing dependencies of the British crown.

English speech is now almost everywhere predominant in the British Isles, but four Celtic tongues – Irish Gaelic, Scottish Gaelic (in north-western Scotland), Welsh and Manx (in the Isle of Man) are still spoken, as is Norman French in the Channel Islands. The climate of Great Britain is temperate and maritime. Great Britain has highly industrialized areas and major seaports. In the south it has a mixed agriculture. Most of the regions of the British Isles are essentially pastoral.

Saltmarsh, J. (1972) *The Encyclopaedia Americana*, Vol 4, Danbury CT: Grolier, 579.

The British Isles consists of England, Scotland, Wales and Northern Ireland, which make up the United Kingdom, and the Republic of Ireland (Eire). It is situated between latitude 50°N and 61°N, and has a great variety of natural landscapes which have developed from underlying rocks...

Variability is the most striking feature of the British weather... The climate of the British Isles is *temperate*; the summers are warm and the winters are mild. There is a lack of extremes and the climate is equable.

The location of the British Isles (on the northwest edge of the European continental shelf where it meets the Atlantic Ocean) explains the climate.

Punnett, N. and Webber, P. (1987) *The British Isles*, Oxford: Basil Blackwell, 6–8.

Bibliography

A Child in Mind (1987) Report of the Commission of Inquiry into the Circumstances Surrounding the Death of Kimberley Carlile. London: London Borough of Greenwich.

A Child in Trust (1985) The Report of the Panel of Inquiry into the Circumstances Surrounding the Death of Jasmine Beckford. London: London Borough of Brent.

Accounts Commission for Scotland (1999) *A Shared Approach. Developing adult mental health services.* Edinburgh: Accounts Commission for Scotland.

Adams, A. (2000) 'The challenge of globalisation.' In A. Adams, P. Erath and S. M. Shardlow (eds) *Fundamentals of Social Work in Selected European Countries.* Lyme Regis: Russell House.

Adams, A., Erath, P. and Shardlow, S. M. (eds) (2000) *Fundamentals of Social Work in Selected European Countries: Present Theory, Practice, Perspectives, Historical and Practice Contexts.* Lyme Regis: Russell House.

Adoption (2000) *A performance and evaluation report.* http://www.cabinetoffice.gov.uk/innovation/2000/adoption/adindex.htm

Agyeman, J., (1993) 'Black people in a white landscape: social and environmental justice.' *Built Environment 6*, 1, 232–6.

Aitchison, J. and Carter, H. (1994) *A Geography of the Welsh Language 1961–1991.* Cardiff: University of Wales Press.

Ardagh, J. (1995) *Ireland: Portrait of a Changing Society.* Harmondsworth, Middlesex: Penguin.

Association of Directors of Social Services (1997) *The Foster Care Market: A National Perspective.* London: ADSS.

Audit Commission (1986) *Making a Reality of Community Care.* London: HMSO.

Auld, J. (1997) *Designing a System of Restorative Community Justice in Northern Ireland: A Discussion Document.* Belfast: QUB.

Bacik and O'Connell (eds) (1998) *Crime and Poverty in Ireland.* Dublin: Round Hall, Sweet and Maxwell.

Bagley, C. (1993) 'Trans-racial adoption in Britain.' *Child Welfare 72,* 3, 258–99.

Baldwin, S. (1926) *On England.* London: Hodder and Stoughton.

Bamford, D. R. (1996) 'Partnership in social work education: A Northern Irish experience.' *International Journal of Educational Management 510,* 3, 21–9.

Barber, B. J. (1998) 'More democracy, more revolution'. *The Nation* 26th October.

Barclay, P. M. (1982) *Social Workers: Their Role and Tasks (The Barclay Report).* London: Bedford Square Press.

Beardshaw, V. and Towell, D. (1990) *Assessment and Case Management: Implications for the Implementation of 'Caring for People'.* London: King's Fund Institute, Briefing Paper 10.

Beck, U. (1992) *The Risk Society.* London: Sage.

Beck, U., Giddens, A. and Lash, S. (1994) *Reflexive Modernization.* Cambridge: Polity.

Becker, S. (1997) *Understanding Poverty.* London: Longman.

Berridge, D. (1997) *Foster Care– a Research Review.* London: Stationery Office.

Blake, W. (1958) 'Milton: a poem in two books, 1804–1808.' In J. Bronowski (ed.) *William Blake.* Harmondsworth, Middlesex: Penguin, 162.

Bland, R. (1994) 'EPIC – a Scottish case management experiment.' In M. Titterton, (ed.) *Caring for People in the Community: the new welfare.* London: Jessica Kingsley.

Bland, R. (1996) 'On the margins: care management and dementia.' In J. Phillips and B. Penhale (eds) *Reviewing Care Management for Older People.* London: Jessica Kingsley.

Bogues, S. and Falconer, T. (1998) *Employment Survey of Newly Qualified Social Workers in Northern Ireland 1996.* Belfast: Care Sector Consultancy.

Bogues, S. and Lindsay, B. (1998) *Evaluation of Family Support.* Derry: Partnership Care West.

Bogues, S. and McColgan, M. (1997) *Evaluation of the Family Support Service.* Belfast: Bryson House.

Borooah, V. (1993) 'Northern Ireland – typology of a regional economy.' In P. Teague (ed.) *The Economy of Northern Ireland.* London: Wishart.

Boyne, G., Griffiths, A., Lawton, A., and Law, J. (1991) *Local Government in Wales: its role and function.* York: Joseph Rowntree Foundation.

Bradley, M. and Aldgate, J. (1994) 'Short term family based care for children in need.' *Adoption and Fostering 18,* 4, 24–9.

Brandon, T. (1998) 'Power and Disabled people: a comparative case study of three community care services in London.' PhD Thesis, London School of Economics.

Breen, R., Hannan, D. F., Rottman, D. B. and Whelan, C. T. (1991 *Understanding Contemporary Ireland.* Cambridge: Polity.

Brewer, J. (1991) 'The parallels between sectarianism and racism.' In CCETSW *One Small Step Towards Racial Justice: The Teaching of Antiracism in Diploma in Social Work Programmes.* London: CCETSW.

Brindle, D. (1999) 'Minister's warning over poor social services.' *Guardian,* London, 24/11/1999, 6.

Bryson, B. (1996) *Notes From a Small Island.* London: Black Swan.

Buckley, H. (1996) 'Child abuse guidelines in Ireland: For whose protection?' In H. Ferguson and T. McNamara (eds) *Protecting Irish children: Investigation, protection and welfare, special edition of administration.* Dublin: Institute of Public Administration, 37–56.

Buckley, H., Skehill, C. and O'Sullivan, E. (1997) *Child protection practices in Ireland: A case study.* Dublin: Oaktree Press.

Bunreacht na hEireann (1937) *Constitution of Ireland.* Dublin: Government Stationery Office.

Butler, I., Drakeford, M., and Pithouse, A., (1998) 'Social services.' In J. Osmond (ed.) *The National Assembly Agenda: a handbook for the first four years.* Cardiff: Institute of Welsh Affairs.

Cameron, L. and Freeman, I. (1996) 'Care Management: Meeting Different Needs.' In C. Clark and I. Lapsley (eds) *Planning and Costing Community Care.* London: Jessica Kingsley.

Campbell, J. (1998) 'Mental health social work and the law in Northern Ireland.' In J. Campbell and R. Manktelow (eds) *Mental Health Social Work in Ireland: Comparative Issues in Policy and Practice.* Aldershot: Avebury.

Campbell, J. and Donnelly, M. (1996) 'Service users' views of a mental health social work team in Belfast.' *Social Services Review, 1,* 1–14.

Campbell, J. and Pinkerton, J. (1997) 'Embracing change as opportunity: reflections on social work from a Northern Ireland perspective.' In B. Lesnik (ed.) *International Perspectives in Social Work: Change in Social Work.* Aldershot: Arena.

Carstairs, V. and Morris, R. (1991) *Deprivation and Health in Scotland.* Aberdeen: Aberdeen University Press.

Carvel, J. (2000) 'Blair vows to increase number of adoptions.' *Guardian,* London: 21/12/2000.

Caul, B. and Herron, S. (1992) *A Service for People.* Belfast: December.

Cavanagh, P. (1998) *Partnership for Families: A Community and Voluntary Sector Perspective.* Paper presented at Stronger Families – Stronger Communities Conference, Derry, 23 September 1998.

CCETSW (1987) *Care for Tomorrow.* London: Central Council for Education and Training in Social Work.

CCETSW (1989) *DipSW: Rules and Requirements for the Diploma in Social Work* (Paper 30), 2nd edn. London: Central Council for Education and Training in Social Work.

CCETSW (1990a) *The Requirements for Post-Qualifying Education and training in the personal Social Services: a framework for continuing professional development* (Paper 31). London: Central Council for Education and Training in Social Work.

CCETSW (1990b) *National Vocational Qualifications in Social Care: Requirements for the Approval of Assessment Centres and Award of Qualifications by CCETSW* (Paper 29). London: Central Council for Education and Training in Social Work.

CCETSW (1991) *One Small Step towards Racial Justice: The Teaching of Anti-Racism in Diploma of Social Work Programmes.* London: Central Council for Education and Training in Social Work.

Chamberlayne, P., Cooper, A., Freeman, R. and Rustin, M. (eds) (1999) *Welfare and Culture in Europe: Towards a New Paradigm in Social Policy.* London: Jessica Kingsley.

Charles, N. (1995) 'The refuge movement and domestic violence.' In J. Aaron, T. Rees, S. Betts, and M. Vincentelli (eds) *Our Sisters' Land.* Cardiff: University of Wales Press.

Children Act, The (1989) London: HMSO.

Children Board and Education Council (1992) *Internal Document.* Guernsey: Children Board.

Children in Scotland (1995) *Scotland's Families Today.* Edinburgh: HMSO.

Ching Leong, F. (1997) 'The Race Relations (NI) Order 1997: Implications for work with children.' *Child Care in Practice 3,* 3, 84–8.

CIPFA (1997) *Local Government Comparative Statistics.* London: HMSO.

Clark, C. and Lapsley, I. (eds) (1996) *Planning and Costing Community Care.* London: Jessica Kingsley.

Clarke, M. (1998) *Lives in Care.* Dublin: Trinity Children's Centre.

Cleland, A. (1995) *Guide to the Children (Scotland) Act 1995.* Glasgow: Scottish Child Law Centre.

Cloke, P., Goodwin, M. and Milbourne, P. (1997) *The Condition of Rural Wales: Marginalisation in the Welsh Countryside.* Cardiff: University of Wales Press.

Cohen, N. (1999) 'Last Rotten Borough.' *Observer,* London 27/6/1999.

Colley, L. (1994) *Britons: Forging the Nation, 1707–1837.* London: Vintage.

Colton, M. (1999) *Stigma and Child Welfare in Wales.* Occasional Paper No. 4, Plant Nghymru/Children in Wales.

Colton, M., Drury, C. and Williams, M. (1995) *Staying Together – Supporting Children Under the Children Act.* Aldershot: Arena.

Community Care and Health (Scotland) Bill, the (2001). Edinburgh: HMSO.

Cotter, A. (1999) 'The Criminal Justice System in Ireland: Towards Change and Transformation.' In S. Quin, P. Kennedy, A. O'Donnell and G. Kiely (eds) *Contemporary Irish Social Policy.* Dublin: University College Dublin Press.

Crickley, A. and Devin, M. (1990) *In Community Work in Ireland: Trends in the 80s, Options for the 90s.* Combat Poverty Agency: Dublin.

Crook, S. Kakulski, J. and Walters, M. (1992) *Postmodernization: Change in Advanced Society.* Sage: London.

Crosby, C. and Barry, M. (1995) *Community Care: Evaluation of the Provision of Mental Health Service.* Aldershot: Avebury.

Davies, B. (1998) 'Shelter-with-care and the community care reforms – notes on the evolution of essential species.' In R. Jack, (ed) *Residential Versus Community Care: the role of institutions in welfare provision.* Houndmills, Basingstoke: Macmillan.

Davies, E. (1994) *They All Speak English Anyway.* Cardiff: CCETSW/Open University Press.

Davies, J. (1993) *A History of Wales* (English edition of Hanes Cymru, 1990). London: Penguin.

Davies, N. (1999) *The Isles: A History.* Houndmills, Basingstoke: Macmillan.

Davies, R. (1994) *The Cost of Unaccountability: A Survey of the Administrative Costs of Welsh Quangos.* Cardiff: Wales Labour Party.

Day, G., (1998) 'A community of communities? Similarity and difference in Welsh rural community studies.' *Economic and Social Review 29,* 233–58.

Department of Health (1987) *Child abuse guidelines: Guidelines on procedures for the identification, investigation and management of child abuse.* Dublin: Department of Health.

Department of Health (1988) *Protecting Children: A Guide for Social Workers Undertaking a Comprehensive Assessment.* London: HMSO.

Department of Health (1991a) *A Study of Enquiry Reports (1980–89).* London: HMSO.

Department of Health (1991b) *The Children Act 1989: Regulations and Guidance Volume 2 – Family Support.* London: HMSO.

Department of Health (1991c) *Working Together.* London: HMSO.

Department of Health (1992) *Memorandum of Good Practice for Interviewing Children.* London: Department of Health.

Department of Health (1995) *Child Protection: Messages From Research.* London: HMSO.

Department of Health (1996) *Building Bridges: a guide to arrangement for inter-agency working for the care and protection of severely mentally ill people.* London: Department of Health.

Department of Health (1998) *Quality Protects.* London.

Department of Health (1999) *Children first: National guidelines for the protection and welfare of children.* Dublin: Department of Health.

Department of Health (2000) *Assessing Children in Need.* London: The Stationery Office.

Department of Health, Department for Education and Employment, *et al.* (2000) *Framework for the Assessment of Children in Need and their Families.* London: Stationery Office.

Department of Health (2000) *Adoption a New Approach.*
http://www.doh.gov.uk/adoption/index.htm

Department of Social Welfare (1997) *Green Paper on The Voluntary and Community Sector and its Relationship with the State*. Dublin: Department of Social Welfare.

DHSS(NI) (1972) *Health and Social Services (NI) Order*. Belfast: HMSO.

DHSS(N1) (1981) *Northern Ireland Review Committee on Mental Health Legislation (McDermott Committee)* Belfast: HMSO

DHSS(NI) (1986) *Mental Health (NI) Order*. Belfast: HMSO.

DHSS(NI) (1990) *Common Criteria for Assessing Practice Learning within Qualifying Training*. Belfast: Regional Document.

DHSS(NI) (1991) *People First*. Belfast: HMSO.

DHSS(NI) (1993) *Health and Personal Social Services (NI) Order*. Belfast: HMSO.

DHSS(NI) (1995) *The Children (NI) Order*. Belfast: HMSO.

DHSS(NI) (1996) *Health and Wellbeing: Into the Next Millennium*. Belfast: HMSO.

DHSS(NI) (1997a) *Wellbeing in 2000*. Belfast: HMSO.

DHSS(NI) (1997b) *Race Relations (NI) Order*. Belfast: HMSO.

DHSS(NI) (1998) *Fit for the Future*. Belfast: DHSS(NI).

Ditch, J. and Morrissey, M. (1992) ' Northern Ireland: review and prospects for social policy.' *Social Policy and Administration 26*, 1, 18–39.

Doherty, D. (1996) 'Child care and protection: protecting children – supporting their service providers.' In H. Ferguson and T. McNamara (eds) *Protecting Irish children: Investigation, protection and welfare, Special edition of administration*. Dublin: Institute of Public Administration.

Dominelli, L. (1999) 'Neo-liberalism, social exclusion and welfare clients in a global economy.' *International Journal of Social Welfare 8*, 1, 14–22.

Drakeford, M. (1995) 'Cultural sensitivity.' In M. Preston-Shoot and S. Jackson (eds) *Educating Social Workers in a Changing Policy Context*. London: Whiting and Birch.

Drakeford, M. and Lynn, E. (1999) 'Educating social workers in the Welsh context.' *Journal of Inclusive Education 3*, 2, 151–67.

Dunlop, L. A. (1999) 'Partnership or Token Gesture? (A Study of Parental Participation in Initial Child Protection Case Conference).' Social Work Monograph, University of Ulster (unpublished).

English J. (ed.) (1998a) *Social Services in Scotland*. 4th edn. Edinburgh: Mercat Press.

English, J. (1998b) 'Central and local government.' In J. English (ed.) *Social Services in Scotland*. Edinburgh: Mercat.

Esping-Andersen, G. (1990) *The Three Worlds of Welfare Capitalism*. Cambridge: Polity Press.

Fahy, B. (1999) *Freedom of angels: Surviving Goldenbridge Orphanage*. Dublin: O'Brien Press.

Faughan, P. and Kelleher, P. (1993) *The Voluntary Sector and the State*. CMRS: Dublin.

Fay, M., Morrissey, M. and Smyth, M. (1999) *The Cost of the Troubles*. London: Zed.

Felce, D., Grant, G., Todd, S., Ramcharan, P., Beyer, G., McGrath, M., Perry, J., Shearn, J., Kilsby, M. and Lowe, K. (1998) *Towards a Full Life: Researching Policy Innovation for People with Learning Disabilities.* Oxford: Butterworth Heinemann.

Ferguson, H. (1994) 'Child abuse inquiries and the report of the Kilkenny incest investigation: A critical analysis.' *Administration 41*, 4, 385–410.

Ferguson, H. (1995a) 'Child Welfare, Child Protection and the Child Care Act 1991: key issues for policy and practice.' In H. Ferguson and P. Kenny (eds) *On behalf of the child: Child welfare, child protection and the Child Care Act 1991.* Dublin: A. & A. Farmar.

Ferguson, H. (1995b) 'The paedophile priest: a deconstruction.' *Studies 84*, 247.

Ferguson, H. (1996) 'Protecting Irish Children in Time: Child abuse as a social problem and the development of the Irish child protection system.' In H. Ferguson and T. McNamara (eds) *Protecting Irish children: Investigation, protection and welfare, Special edition of administration.* Dublin: Institute of Public Administration.

Ferguson, H. (1997) 'Protecting children in new times: Child protection and the risk society.' *Child and Family Social Work 2*, 4, 221–34.

Ferguson, H. (2001a) 'Social work, individualization and life politics.' *British Journal of Social Work 31*, 1, 41–55.

Ferguson, H. (2001b) 'Ireland.' In B. Schwartz-Kenny, M. MaCauley and M. A. Epstein (eds) *Child Abuse: A global view.* Westport CT: Greenwood Press.

Ferguson, H. and Kenny, P. (eds) (1995) *On behalf of the child: Child welfare, child protection and the Child Care Act 1991.* Dublin: A. & A. Farmar.

Ferguson, H. and O'Reilly, M. (2001) *Keeping children safe: Child Abuse, child protection and the promotion of welfare.* Dublin: A. & A. Farmar.

Ferguson, H. and Synott, P. (1995) Intervention into domestic violence in Ireland: Developing policy and practice with men who batter. *Administration 43*, 3, 57–81.

Fitzpatrick, S. (1995) *Services for Elderly Patients Following Discharge from Acute Hospital Care.* Glasgow: University of Glasgow, Department of Social Policy and Social Work.

Flanders, M. and Swann, D. (1977) 'A Song of Patriotic Prejudice.' In C. Flanders (ed.) *The Songs of Michael Flanders and Donald Swann.* London, Elm Tree/St George's.

Forbes, J. and Sashidharan (1997) 'User Empowerment in Services – Incorporation or challenge' *British Journal of Social Work 27*, 4, 481–498.

Forde, C. (1996) 'History of Community Work.' In P. Burgess (ed) *Youth and Community Work.* Cork: UCC.

Forrester-Jones, R., and Grant, G. (1997) *Resettlement from Large Psychiatric Hospital to a Small Community Residence.* Aldershot: Avebury.

Fox Harding, L. (1991) *Perspectives in Child Care Policy.* London: Longman.

Foyle Health and Social Services Community Trust (1997) *Children of Creggan: Report on the Social and Health Needs of the Under Fives*, Volume 1, Derry. Foyle Health and Social Services Community Trust.

Fratter, J., Rowe, R. *et al.* (1991) *Permanent Family Placement: A Decade of Experience.* London: BAAF.

Gadd, B. (1996) 'Probation in Northern Ireland. ' In G. McIvor *Working with Offenders.* London: Jessica Kingsley Publishers.

Gaffikin, F. and Morrissey, M. (1990) *Northern Ireland: The Thatcher Years.* London: Zed.

Gibbons, J., Conroy, S. and Bell, C. (1995) *Operating the Child Protection System.* London: HMSO.

Gibson, F. and Michael, G. (1993) *Perspectives on Discrimination in Northern Ireland.* London: CCETSW.

Giddens, A. (1990) *The Consquences of Modernity.* Cambridge: Polity Press.

Giddens, A. (1998) *The Third Way.* Cambridge: Polity.

Giddens, A. (1999) *Runaway World.* BBC Reith Lectures, http://news.bbc.co.uk

Goodman, A., Johnson, P. and Webb, S. (1997) *Inequality in the UK.* Oxford: Oxford University Press.

Grant, G., (1978) 'The provision of social services in rural areas.' In G. Williams (ed.) *Social and Cultural Change in Contemporary Wales.* London: Routledge and Kegan Paul.

Grant, G. (1994) 'What can care management learn from individual planning?' *Centre for Social Policy Research and Development Newsletter,* 11, summer, 12–17.

Griffiths Report (1988) *Community Care: Agenda for Action.* London: HMSO.

Hadden, T. and Boyle, K (1989) *The Anglo-Irish Agreement.* London: Sweet and Maxwell.

Hadfield, B. (1989) *The Constitution of Northern Ireland.* Belfast: SLS.

Hadley, R. and Clough, R. (1996) *Care in Chaos: frustration and challenge in community care.* London: Cassell.

Hallett, C. and Hazel, N. (1998) *The Evaluation of the Children's Hearings in Scotland. Volume 2. The International Context: Trends in Juvenile Justice and Child Welfare.* Edinburgh: Scottish Office Central Research Unit. The Stationery Office.

Hallett, C. and Murray, C. with Jamieson, J. and Veitch, B. (1998) *The Evaluation of the Children's Hearings in Scotland. Volume 1. Deciding in Children's Interests.* Edinburgh: Scottish Office Central Research Unit. The Stationery Office.

Hayes, D. (1997) 'Parental Participation at the Child Protection Case Conference: An Evaluation of Practice in North and West Belfast.' *Child & Practice 4,* 2, 159–80.

Healy, S. and Reynolds, B. (1985) *Ireland Today: Reflecting in the Light of the Gospel.* Dublin: CORI.

Healy, S. and Reynolds, B. (eds) (1999) *Social Partnership in a New Century,* Dublin: Conference of Religious in Ireland. Justice Commission.

Higgins, K., Pinkerton, J. and Switzer, V. (1997) *Family Support in Northern Ireland.* Belfast: Centre for Child Care Research, QUB.

Hill, M., Murray, K. and Rankin, J. (1991) 'The early history of Scottish child welfare.' *Children and Society 5,* 2, 182–195.

Hills, J. (1995) *Joseph Rowntree Inquiry into Income and Wealth*. Volume 2. York: Joseph Rowntree Foundation.

Himsworth, C. M. G. and Munro, C. R. (1999) *Greens Annotated Acts: The Scotland Act 1998*. Edinburgh: W. Green/Sweet and Maxwell.

Hogg, K. (1999) *Youth Crime in Scotland. A Scottish Executive Policy Unit Review*. Edinburgh: Scottish Executive.

Home Office (1995) *Strengthening Punishment in the Community: A Consultative Document*. London: Home Office.

Home Office (1996) *Three Year Plan for the Probation Service*. London: Home Office.

Home Office (1998) *Prisons, Probation: Joining Forces to Protect the Public*. London: Home Office.

Horgan, G. (1997) 'The Children (Northern Ireland) Order.' *National Children's Bureau Highlight*, 153, July.

Horgan, G. and Sinclair, G. (1997) *Planning for Children in Care in Northern Ireland*. London: NCB.

Hornsby-Smith, M. (1999) 'The Catholic church and social policy in Europe.' In P. Chamberlayne, A. Cooper, R. Freeman, and M. Rustin, (eds) *Welfare and Culture in Europe: Towards a New Paradigm in Social Policy*. London: Jessica Kingsley.

House of Commons (1998) *The Barnett Formula*. Research Paper 88/9. London: House of Commons.

Howe, D. (1992) 'Child abuse and the bureaucratisation of social work.' *Sociological Review 40*, 3, 490–508.

Hunter, D. J. and Wistow, G. (1987) *Community Care in Britain: variations on a theme*. London: King Edward's Hospital Fund.

Hutton, W. (2001) 'The Saxon tigers roar back.' *Observer*. London, 30.

Ife, J. (1997) *Rethinking Social Work*. Longman: Melbourne.

Jack, R. (ed) (1998) *Residential Versus Community Care: the role of institutions in welfare provision*. London: Macmillan.

Jarvie, G. (1989) 'Culture, social development and the Scottish Highland Gatherings.' In D. McCrone, S. Kendrick and P. Straw (eds) *The Making of Scotland: Nation, Culture and Social Change*. Edinburgh: Edinburgh University Press/British Sociological Association.

Jay, E. (1992) *Keep them in Birmingham*. London: CRE.

Jenkins, O. (1994) Cardiff: South Glamorgan County Council.

Jones, B. J. (1994) 'Welsh politics come of age: the transformation of Wales since 1979.' In J. Osmond (ed) *A Parliament For Wales*. Llandysul: Gomer Press.

Jones, C. (1993) 'Distortion and demonisation: the Right and anti-racist social work education.' *Social Work Education 12*, 2, 9–16.

Jones, C. (1996) 'Anti-intellectualism and the peculiarities of British social work education.' In N. Parton (ed) *Social Theory, Social Change and Social Work.* London: Routledge.

Jones, G., (1999) 'Shaping the Future in Wales.' *Professional Social Work.*

Jordan, B. (1997) 'Partnership with service users in child protection and family support.' In N. Parton (ed.) *Child Protection and Family Support: Tensions, contradictions and possibilities.* London: Routledge.

Keenan, O. (1996) *Kelly: A child is dead. Interim report of the Joint Committee on the Family.* Dublin: Government Publications Office.

Kelly, G. and Pinkerton, J. (1996) 'The Children (Northern Ireland) Order 1995: Prospects for Progress?' In M. Hill and J. Aldgate (eds) *Child Welfare Services: Developments in Law, Policy, Practice and Research.* London: Jessica Kingsley.

Kent, R. (1997) *Children's Safeguards Review* Edinburgh: Stationery Office.

Kilbrandon, L. (1964) *Children and Young Persons, Scotland.* Cmnd 2306, Edinburgh: Scottish Office, HMSO.

Kilbrandon Report (1973) *Report of the Royal Commission on the Constitution.* Cmnd 5460, London: HMSO.

Kincraig Report (1988) *Parole and Related Issues in Scotland.* Cmnd 598, Edinburgh: HMSO.

Kinealy, C. (1999) *A Disunited Kingdom? England, Ireland, Scotland and Wales, 1800–1949.* Cambridge: Cambridge University Press.

Labour Party (1999) *Working Hard for Wales: Labour's Election Manifesto for the National Assembly for Wales.* Cardiff: Labour Party.

Lambeth, London Borough (1987) *Whose Child?* London: Lambeth Borough Council.

Lamont, N. (1999) *In Office.* London: Tribune Books.

Lavan, A. (1998) ' Social work in Ireland.' In S. M. Shardlow and M. Payne (eds) *Contemporary Issues in Social Work: Western Europe.* Aldershot: Arena.

Levitt, I. (1988) *Poverty and Welfare in Scotland, 1890–1948,* Edinburgh: Edinburgh University Press.

Levitt, I. (1989) 'Welfare, government and the working class: Scotland, 1845–1894.' In D. McCrone, S. Kendrick, and P. Straw (eds) *The Making of Scotland: Nation, Culture and Social Change.* Edinburgh: Edinburgh University Press/British Sociological Association.

Lewis, J. and Glennerster, H. (1996) *Implementing the New Community Care.* Buckingham: Open University Press.

Lindsay, T. and Chapman, T. (2001) *Youth Justice in Northern Ireland.* Milton Keynes: Open University Press.

Lorenz, W. (1994) *Social Work in a Changing Europe.* London: Routledge.

Lorenz, W. (1999) 'Social work and cultural politics: the paradox of German social pedagogy.' In P. Chamberlayne, A. Cooper, R. Freeman and M. Rustin (eds) *Welfare and Culture in Europe: Towards a New Paradigm in Social Policy*. London: Jessica Kingsley.

Loucks, N. (1996) *HMPI Cornton Vale; research into Drugs and Alcohol, Violence and Bullying, Suicides and Self-Injury, and Backgrounds of Abuse*. Edinburgh: Scottish Prison Service Occasional Papers. Report No. 1/98.

MacKay, C. (1997) 'Community Care. Division E.' In R. Mays (ed) *Scottish Social Work Legislation*. Edinburgh: W. Green/Sweet and Maxwell.

Mackay, F. and Bould, C. (eds) (1997) *Engender: Gender Audit 1997*. Edinburgh: Engender.

Mackay, F., Chrisma, B. and Young, G. (1999) *Gender Audit 1998–99: Putting Scottish Women in the Picture*. Edinburgh: Engender.

Mallett, J. (1997) *The Hidden Troubles*. Derry: CPAG.

Mandelstam, M. (1999) *Community Care Practice and the Law*, 2nd edn. London: Jessica Kingsley.

Mannkler, J. (1997) *Out of the Shadows: An Action Research Report into Families, Racism and Exclusion in Northern Ireland*. Belfast: University of Ulster.

Marshall, K., Jamieson, C. and Finlayson, A. (1999) *Edinburgh's Children: The Edinburgh Inquiry into Abuse and Neglect of Children in Care*. Edinburgh: City of Edinburgh Council.

Martin, F. M., Fox, S. J. and Murray, K. (1981) *Children Out of Court*. Edinburgh: Scottish Academic Press.

Mays, R. (ed.) (1997) *Scottish Social Work Legislation*. Edinburgh: W. Green/Sweet and Maxwell.

McAra, L. (1998) *Social Work and Criminal Justice, Volume 5. Parole Board Decision Making*. Edinburgh: The Stationery Office.

McBoyle Report (1963) *Report of the Committee on the Prevention of Neglect of Children*. Edinburgh: HMSO.

McColgan, M. (1995) 'The Children (NI) Order 1995: Considerations of the Legislative, Economic and Political, Organisational and Social Policy Contexts.' *Children and Youth Services Review 17*, 5/6, 637–49.

McColgan, M. (1998) 'Western Area Child Protection Committee Multi-Professional Audit.' University of Ulster/Western Health and Social Services Board (unpublished).

McCoy, K. (1993) 'Integration – a changing scene.' In *Perspectives on Integration*, DHSS(NI)/SSI, 7–19.

McCrone, D. (1992) *Understanding Scotland: The Sociology of a Stateless Nation*. London: Routledge.

McCrone, D. (1996) 'Autonomy and National Identity in Stateless Nations: Scotland, Catalonia and Quebec.' *Scottish Affairs 17*, autumn, 42–8.

McCullagh, C. (1996) *Crime in Ireland: A sociological introduction.* Cork: Cork University Press.

McGarry, J. and O'Leary, B. (1995) *Explaining Northern Ireland.* Oxford: Blackwell.

McGhee, J. (1995) 'Consumers' views of a post-placement support project.' *Adoption and Fostering 19,* 1, 41–45.

McGhee, J., Waterhouse, L. and Whyte, B. (1996) 'Children's hearings and children in trouble.' In S. Asquith (ed) *Children and Young People in Conflict with the Law.* London: Jessica Kingsley.

McGinley, M. (1995) 'A programme manager perspective.' In H. Ferguson and P. Kenny (eds) *On behalf of the child: Child welfare, child protection and the Child Care Act 1991.* Dublin: A. & A. Farmar.

McGuinness, C. (1993) *Report of the Kilkenny incest investigation.* Dublin: Government Stationery Office.

McIntosh Commission (1999) *Moving forward: Local Government and the Scottish Parliament. The Report of the Commission on Local Government and the Scottish Parliament.* Edinburgh: The Scottish Office.

McIvor, G. and Barry, M. (1998a) *Social Work and Criminal Justice, Volume 7. Community Based Throughcare.* Edinburgh: The Stationery Office.

McIvor, G. and Barry, M. (1998b) *Social Work and Criminal Justice, Volume 6. The Process and Outcomes of Probation Supervision.* Edinburgh: The Stationery Office.

McKay, S. (1998) *Sophia's Story.* Dublin: Gill and Macmillan.

McKendrick, J. (1995) 'Poverty in the United Kingdom: The Celtic divide.' In C. Philo (ed.) *Off the Map: The Social geography of poverty in the UK.* London: CPAG.

McLaughlin, B. (1985) *Deprivation in Rural Areas.* Department of the Environment: London.

McManus, J. J. (1997) *Report on Investigation into Aberdeen City Council Social Work Department's Handling of the Case of Mr. Steven Leisk.* Aberdeen: Aberdeen City Council.

McVeigh, R. (1992) 'The Specificity of Irish Racism.' *Race and Class 33,* 4, 31–45.

Midgley, J. (2001) 'Issues in International Social Work.' *Journal of Social Work 1,* 1, 21–35.

Midwinter, E. (1994) *The Development of Social Welfare in Britain.* Buckingham, Open University Press.

Mikes, G. (1946) *How to be an Alien.* London: Penguin André Deutsch.

Miles, R. and Dunlop, A. (1987) 'Racism in Britain: The Scottish Dimension.' In P. Jackson (ed) *Race and Racism.* London: George Allen Unwin.

Millham, S., Bullock, R. *et al.* (1986) *Lost in Care.* London: Gower.

Moore, C. (1995) *Betrayal of trust: The Father Brendan Smyth affair and the Catholic Church.* Dublin: Marino.

Moore, G. and Whyte, W. (1998) *Moore and Wood's Social Work and Criminal Law in Scotland.* 3rd edn. Edinburgh: Mercat Press.

Moorhouse, H. F. (1989) '"We're off to Wembley!" The history of a Scottish event and the sociology of football hooliganism.' In D. McCrone, S. Kendrick and P. Straw (eds) *The Making of Scotland: Nation, Culture and Social Change.* Edinburgh: Edinburgh University Press/British Sociological Association.

Morgan, B. and Morgan, K. (1998) 'Economic development.' In J. Osmond (ed.) *The National Assembly Agenda: a handbook for the first four years.* Cardiff: Institute of Welsh Affairs.

Morgan, K. and Roberts, E. (1993) 'The Democratic Deficit: A Guide to Quangoland.' *Papers in Planning and Research No. 144.* Department of City and Regional Planning, University of Wales: Cardiff.

Morris, J. (1993a) *Community Care or Independent Living?* York: Joseph Rowntree Foundation.

Morris, J. (1993b) *Independent Lives? Disabled People and Community Care.* Basingstoke: Macmillan.

Morris, K. and Tunnard, J. (1996) *Family Group Conferences.* London: Family Rights Group.

Moxley, D. P. (1989) *The Practice of Case Management.* Newbury Park, CA: Sage.

Murphy, M. (1996) 'From prevention to "family support" and beyond: Promoting the welfare of Irish children.' In H. Ferguson and T. McNamara (eds) *Protecting Irish children: Investigation, protection and welfare, special edition of administration.* Dublin: Institute of Public Administration.

Myers, F. (1999) 'Social Workers as Mental Health Officers: Different Hats, Different Roles?' In M. Ulas and A. Connor (eds) *Mental Health and Social Work.* London: Jessica Kingsley.

National Assembly for Wales (2000a) 'Record Spending Plans Backed by Assembly.' *Press Release 1079,* October.

National Assembly for Wales (2000b) *Putting People First: a Partnership Government for Wales.* National Assembly for Wales: Cardiff.

News (2000) 'Platt defends frameworks.' *Community Care* 1304, 9.

NIO (Northern Ireland Office) (1982) *The Probation Order (NI) 1982.* Belfast: NIO.

NIO (Northern Ireland Office) (1998a) *The Agreement.* Belfast: NIO.

NIO (Northern Ireland Office) (1998b) *We Will Remember Them: Report of the Northern Ireland Victims Commissioner.* Belfast: NIO.

NIO (Northern Ireland Office) (1998c) We Will Remember Them: Report of the Northern Ireland Victims Commissioner Sir Kenneth Bloomfield. Belfast: HMSO

NIO (Northern Ireland Office) (1999b) *The Criminal Justice (Children) Order 1999.* Belfast: HMSO.

NISW (1997) *The Northern Ireland Social Services Workforce in Transition.* London: NISW.

Norrie, K. M. (1999) 'Improving Scottish Family Law: response to the Scottish Office Consultation Paper.' *Scottish Law and Practice Quarterly 4,* 3, 157–71.

North Western Health Board (1998) *Report of the inquiry into the West of Ireland farmer case.* Manorhamilton, Co. Leitrim, Ireland: North Western Health Board.

Northern Health and Social Services Board (1999) *Northern Area Children and Young People's Committee, Children's Services Plan 1999–2002.*

O'Connor, P. (1998) *Women in Irish Society.* Dublin: IPA.

O'Hagan, K. (ed.) (1996) *Competence in Social Work Practice: A practical guide for professionals.* London: Jessica Kingsley Publishers.

O'Hagan, K. (1997) 'Parental Participation in Emergency Child Protection.' *Child Care in Practice 3,* 3, 22–41.

O'Loughlin, A. (1999) 'Social Policy and Older People in Ireland.' In S. Quinn, P. Kennedy, A. O'Donnell and G. Kiely (eds) *Contemporary Irish Social Policy.* Dublin: University College Dublin Press.

O'Mahony, P. (1993) *Crime and Punishment in Ireland.* Dublin: Round Hall Press.

O'Morain, P. (1999) 'EHB Child Care Workers, Leaving Due to Threats.' *Irish Times,* 8 October.

Offe, C. (1984) *Contradictions of the Welfare State.* Hutchinson: London.

Orwell, G. (1941) *The Lion and The Unicorn.* London: Penguin.

Orwell, G. (1947) *The English people.* London: Collins.

Orwell, G. (1949) *Nineteen eighty-four: a novel.* London: Secker and Warburg.

Osmond, J. (1994) 'Re-Making Wales.' In J. Osmond (ed.) *A Parliament For Wales.* Llandysul: Gomer Press, 5–35.

Osmond, J. (ed.) (1998) *The National Assembly Agenda: a handbook for the first four years.* Cardiff: Institute of Welsh Affairs.

Packman, J. and Jordon, B. (1991) 'The Children Act: Looking Forward, Looking Back.' *British Journal of Social Work 21,* 4, 315–27.

Packman, J., Randall, R. *et al.* (1986) *Who Needs Care?* Oxford: Blackwell.

Parker, R. and Charles, H. (1939) *There'll Always be an England.* London: Irwin Dash Music.

Parry Jones, B. (1998) *Care management in Wales: The strain of front-line practice.* Research Summary No. 4, CSPRD, April.

Parry Jones, B., Robinson, C., Ramcharan, P. and Grant, G. (1998) *Assessment and Care Management in Wales: Summary Report.* Bangor: Centre For Social Policy Research and Development, University of Wales.

Paterson, F. and Tombs, J. (1998) *Social Work and Criminal Justice, Volume 1. The Impact of Policy.* Edinburgh: The Stationery Office.

Paxman, J. (1998) *The English.* Harmondsworth, Middlesex: Penguin.

Payne, M. (1995) *Social Work and Community Care.* Basingstoke: Macmillan.

Payne, M. (1996) *What is Professional Social Work?* Birmingham: Venture.

Payne, M. (1998) 'Care management and social work.' In J. Bornat, J. Johnson, C. Pereira, D. Pilgrim and F. Williams (eds) *Community Care: A Reader* (2nd edn). Basingstoke: Macmillan.

Payne, M. (1998a) 'United Kingdom' In N. S. Mayadas, T. D. Watts and D. Elliot (eds) *International Handbook on social work theory and practice.* Westport, CT: Greeenwood Press.

Percy Commission (1957) *Report of the Royal Commission on the Law Relating to Mental Illness and Mental Deficiency* (Cmnd 169). London: HMSO.

Pilling, D. (1993) *Approaches to Case Management for People with Disabilities.* London: Jessica Kingsley.

Pinkerton, J. Higgins, K. and Devine, P. (2000) *Family Support: Linking Project Evaluation to Policy Analysis.* Aldershot: Ashgate.

Pittock, M. G. H. (1999) *Celtic Identity and the British Image.* Manchester: Manchester University Press.

Pollitt, C. (1993) *Managerialism and the Public Services: cuts or cultural change in the 1990s?* Oxford: Blackwell.

Potter, M. (1995) 'Mental Disorder.' In C. White (ed.) *Law for Social Workers in Northern Ireland.* Dublin: Gill and Macmillan.

Powell, F. (1992) *The Politics of Irish Social Policy 1600–1990.* New York: Edwin Mellen Press.

Powell, F. (1998) 'The professional challenges of reflexive modernization: social work in Ireland.' *British Journal of Social Work, 28,* 311–28.

Powell, F. and Guerin, D. (1997) *Civil Society & Social Policy: Voluntarism in Ireland.* Dublin: A. A. Farmer.

Prior, P. (1993) *Mental Health and Politics in Northern Ireland.* Aldershot: Avebury.

Prison Reform Trust (1997) *The Prison Population in Britain, Europe and the Rest of the World.* London: Prison Reform Trust.

Probation Board for Northern Ireland (1996) *A Challenging Future, Probation Board for Northern Ireland Annual Report 1995/96 and Business Plan 1997/97.* Belfast: PBNI.

Quinn, P. (2000) 'Britain projected.' *Tate: The Art Magazine,* Spring 2000, 34–7.

Quin, S. and Redmond, B. (1999) 'Moving from needs to rights: social policy for people with disability in Ireland.' In S. Quinn, P. Kennedy, A. O'Donnell and G. Kiely (eds) *Contemporary Irish Social Policy.* Dublin: University College Dublin Press.

Ramsbotham, D. Sir (HM Chief Inspector of Prisons) (2000) *Report on Inspection of HM Young Offender Institution Portland.* London: Home Office.

Raftery, M. and O'Sullivan, E. (1999) *Suffer the Little Children: The inside story of Ireland's industrial schools.* Dublin: New Island Books.

Rea, E. (1996) *Readiness to Practice (Northern Ireland), A Study of Professional Social Work Training.* Belfast: DHSS (NI).

Regulation of Care (Scotland) Act (2001) Edinburgh: HMSO.

Reilly, I. (1997) 'The Central Council for Education and Training in Social Work.' *Child Care in Practice 3*, 1, 1–10.

Reith, M. (1998) *Community Care Tragedies: a practice guide to mental health inquiries.* Birmingham: Venture.

Report of the Committee of Inquiry into the care and supervision provided in relation to Maria Colwell (1974). London: HMSO.

Report of the Inquiry into Child Abuse in Cleveland (1988). London: HMSO (Cmnd 412)

Richardson, V. (1999) 'Children and social policy.' In S. Quinn, P. Kennedy, A. O'Donnell and G. Kiely (eds) *Contemporary Irish Social Policy*, Dublin: University College Dublin Press, 174–200.

Rigg, D. (ed.) (1982) *No Turn Unstoned: the worst ever theatrical reviews.* London: Elm Tree Books.

Ritchie, J., Dick, D. and Lingham, R. (1994) *The Report of the Inquiry into the Care and Treatment of Christopher Clunis.* London: HMSO.

Roberts, B. (1994) 'Welsh Identity in a Former Mining Valley: Social Images and Imagined Communities.' *Contemporary Wales 7*, 77–96.

Robinson, C. A. (ed) (1994) *Welsh Office Elderly Initiative: A selection of projects.* CSPRD, University of Wales: Bangor.

Robinson, C. and Stalker, K. (1993) 'Patterns and Provisions of Respite Care and the Children Act.' *British Journal of Social Work 23*, 1, 45–63.

Rowe, J. and Lambert, L. (1973) *Children Who Wait.* London: Association of British Fostering and Adoption Agencies.

Rushton, A. and H. Minnis (1997) 'Transracial family placements.' *Journal of Child Psychology and Psychiatry 38*, 2, 147–59.

Ryan, P., Ford, R., Beardsmore, A. and Muiden, M. (1999) 'The enduring relevance of case management.' *British Journal of Social Work 29*, 1, 97–125.

Scottish Culture (2001)
http://scottishculture.about.com/culture/scottishculture/library/blquotesall.htm

Scottish Executive (1999a) *Making the Right Moves: Rights and protection for adults with incapacity.* Cmnd SE/1999/24. Edinburgh: The Stationery Office.

Scottish Executive (1999b) *Statistical Bulletin. Social Work Series.* SWK/S/1999/21. Edinburgh: Government Statistical Service.

Scottish Executive (2000) *Parents and Children.* Edinburgh: Scottish Executive.

Scottish Executive Education Department (1999) *Information on Children in Residential Accommodation in the Year to 31 March 1998.* Edinburgh: Scottish Executive.

Scottish Law Commission (1995) *Report on Incapable Adults.* No. 151. Edinburgh: HMSO (Cmnd 2962).

Scottish Office (1966) *Social Work and the Community.* Edinburgh: HMSO (Cmnd 3065).

Scottish Office (1991) *The Report of the Inquiry into the Removal of Children From Orkney in February 1991. The Clyde Report.* Edinburgh: HMSO.

Scottish Office (1995) 'The New Councils.' In J. English (ed) (1998) *Social Services in Scotland.* 4th edn. Edinburgh: Mercat Press.

Scottish Office (1996) *Health in Scotland 1995.* Edinburgh: HMSO.

Scottish Office (1997a) *Framework for Mental Health Services in Scotland.* SWSG/30/97. Edinburgh: Scottish Office.

Scottish Office (1997b) *Statistical Bulletin, Social Work Series, Referrals of children to Reporters and Children's Hearings 1995–1996.* SWK/CH/1997/20. Edinburgh: Scottish Office.

Scottish Office (1998a) *Community Sentencing. The Tough Option: Review of Criminal Justice Social Work Services.* Edinburgh: Scottish Office.

Scottish Office (1998b) *Scottish Abstract of Statistics No. 26.* Edinburgh: Scottish Office.

Scottish Office (1998c) *Statistical Bulletin, Education Series.* J2/1998/7. Edinburgh: Scottish Office.

Scottish Office (1998d) *Statistical Bulletin, Social Work Series, Community Care.* SWK/CMC/1998/7. Edinburgh: Scottish Office.

Scottish Office (1998e) *Women Offenders – A Safer Way: A Review of Community Disposals and the Use of Custody for Women Offenders in Scotland.* Edinburgh: Social Work Services and Prisons Inspectorate for Scotland.

Scottish Office (1999) *Aiming for Excellence: Modernising Social Work Services in Scotland.* Edinburgh: The Stationery Office (Cmnd 4288).

Scottish Office Home Department (1999) *Looking After Children in Scotland: Good Parenting, Good Outcomes.* Edinburgh: The Scottish Office.

Scottish Poverty Information Unit (1998) *Scottish Poverty Information Unit Submission on Social Exclusion to the Scottish Affairs Committee.* Glasgow: Glasgow Caledonian University.

Seebohm Report (1968) *Report of the Committee on Local Authority and Allied Personal Social Services.* London: HMSO (Cmnd 3703).

Shardlow, S.M., and Payne, M., (1998) *Contemporary Issues in Social Work: Western Europe.* Aldershot: Arena.

Sheppard, M. (1991) *Mental Health Work in the Community: theory and practice in social work and community psychiatric nursing.* London: Falmer.

Sheppard, M. (1995) *Care Management and the New Social Work: a critical analysis.* London: Whiting and Birch.

Skehill, C. (1999) *The Nature of Social Work in Ireland.* New York: Edwin Mellen Press.

Smith, C. (1997) *The Scottish Voluntary Sector Report.* Edinburgh: Scottish Council for Voluntary Organisations.

Smyth, M. and Campbell, J. (1996) 'Social work, sectarianism and anti-sectarian practice in Northern Ireland.' *British Journal of Social Work 26*, 1, 77–92.

Smyth, M., Schlindwein, H. and Michael, G. (1993) *Implementing Anti-Discriminatory Practice in Northern Ireland.* Ulster: University of Ulster.

Social Work Services Group (1991) *National Objectives and Standards for Social Work Services in the Criminal Justice System.* Edinburgh: Scottish Office.

Social Work Services Group (1999) *Adoption Applications in Scotland, Information Note.* Edinburgh: Scottish Office.

Social Services Inspectorate (1996) *Inspection of Local Authority Fostering.* London: SSI.

Southern Health and Social Services Board (1999) *Children's Services Plan 1999–2002.* Armagh: SH&SSB.

Spence, L. (1996) *'All Alone? The Health & Social Care Needs of Lone Parents.'* Belfast: Gingerbread and Northern Health & Social Services Board.

Spratt, T. (1998) *Constructing Child Abuse: Patterns and Possibilities.* Belfast: University of Ulster and South & East Belfast Trust.

SSI(NI) (1997) *Report of the Chief Inspector for Social Services* (NI). Belfast: DHSS(NI).

SSI/SWSG (1991a) *Care Management and Assessment: managers' guide.* London: DH SSI/SWSG.

SSI/SWSG (1991b) *Care Management and Assessment: practitioners' guide.* London: DH SSI/SWSG.

Stalker, K. (1993) *The efficiency and effectiveness of community care: evaluation of pilot projects: (1) Tayside region in Social Work research centre, Stirling, Is Social Work Effective?* Research Findings form the Social Work Research Group. Stirling: Social Work Research Centre.

Stalker, K., Taylor, C. and Petch, A. (1994) *Implementing Community Care in Scotland: Early Snapshots.* Stirling: University of Stirling, Social Work Research Centre.

Steinberg, R. M. and Carter, G. W. (1983) *Case Management and the Elderly.* Boston MA: Lexington.

Sutherland Report (1999) *With Respect to Old Age: A Report by the Royal Commission on Long Term Care.* London: The Stationery Office.

Switzer, V. (1997) *Child Care Statistics in Northern Ireland: The Last Decade 1986–1995.* Belfast: Centre For Child Care Research: Queens University Belfast.

SWSI (1992) *Another Kind of Home: A Review of Residential Child Care. A Report by the Chief Inspector of Social Work Services for Scotland.* Edinburgh: HMSO.

SWSI (1996) *Rebuilding Confidence: Social Work Services in Orkney.* Edinburgh: The Stationery Office.

SWSI (1997a) *A Commitment to Protect. Supervising Sex Offenders: Proposal for More Effective Practice.* Edinburgh: Scottish Office.

SWSI (1997b) *Children's Safeguards Review.* Edinburgh: The Stationery Office.

SWSI (1998) *Sensing Progress: Social Work Services for People with a Sensory Impairment. Report by the Social Work Services Inspectorate.* Edinburgh: The Stationery Office.

Teague, P. (1993) 'Discrimination and fair employment in Northern Ireland.' In P. Teague (ed) *The Economy of Northern Ireland.* London: Wishart.

Thoburn, J., A. Murcoch *et al.* (1997) *Permanent family placement for children of minority ethnic origin: a report to the Department of Health.* Norwich: University of East Anglia.

Thomas, M. and Pierson, J. (1995) *Dictionary of Social Work.* London:Collins Educational.

Thompson, N. (1997) 'Anti-discriminatory practice.' In M. Davies (ed.) *The Blackwell Companion of Social Work.* Oxford: Blackwell.

Thorpe, D. (1997) 'Regulating late-modern childrearing in Ireland.' *Economic and Social Review 28,* 2, 63–84.

Titterton, M. (1990) 'Caring for People in Scotland.' Evidence to the House of Commons Social Services Committee (unpublished).

Traynor, C. (1998) 'Adapt and Service: Social Work in a Sectarian Society.' *Professional Social Work,* January.

Triseliotis, J., Borland, M. and Hill, M. (1999) *Fostering Good Relations: A Study of Foster Care and Foster Carers in Scotland.* Edinburgh: Scottish Office Central Research Unit/The Stationery Office.

TUC Cymru (1999) *Poverty and Ill Health – Our Greatest Challenge.* Cardiff: TUC.

Turner, M. (1998) 'Health Services.' In J. English (ed)*Social Services in Scotland.* 4th edn. Edinburgh: Mercat Press.

Ulas, M., Myers, F. and Whyte, B. (1994) *The Role of the Mental Health Officer.* Edinburgh: Scottish Office Central Research Unit/HMSO.

Utting, W. (1997) *People Like Us: the report of the review of the safeguards for children living away from home.* London: Stationery Office/Department of Health.

Vourlekis, B. S. and Greene, R. S. (eds) (1992) *Social Work Case Management.* New York: Aldine de Gruyter.

Wagner Report (1998) *Residential Care: a positive choice (Report of the Independent Review of Residential Care).* London: HMSO.

Walsh, T. (1999) 'Changing expectations: The impact of "child protection" on social work in Ireland.' *Child and Family Social Work 4,* 1, 33–42.

Warren, D. (1999) *National Standards in Foster Care.* The RHP Companion to Foster Care. Lyme Regis: Russell House.

Waterhouse, L., McGhee, J., Whyte, B., Loucks, N., Kay, H. and Stewart, R. (2000) *The Evaluation of the Children's Hearings in Scotland. Children in Focus. Social Work Research Findings No. 31.* Edinburgh: Scottish Office Central Research Unit/The Stationery Office.

Waterhouse, S. (1997) *The Organisation of Fostering Services: A Study of the Arrangements for the Delivery of Fostering Services in England.* London: National Foster Care Association.

Weil, M., Karls, J. M. and associates (1985) *Case Management in Human Service Practice: a systematic approach to mobilising resources for clients.* San Francisco: Jossey-Bass.

Welsh Office (1983) *All Wales Strategy for the Development of Services for Mentally Handicapped People.* Cardiff: Welsh Office.

Welsh Office (1985) *A Good Old Age: An Initiative in the Care of the Elderly in Wales.* Cardiff: Welsh Office.

Welsh Office (1989) *Mental Illness Services: A Strategy for Wales.* Cardiff: Welsh Office.

Welsh Office (1995) *Wales in Figures.* Cardiff: Welsh Office.

Welsh Office (1996) *A Statistical Focus on Wales.* Cardiff: Welsh Office.

Welsh Office (1997) *An Economic Strategy for Wales: a consultation document.* Cardiff: Welsh Office.

Welsh Office (1998) Digest of Welsh Statistics. Cardiff: Welsh Office.

Welsh Office (1999) 'Alun Michael Welcomes "Unique Opportunity" of Objective One Status for West Wales and the Valleys.' *Press release W99–276,* 26 March.

Welsh Office and the Department of Health (1998) *Social Services: Building for the future.* Cardiff: Welsh Office.

Wenger, C., (1995) 'Ageing in Rural North Wales: Twelve Years of Domiciliary Visiting Services.' *Contemporary Wales,* 7, 153–71.

Western Health and Social Services Board (1999) *Western Area Children and Young Person's Committee, Children's Services Plan 1999–2002.* Derry: WH&SSB.

White, M. (2000) Fair and Effective. *Guardian.* London: 10/1/2000, 8.

White, V. and Leonick, B. (1999) in *Social Work and the State.* Brighton: Pavillion.

Whyte, J. (1991) *Understanding Northern Ireland.* Oxford: Clarendon Press.

Whyte, J. H. (1980) *Church and State in Modern Ireland. 1923–1979,* 2nd edn. Dublin: Gill and Macmillan.

Williams, C. (1995) '"Race" and Racism: Some Reflections on the context of Wales.' *Contemporary Wales 8,* 113–31.

Williams, C. (1998) *European Year Against Racism: The Torfaen Project.* Torfaen: County Borough Council Report to the European Commission.

Williamson, A. and Darby, J. (1978) 'Social welfare services.' In J. Darby and A. Williamson (eds) *Violence and the Social Services in Northern Ireland.* London: Heinemann.

Winchester, R. (2000) 'What's wrong with Wales?' *Community Care, 1347,* 9–15 November, 22–3.

Winrow, M. and Priestley, M. M. (1976) *Social and Economic Stress in Wales: A study of social deprivation and economic imbalance.* Lampeter: Geography Department, St David's College.

Younghusband, E. (1981) *The Newest Profession: A Short History of Social Work.* Sutton, Surrey: Community Care/IPC Business Press.

The Contributors

Jim Campbell is a senior lecturer in the School of Social Work at Queen's University, Belfast. Previously, he was a mental health social worker. His current teaching and research interests are in mental health, social work and social policy, as well as social work and social conflict in Northern Ireland and other troubled regions. He has published extensively in these areas.

Mark Drakeford is a senior lecturer in social policy and social work at the University of Wales, Cardiff. He is currently seconded to the National Assembly for Wales as the Cabinet social policy adviser.

Harry Ferguson is Professor of Social Work at the University of the West of England, Bristol. Previousle, he was Professor of Social Policy and Social Work at University College Dublin and also worked in the Department of Applied Social Studies, University College, Cork, and the Department of Social Studies, Trinity College, Dublin. He has researched and published extensively in the areas of child abuse and protection, domestic violence, fatherhood, men and masculinities, and on the application of critical social theory to social work. His most recent book is *Keeping Children Safe: Child Abuse, Child Protection and the Promotion Of Welfare* (with M. O'Reilly), published by A&A Farmar, Dublin (2001).

Mary McColgan is a lecturer in social work at the University of Ulster and is based at the Magee campus in Derry. She is currently Programme Director for the postgraduate diploma in social work. Her professional background has been as a social work practitioner and middle manager in fieldwork child care practice. Current research and teaching interests are in child observation training, child and family practice, audits of professional child care practice and the involvement of children in research. She has been involved in contributing to social work education and training in Romania and teaching in Belarus. Her voluntary work interests include family support and community development.

Janice McGhee is a lecturer in the Department of Social Work at the University of Edinburgh. Her main teaching responsibilities include social work law, psychology and human development. She qualified as a social worker in 1979 and has substantial practice experience in local authority fieldwork settings and as a senior social worker in a London teaching hospital. Current research interests are related to child care policy and law, the children's hearings system and the impact of recent child protection legislation.

Malcolm Payne is Professor and Head of Department of Applied Community Studies at the Manchester Metropolitan University, having worked in probation, social services, and the national and local voluntary sector. He is the author of, most recently, *Modern Social Work Theory* (2nd edition), Macmillan (1997) and *Teamwork in Multiprofessional Care*, Macmillan (2000).

Fred Powell is Professor of Applied Social Studies at the National University of Ireland, Cork, and a member of the Royal Irish Academy. Before taking up his current position he worked as a social worker in the London Borough of Newham and a lecturer in social studies at the University of Ulster. He has also taught in the United States and been an adviser to the Council of Europe on adult education and social inclusion. He has published three major books: *The Politics of Irish Social Policy* (1992), *Social Policy and Civil Society* (1997) and *The Politics of Social Work* (2001).

Steven M. Shardlow is Professor of Social Work at the University of Salford and Editor-in-Chief of the *Journal of Social Work*. Previously he has worked as a social work practitioner and manager in both field and residential work. He has been involved in international social work, particularly in Europe, through development work, consultancy and research. Current research interests are: professional ethics, comparative social practice in the social professions, and professional social work education and practice – especially practice learning. He has published widely in these fields and his work has been translated into several languages.

Lorraine Waterhouse is Professor in the Department of Social Work at the University of Edinburgh and a member of the University Court. Her research focuses on children and families, their health and development. Educated in Canada, she came to Scotland in 1972 where she worked successively as a social worker and senior social worker in the Department of Child and Family Psychiatry at the Royal Hospital for Sick Children, Edinburgh.

Charlotte Williams is a lecturer in social policy at the University of Wales, Bangor. She has been involved in social work education, training and practice for over twenty years, nationally and internationally. She is co-editor of the book *Social Work and Minorities: European Perspectives* and has published widely on issues of anti-discriminatory practice. Her current research interests include social policy in Wales following devolution, in particular the participation of minorities in the policy process.

John Wolfe moved to Guernsey in 1974, owning and running a large horticultural business for six years. In 1980 he took up a post in child care social work before undertaking professional training at Bristol Polytechnic where he obtained his CQSW. John held the posts of manager in a residential unit for adolescents, field social worker in child protection, and adoption and fostering officer working with NCH. In 1990 he moved from the Channel Islands to work for SSAFA in Germany as an area social worker, adoption and fostering specialist, and senior social worker. During this period he also spent a year living in the Netherlands attached to NATO and other forces. In 1994 he worked as a social worker in Cyprus while working for SSAFA. He returned to the Channel Islands in 1995 as Assistant Director of the Children Board, becoming Deputy Director in 1998. He is married with two daughters and has a (small) smallholding specialising in rare ducks and hens – this occupies his leisure time.

Subject index

Author index